Kansas Matters

Kansas Matters

Twenty-First-Century Writers on the Sunflower State

Edited by Thomas Fox Averill and
Leslie VonHolten

 University Press of Kansas

Published by the University Press of Kansas (Lawrence, Kansas 66045), which was organized by the Kansas Board of Regents and is operated and funded by Emporia State University, Fort Hays State University, Kansas State University, Pittsburg State University, the University of Kansas, and Wichita State University.

Library of Congress Cataloging-in-Publication Data

Names: Averill, Thomas Fox, editor | VonHolten, Leslie, editor
Title: Kansas matters / edited by Thomas Fox Averill and Leslie VonHolten.
Description: Lawrence : University Press of Kansas, 2025.
Identifiers: LCCN 2025008525 (print) | LCCN 2025008526 (ebook)
  ISBN 9780700640508 cloth
  ISBN 9780700640515 epub
Subjects: LCSH: American literature—Kansas | American literature—21st
  century | Kansas—Literary collections | BISAC: LITERARY COLLECTIONS /
  Subjects & Themes / Places | POETRY / American / General | LCGFT:
  Literature
Classification: LCC PS571.K2 K36 2025 (print) | LCC PS571.K2
  DDC 810.9/97810905—dc23/eng/20250423
LC record available at https://lccn.loc.gov/2025008525.
LC ebook record available at https://lccn.loc.gov/2025008526.

British Library Cataloguing-in-Publication Data is available.

Cover design by Karl Janssen
Cover art: *Like a Bell Rung Deep* by Angie Pickman, Rural Pearl Studio

Contents

Introduction

"Dear Old Kansas!"

Thomas Fox Averill

In 1990 I edited *What Kansas Means to Me: Twentieth-Century Writers on the Sunflower State.* I titled my introduction "Afflicted by Affection." The process of selecting the contents of that anthology, after a year-long dive into essays and poems, reinforced in me a lifetime of feeling at home in Kansas. That deep sense of home is, in some ways, an affliction. It caused me to stay put, grounded in both senses of the word—"grounded in a place" and "grounded" in range, not cleared for liftoff, though I've taken flight anyway, happily finding my home on this range. But the affliction made me defensive about any derision of this place so dear to my heart. It made me a bit of a zealot, passionate enough to shape university courses in Kansas literature, Kansas folklore, and Kansas film throughout my career at Washburn University. It also made me a collector and bibliographer; the many books and magazines, CDs, films, and paraphernalia I gathered over forty years— around twenty-five hundred items—became the bedrock of the Thomas Fox Averill Kansas Studies Collection, now with more than nine thousand catalogue entries and housed in the Washburn University Library. In short, Kansas has inspired and shaped my teaching career, my travels, my reading, and my thinking.

Since the publication of *What Kansas Means to Me*, I have learned to moderate my affliction of affection. Yes, I'm still passionate about Kansas. Yes, I'm still avidly reading Kansas writers and collecting Kansas books. But I'm also more balanced in my view, more philosophical, more wary of sentimentality about place. I credit some of that change to William Jennings Bryan Oleander, a crusty old character from Here, Kansas, that I created to give voice to radio commentaries for Kansas Public Radio. For nearly thirty years, Mr. Oleander allowed me to be whimsical, critical—and sometimes even cynical—about the Sunflower State. Mostly with humor, of course. From Oleander's Three-Minute History:

We came out of the 1880s poor and crazy, we prohibited liquor and . . . gave power to the scraggly farmers in the Populist Party just long enough for William Allen White to get famous writing "What's the Matter with Kansas?" even though everyone had known what was wrong since Coronado (who killed the guide who lured him here to find the seven cities of gold)—and not being able to fortify with a stiff drink didn't help.

I added some much-needed state symbols:

State Weather: The tornado.
State Greeting: The Western Kansas one-finger salute (finger raised
     slightly from the hand on the top of the steering wheel).
State Headwear: Feed cap.
State Modifier: "Pretty," as in "pretty much."
State Sentence Opener: "Well," as in "Well, what do you know?"
State Affirmative: "Yep."
State Negative: "Nope."
State Scenery: Level.

Here's how these symbols would work. Let's say it's the day after a devastating tornado. Two Kansas farmers give a one-finger greeting and stop their pickup trucks to talk.

"Well," says one, "pretty good storm last night."
"Yep," says the other, taking off his feed cap and wiping his shockingly
     white forehead. "You got anything left?"
"Nope," says the first one. "It was pretty much level when I came to
     Kansas, and now it's pretty much leveled again."

Through Oleander commentaries I expressed what I always knew: we Kansans love our stereotypes as much as we love those who stereotype against us.

A second cure for the affliction of affection was a large dose of alarming post-1990 politics. An anti-evolutionary Kansas State Board of Education, along with the short-sighted economic policies of the Kansas right wing, made Kansas a laughingstock and a poster child for budget woes. Our highways deteriorated, our educational system lacked support, our arts commission was gutted. In short, our physical, educational, economic, and artistic infrastructures were failing us. Fortunately, much of that dark period has been brightened by recent policies, and those of us with affection for the best of Kansas have remained in the state and worked hard for change, because we know that Kansas matters: to us, and to the nation and world.

So, when the University Press of Kansas was ready for an updated anthology of writing from Kansas essayists, playwrights, novelists, and poets, I was pleased to accept the call. This was not to be a sequel, and *What Kansas Means to Me* would remain in print, valuable for its careful look at the history and culture of Kansas. *Kansas Matters* would be a twenty-first-century book, reflecting all the richness, diversity, and contemporary issues that have made Kansas anew in the past thirty-five years. I have always believed Kansas to be a bellwether state, the very name conjuring up definite images, positive and negative: of exploration and trails; of Abolition, Prohibition, and Populism; of our election of the first female mayor in the United States; of our place in cowboy culture and the Wild West; of our connection to the *Wizard of Oz* and to basketball; of our prairies, plains, and monumental rock formations. All of these things, along with less positive thoughts, cross the minds of people who hear about Kansas. In his 1896 editorial diatribe against Populism, *What's the Matter With Kansas?*, William Allen White gave us a lasting question, a phrase used over and again in essays and book titles. His writing also showed that Kansas mattered to the nation, and that those things that matter to Kansas, those "Kansas matters," were far-reaching then, and remain so today. Not that Kansas is alone as bellwether: other states conjure important associations. Still, what other of the fifty states conjures such a host of associations? Massachusetts for everything from Plymouth Rock to liberal politics. Virginia for its Washington and Jefferson, for its embodiment of the Old South. Texas for its many flags, its Alamo, and its sheer size. California for its experimentation, fertility, its Hollywood. Include Kansas, and you have my own list of conjure states.

As happy as I am to engage Kansas and Kansas writing once again, I have reached an age that makes me suspicious of myself as authority. Or as *the* authority. So, I asked Leslie VonHolten to join me in the editing of *Kansas Matters*. She has added knowledge, insight, and connections. She has been an equal partner in planning, shaping, soliciting, and editing the work you will find in this book. Early on, we agreed that this would be an evocative book, and I want to outline our thinking.

Carl Becker's 1910 essay "Kansas" is the first selection in *What Kansas Means to Me*. He opens with his own introduction to the Sunflower State.

Traveling from New England by train to begin his teaching career in history at the University of Kansas, he observes two young women, full of what he calls "ceaseless chatter." As they cross the Kansas border, they quiet themselves, and, after a long silence, one turns to the other and says, "Dear old Kansas!" Becker's essay explores that utterance. He writes: "To understand why people say 'Dear old Kansas!' is to understand that Kansas is no mere geographical expression, but a 'state of mind,' a religion, and a philosophy in one."

His "Kansas" is a spot-on analysis of the state in terms of our history and culture, our individualism, our idealism, our sense of equality, our belief in government as a powerful tool that seeks to do the will of the people. In this, he foresees our progressive, common-sense history of bettering the lives of all Kansans. He also points out that for all our individualism and self-reliance—attributable to pioneering, hard work, survival, to doggedness in the face of the *aspera*, the "difficulties" of the early Kansas years—we are also communal, and conforming, with a strong reliance on each other.

But as insightful as Becker is about the state, he never examines the *feeling* behind "Dear old Kansas." The two young women are not likely as privy to the historical and cultural factors Becker uses to discuss Kansas as a state of mind. They were looking at the landscape. They were returning home. They felt something intangible, and they blessed that emotion with a simple sigh, a moment of contentment. I have my own "dear" homecoming moment, often upon returning from the airport after time away. Traveling west on I-70, just past the Lecompton exit, I am always awed by a sudden opening of the horizon, north, down to the Kansas River valley, rolling hills, cattle ponds, tree-lined creeks: miles and miles of open beauty that says, "home again."

In *Kansas Matters*, Leslie and I offer the work of writers with great insight into the *feelings* Kansas evokes. This collection is not meant to be a history lesson, although our rich history is both explained and alluded to. Nor is it an attempt to tell *the* story of Kansas, as we are each a single story that contributes to the story of our state. Nor is it a sentimental rendering of some unblemished version of who we are as a people and politic. *Kansas Matters* is what one of our writers calls "a living map." Personal geographies and histories join with the richness of memory and emotion, and our individual landscapes reveal their deepest richness, what we feel in our hearts rather than our heads. We give you the Kansas River, the county lakes, the strip mine pits, and the creek walks. We experience the Flint Hills, the "minimalist" High Plains, the chalk outcrops, and always the sky, with its beauty and terrorizing tornadoes. We visit Dodge City, Ashland, Parsons, Topeka, and Lawrence, among other towns and cities.

To outsiders, our personal landscapes, though incredibly rich to us, may seem unimpressive. In his poem "In Response to a Question," William Stafford makes a parenthetical statement: "(Some people call their scenery flat, / their only pictures framed by what they know: / I think around them rise a riches and a loss / too equal for their chart—but absolutely tall.)" As these essays celebrate our living maps, they also describe those riches and losses embedded in our "absolutely tall" experience of place.

Familiarity is also embedded in that echoing word: family. And home. Many of us are here, or our hearts are here, because of generational ties. But if Kansas pulls people, and keeps them here, in part because of family traditions, it also lures people with generosity: newcomers welcomed, friendships forged, democratic openness observed.

Kansas history, culture, and traditions also serve our Kansas writers as inspiration, from John Brown to Nicodemus, from the beginnings of basketball to the roots of art therapy.

From sunflowers to buffalo/bison (those actual state symbols), the iconography of Kansas threads through all this fine writing. After all, Carl Becker, in his essay, speculates that the young women on the train had their attention fixed "upon something in the scene outside—fields of corn, or it may have been the sunflowers that lined the track." Our writers have their attention in more than one place: what is outside them, yes, but also what is inside; on the past, of course, but also on the future. This hybrid attention serves us well as we contemplate what it is that makes Kansas matter.

Another nod to *What Kansas Means to Me*: Milton Eisenhower, in his 1949 essay "The Strength of Kansas," wrote, "We have a state spirit which is a unique mingling of Puritan morality, Southern chivalry, and Western individualism."

Eisenhower concluded his essay: "Sacrificing none of her devotion to political and intellectual freedom, nor to democratic concepts of human dignity and equality . . . I say, Kansas is . . . ready to serve as the sane moderator of ideological extremes, the firm core of the American culture and the vital center of creative compromise."

That is an ambitious task, but many of the writers in *Kansas Matters* are showing us the way. They write of just such a balance in Kansas. A tolerance for differences, a reliance on community, a sense of justice, a need to be welcoming and productive together. Kansas needs this balance, this "hybrid vigor," as Eisenhower called it: idealism, neighborliness, independent thinking. Kansas needs vigor to keep us from extremes. Extreme Western individuality might promote private rights over public responsibility. Unchecked Southern influence might lead to the same fissures and extremes that once fostered prejudice and racism. Narrow Puritanism might undermine our tolerance for anyone's right to live life as they want to, not how we wish them to.

Recently, these three elements of the Kansas historical character have too often been factions of our population—some of us Puritan-influenced, some Southern-influenced, some Western-influenced. As a result, we have drawn political and cultural battle lines between and among us. The writers in *Kansas Matters* inspire us to blend all three into each of ourselves, to make them the fabric of our lives. When we strive to integrate everyone into our politics and culture, we are, finally, integrating ourselves. In this book, we give you the Kansas we know it can be, and Kansas as we want it to be. During the Kansas Sesquicentennial of Statehood in 2011, the State Library chose *What Kansas Means to Me* as a book for libraries to feature and to create programming around. As editor, I was able to visit twenty-five libraries that spring, having conversations about Kansas with amazing patrons. They were well-educated, well-traveled, community-minded, volunteer-oriented, welcoming, articulate citizens. After the experience I often told people that if I could have chosen five people from each library and sent them to the Statehouse, we'd have the Kansas that reflects our very best. When editing an anthology, we can make those choices, giving you our best version of the state.

Carl Becker ended his "Kansas" with: "The Kansas spirit is the American spirit double distilled." In *Kansas Matters*, we offer a fresh distillation of the Kansas spirit.

Ad Astra
Traci Brimhall

The story we tell the future will have windmills
and the quiet clap of cottonwood leaves, annual

festivals and old streams elbowing their way into
fields that many histories ago were shallow seas.

The story will be what we make of it, with our corn
mazes and street corners, dirt roads and art districts,

block parties and community gardens. Our chapters
will be like our seasons—reliable in their surprises.

The busy plots of star-baked summers and the slow
conclusion of winter with its catalog of snowflakes.

In the story we are writing into the future there are
kids biking through the neighborhood and a great

blue heron at the pond hunting in its own shadow.
The story has the People of the Wind and people

of the wandering. The rooted and the transplanted.
What comes next, we can almost see—rain's

brief signature on the sidewalk and a chevron of
migrating geese breaking up the wide open blue.

A story where wind romances a dandelion, and bees
lounge at their favorite goldenrod saloons. The story

we are writing to the future has facts, like how
a sunflower's face is a union of individual seeds all

leaning towards the sun together. This story grows.
It changes with each day. It's full of possibilities,

like how, before dawn ripens the horizon, the night
sky dreams one more story for the library of stars.

Section I: Oh Give Me a Home

I would not exchange, my home here to range / forever in azure so bright.

> — Brewster Higley, "My Western Home"

"And oh, Aunt Em! I'm so glad to be at home again!"

> —L. Frank Baum, *The Wonderful Wizard of Oz*

Kansas and home often seem synonymous. Our state song is "Home on the Range." Dorothy's "There is no place like home" became famous with the popularity of Hollywood's *The Wizard of Oz*. *Little House on the Prairie* reinforces the pioneering trials and virtues associated with making a home. These three iconic references, interestingly, emerged around the same time.

"Home on the Range" was not always associated with Kansas. It was widely sung as a cowboy folk song. Then, during the Great Depression and Dust Bowl, the worst of times, Franklin Roosevelt named it his favorite song. Because of a copyright dispute, the origin of the song was researched. The lyrics, as it turned out, were first published as "My Western Home" by Brewster Higley in the *Smith County Pioneer* in 1873. Daniel Kelley, of Gaylord, Kansas, composed the music that same year. Kansas enshrined it as the state song in 1947—and no wonder, with its "buffalo roam," its "deer and the antelope play," its "seldom is heard, a discouraging word / And the sky is not clouded all day."

The Wizard of Oz, based on L. Frank Baum's *The Wonderful Wizard of Oz* (1900), was first released in 1939, then re-released in 1949, then broadcast on television beginning in 1956. An annual showing catapulted it to the most watched of any film. Also in 1956, the novel's copyright expired, and it was reprinted in many editions, re-illustrated and often abridged.

Around this same time, in 1953, the *Little House* series, by Laura Ingalls Wilder, was re-reissued with illustrations by Garth Williams. *Little House on the Prairie*, describing the difficult year of 1870, when the Ingalls family pioneered in southeastern Kansas, became a favorite and, along with the other eight *Little House* books, made their way into school curriculums, libraries, and popular culture.

I was in elementary school in Kansas during those years. Mrs. Shellhorn, my third-grade teacher, read all the *Oz* and *Little House* books to us. In kindergarten, we had celebrated the 1954 Kansas Territorial Centennial by growing wheat in buckets. Abilene's own Dwight D. Eisenhower was in the White House. The first miles of interstate were laid in Kansas. William Inge of Independence, Kansas, was on Broadway. Kansas was the right place to call home. For many, it still is.

When Dorothy meets the scarecrow and he asks her about Kansas, she reports on the gray landscape, the cyclone that swept her to Oz. He listens carefully, then says, "I cannot understand why you should wish to leave this beautiful country and go back to the dry, gray place you call Kansas." Dorothy chastises him: "That is because you have no brains. . . . No matter how dreary and gray our homes are, we people of flesh and blood would rather live there than in any other country, be it ever so beautiful. There is no place like home."

This Home section offers writers "of flesh and blood" as they speak to the dreary, to the gray, to the challenges, but also to the beauty of a sometimes-underappreciated landscape, and to experiences that make Kansas like no other place. All of them speak to migration, to immigration, to adoption of place, to that feeling that their hearts are in Kansas, the quintessential Heartland. Here, we have the suffering and healing of Kevin Young's Nicodemus settlers. Josh Svaty tells of his Smoky Hills landscape and a loved one buried on that "lone prairie." We witness the love for an industrially ruined landscape being reclaimed by nature in Al Ortolani's southeastern Kansas strip pits. Traci Brimhall realizes that she is surprisingly at home. Jeffrey Ann Goudie's northeast Kansas pilgrimages turn into her permanent and proud residence in a subtly beautiful and politically practical place. Armando Minjárez Monárrez chronicles a migration to southwestern Kansas, a land of many landscapes, skyscapes, and cultures. And Becky Mandelbaum's character returns to Kansas to be picked up at the Wichita airport by a mother who squeezes her three times, just as Dorothy clicks her heels three times.

Kansas poet William Stafford begins his poem "Allegiances" (1970) with an injunction: *It is time for all the heroes to go home / if they have any, time for all of us common ones to locate ourselves by the real things / we live by.* These writers tell us about those real things we live by.

—Thomas Fox Averill

Nicodemus

Kevin Young

*Being a true account
of the flight of Freedmen
during Redemption
to the Colored Canaan*

*"Why do you wear
Your shroud while you are living, Nicodemus?
And a black shroud at that?"*
—Edward Arlington Robinson

Nicodemus was a slave of African birth
    And was bought for a bag full of gold;
He was reckoned a part of the salt of the earth,
    But he died years ago, very old.
Nicodemus was a prophet, at least he was as wise,
    For he told of the battles to come;
How we trembled with fear, when he rolled up his eyes,
    And we heeded the shake of his thumb.

Soon as I saw the song I knew,
dropped my plow, unhitched
& headed to where Blue sported
two hoes, hauling much as two men.
Said, "I swear Blue it's so good
we're already gone." I couldn't tell him
what it said, just lured him like a moth
from the hot lamp of the field
& pointed. HO KANSAS! the ad
read, he said, good land, good water
& rocks, good wood on the streams
only $5 a passage. "Nicodemus, now
ain't that name the sweetest heard
since your own?" Finished reading aloud,
Blue just sat in his indigo, sweaty
& shook. No one could cover the country mile
of that man's smile, not even
his gals at them dances, but here
he sat shaking his head till blue
as his shirt & name. Didn't say a word

but didn't need to—we'd been brothers
since Big Massa died & told us so,
called me son, tho don't tell that
to the Widow cause she don't
like to hear what she already know.
Me, I just left Blue there, gathered
Lucy & Moses & the rest to say
what I'd heard. We all knew
of the blood in those parts—
the man Carolina hung & made
sure we'd heard about. No one named
anyone Nat for years—
but now we could go & pioneer
our own brand of unbranded
freedom. No more paddyrollers
& nightraiders, only the same stone

welcome of the land, well looky there
settlements along River Solomon.

Most would have none of it.
Moses said Missus needed us
in the House & cussed
"Don't know who this
Nickledemon is, but I'se sure
bout one thing—he ain't here
or home." I argued with Moses
& reminded everyone of bad butter—
how this South's Redemption
didn't want us, how the town tried
to ghost us out the vote. No chords,
words, only nods in the small crowd,
grown men acting like sheep
scared as sin. "My folks done this
here Dixie since you were only
dix," Blue said, sad. Only Black Tom
stood & said "I want to be alive
not yall, who're dead & don't know it."

[**AIR**]

Freedom what we already had,
only we were too dumb
to say it. Speak up girl, the white
man said, but Lucy'd been mostly
mute since they'd taken our son
from her—Sir, I said, I better
tell her myself, & did. They wouldn't
let us cross with Black Tom's trunk
or her daddy's walking stick—
said she'd have to leave them
ashore, or have them sent. "No" needs
no translation & neither did her
sorrow. They sent the stick & trunk
overboard like so much heavy hay.

We'd made Orleans three days
& camped at the bank. I couldn't
sleep or wait for the Committee
of Colored Folks to meet, awake watched
the water carried out to sea—pitchered
slaves shivering, sold, or shucked
overboard like rotten cobs from Missourah
where they say a colored man can't walk.

Next day the boats left bound
for Kentucky & Kansas, coming from far
as Tennessee & St. Louie just to spot
free soil, call it your own. The Committee
& Colony already paid, all we needed
was what we had: one mule, a year
saved up & some backs & hands
unafraid of work. So we set out
without a thought or second
to waste & my Lucy began
to hum—what I hadn't heard
since she found our son, fetched
me quiet to cut his body down.

[**WATER**]

Wyandotte, the Kaw, Saint Joe—
the names came to me like stories
my mother told of her daddy
who flew north one night & could write
with both hands. Say he had
bird & no slave in him, say he went
to find his tribe who knew to swim
& sing. Black as Blue was, he had
no nigger's nose, & I suppose
no need for north or Canaan,
Kansas or Canada. He stayed.
I got that bird in me & Lucy

that stubborn black. Black Tom's body
which made it alive most the way here
all but buried itself—alls I did is dig
a shallow along the Solomon
to stand him down in. Saw the soil,
tasted it, & that was enough. Lucy swayed
into the shallows, teared, drowned
her daddy's spirit stick I swore I'd seen
the men send over. No Liberia here
for her daddy Tom to return to, his body
must find its own precious way.

[EARTH]

That first year heaven
must have hated us, sent
grasshoppers, drought,
then ice & snow that glazed
our one tree, flat-footed light
glaring back. I caught
whatever all I could
along the Solomon; we ate muskrat
& possum & one time deer
which cured us of wanting

to turn tail around.
Few others lasted past frost.
We dug in like the prairie dogs
that scampered in summer,
that, if winter would have trapped,
we would have eaten. By spring
half-starving, sick of each other,
we were studying horizon,
making ready to move on—
& then all a sudden the snow
warmed & the grass
unflattened, stood up, whistled.

Stalks of sun grew tall
& waved. We dug out like potatoes,
planted. Lucy began to grow
sick, unable to keep anything down
but bread—the staler the better.
I grew thin with worry. Lord,
don't take this one from me.
Then, miracle, she sat up & made
me know—her face—she thought
what fought inside her was a child.

I drank. Walked the fields
with their short shoots & thought

of our boy, gone
like a whistle, like weather, & wished
back the snows. At least I knew
how to wait those out (though
that's probably what got us this mess
the first place). Found

her home by the fire, warming,
& bent to hear our future—
far-off—muffled inside her. I slept
there a long time, it seemed, dreaming
of food, of feeling fuller than I'd ever been
or remembered. By harvest
she was carrying high—a girl—& the crops
were almost in, when she flooded
the floor like the Solomon—

our second was coming so I sent
for Miss Nancy who left the schoolhouse
to deliver. Days of pain, too much
sun—I paced a moat outside the door
my wife would not let me in.
Miss Nancy had her chomping
birthroot, a knife under the bed to cut
down the pain. Our last, lost,
had almost killed her. And me.

When the shouting hours stopped
I really got scared. After forever,
Miss Nancy called me in
to see her, our purple
bundle of yawn, my wife singing
Name a Evie—sweetest,
first words she'd let out in years.

[**FIRMAMENT**]

Evie grew up tall & straight—
went to school, taught
me to read, to write
them winter nights

when it wasn't harvest
or time to plant.
The boys I kept
away like the crows

by polishing on the porch
my gun. Word
reached us Blue went
into his name. Lucy went

one night, late,
but that's the Lord's

business, not yours. No last
words, she slipped quiet
& never got to see our child
get older & the vote,

marry, move away as the smart
ones always seem to. That
is that. I have kept
this record for Evie so she won't

forget—but mostly
for my son & Black
& my brother Blue & Lucy—
all the dead who can't.

Palacky Township, September 2023

Joshua Svaty

After my dad had his second heart attack, he told us that when he died he wanted to be buried in a hole in the ground on our farm, without a coffin or fanfare. "The state law says if you do it within twenty-four hours of dying you don't need anything," he said. My siblings and I knew enough about the Bohemian mind to know that despite being in his late seventies, this statement was the full extent of my father's estate planning. We even called our law office in town to check, but without his permission they couldn't tell us whether he had done estate planning. As a general rule, Bohemians never do estate planning; that means we might die. Never mind that the statistical average of death for those who do not plan is extraordinarily identical to those who do.

A few years after my dad's pronouncement—he somehow remained alive—my older brother Seth was diagnosed with colon cancer at the age of forty-four. He underwent significant treatment and aggressive care, but after about a year it became apparent that the cancer was going to take him. He asked that he be put in the ground without a box, just as dad had requested. This pronouncement had a stronger immediacy to it, so I reached out to a friend to ask her the exact laws about putting someone in the ground. We wanted to honor Seth's wishes, but none of us wanted to break the law or mishandle his body.

We were glad we checked. Turns out you don't have to bury a body that soon. One of three things must happen within twenty-four hours: embalming, cremating, or refrigerating. And the law considers ice around the body to be "refrigeration." Once we learned the rules, we haphazardly said, "Oh, this will be fine," and went back to the business of living in the moment with Seth without making any further preparations.

One day in late September we needed to do some work on the corral at Kozicek's, our big pasture in western Ellsworth County where our cattle herd spent the summer. We named it Kozicek's after Don Kozicek, the guy who owned it before we bought it, but he had only owned it since 1967. It was part of the original Doubrava farm and was only a half-mile south of the original Svaty homestead. A century ago, western Ellsworth County was packed with Bohemian families bursting at the seams with kids. All the kids in Palacky Township went to Progress School, the one-room schoolhouse solidly built from Greenhorn limestone in 1911. It still stands on the corner of the township road just across from Doubrava's and Svaty's. My grandfather Garfield was a part of the first class to go all the way through the school, K-8, and that was the extent of his formal education. In 1918 the Progress School teacher, Helen Sekavec, had my grandfather and the rest of the school stand up at the Christmas program and sing "Whispering Hope" for a safe return of all the young men returning from the Great War. Helen Sekavec didn't like war.

This September day I let my kids go out early to work on the corral with my dad. I drove down to Sterling to get Seth. At this point the cancer had spread throughout his body, most noticeably in his lungs, and he struggled to take even a few steps without exhausting himself. Knowing the day was getting closer, I thought I would use the brief drive to talk through any remaining end-of-life issues with him.

We pulled out of Sterling onto Highway 14, on the brand-new Bob Bethell interchange, and I remarked that if anyone ever named a piece of transportation infrastructure after me I would come back from the grave and haunt that person. Seth agreed. Transportation infrastructure is both a blessing and a curse on the Kansas prairie. The first stretch of interstate highway was constructed in Kansas, and we pride ourselves on being able to move people and goods into, out of, and across our state better than anyone else. But the prairie has always been a place to cross, and every piece of transportation infrastructure that is built cuts the pathways that animals, insects, and water have used for millennia. Our shared agreement on an eponymous interchange was the first and last thing we said about end-of-life planning for ten of our forty-minute drive, until I said, "Do you think you'd like a celebration of life?" Seth said "Yes," and that was the last we spoke of any of it.

We spent the remainder of the drive admiring one of our favorite spots in Kansas, the point on Highway 14 north of Highway 4 where the road crosses the divide between the Arkansas River watershed and the Smoky Hill watershed. The Arkansas landscape is flat—as flat as anyone outside of Kansas imagines the entire state to be. During Christmas, the city of Lyons, which is in the Arkansas flats north of Sterling, puts red Christmas lights on their water tower to look like a Christmas bell, and it stands as a giant beacon visible for miles and miles because there is nothing that prevents anyone from seeing it across the flat landscape.

But the Smoky Hill watershed—our home—cuts away north of Lyons like a national park vista. What had been thousands of acres of tabletop fields only a few miles to the south suddenly gives way to the chaos of the Smokys and their Dakota sandstone—bluffs, caves, carvings, and paths in the rock heavily used by tens of thousands of ancient bison that pounded hoofprints into the stone. The grooved marks where their dewclaws slid into the footholds are still visible as if they were made yesterday. My brother and I talked about how much we loved this landscape. How much we understood the cosmic power of that break between the Arkansas and the Smoky—because it isn't just another divide between watersheds. The Smoky Hill River is the southernmost tributary of the Missouri River system, the largest river system in North America. Everything from the Smoky north all the way into Canada flows into the Missouri. Everything from the Arkansas south flows into the Mississippi on its own. Our divide isn't the Continental Divide, which is west of us in the Colorado Rockies, but is a north/south divide of the entire middle of the continent. We were on it.

Seth and I finally made our way into western Ellsworth County, still only a few miles north of the divide between the river systems, and into what my dad called the "high country" of Kozicek's. We drove past Progress School, long silent but still a monument to the Herculean effort to publicly educate every child across the nation, which no doubt helped usher in the American Century. We drove to the crest of the next hill, which was the entrance of Kozicek's, only forty feet in elevation below the highest point in the county a half-mile to the south of us.

The corral we had built was at the crest near the gate. True to our Bohemian roots, we had built the corral using spare parts and items we found lying around. In the pasture, piles of old railroad ties had been pulled up when they took out the Frisco line that ran into Ellsworth from the southwest. The railroad ties had been stacked like Jenga blocks, and many still had their 1930s date pins in them. They were made from ancient oaks, soaked in whatever the railroad was using to soak their ties in the 1930s; left alone, they would probably remain stacked in the pasture for hundreds of years. To build the corral, we had drilled holes in the ground and stood the ties upright as posts. It made for a perfectly functional corral with the cost of almost nothing but our labor. On this September day, we were there to make repairs ahead of moving our cows back home to central Ellsworth County in advance of winter and in preparation for calving season.

As the highest point in the county, Kozicek's is almost never lovely—it is at the very least windy—but on that day in early fall the breeze was light and the sun was warm, and my dad, my two sons, my dying brother, and I spent several hours making repairs, telling stories, and trying to determine the plant species growing near the corral. We were still in one of the worst multi-year droughts on record; the cattle had eaten most of what could be eaten, and it was time for them to go. When pastures get "hit hard" with grazing, opportunity plant species emerge, and we had a significant bloom of broomweed. In its own way, broomweed is beautiful. Its small yellow flowers were the only signs of reproduction and effort at the conclusion of what had been a hellish summer.

We chewed on some sage, chewed on some other plants whose identity we didn't know, and chewed on the reality that we were with my brother and he was dying. In a demonstration of the beauty of the day, he even chewed on a plant, claimed he was cured, and danced around for a few seconds.

Less than two weeks later, my brother died. His lungs were finally unable to provide the oxygen he needed. He died in the Hutchinson hospital late at night and was brought to Ellsworth by our funeral home across the same watershed divide he and I had driven. We retrieved him the next morning to keep him at my parents' house while we made the final preparations.

That afternoon, less than twelve hours after his official death (at which we were all present), my remaining brother, sister, father, and two of Seth's children—his teenage sons—walked down the hill from my parents' house to dig his grave. We had chosen a spot on Schwerdtfeger's, the quarter just to the east of the quarter on which we had grown up.

The Flint Hills get most of the attention in Kansas, but the Smoky Hills and Gypsum or Red Hills are quietly just as scenic, if not more, and my family happens to live and farm in one of the most beautiful parts of the Smoky Hills. Highway 156 cuts diagonally across the home quarter just a few miles southwest of Ellsworth, and our farm is on the south side of the highway facing away from it and toward the Oxhide Creek valley that drops sharply down from our hill then rises to a prominent hill that we call Headley's some two miles distant. Frequent travelers to and from southwest Kansas will know my description and immediately recognize the spot as indeed one of the prettiest in the state, and my eyes have studied it in every season of every year of my life. Seth would be buried at the edge of the Schwerdtfeger hill, overlooking that scene.

If the last day I spent working with my brother at Kozicek's was abnormally lovely for Kansas, the day we dug his grave swung hard in the other direction. The grave-digging crew made quick work of the Harney silt loam—the "official" state soil of Kansas—but there wasn't much of it, and it wasn't more than a powder after multiple years of consecutive drought. Our shovels dug easily, the only force working against us being the wind. It blasted out of the south with gusts upward of forty-five miles per hour. In some areas of the country "gusts" can imply a once-in-a-while uptick in wind, but in central Kansas forty-five miles per hour seemed constant as we worked, and the pathetically dry, worn-out soil instantly went airborne. We had to turn our backs to it to prevent our eyes from being scoured.

Within eighteen inches of digging, we encountered Dakota sandstone, the formation that dominates this landscape. The Dakota was a source of discovery during my childhood running around with Seth—it had given us three box canyons within a quarter mile of our childhood home, a playground unmatched by any other in Kansas—so it was fitting that we would hit the Dakota as we dug his grave. Sandstone varies in hardness, being significantly harder than limestone in some cases and then being so soft you can carve it with your fingernails. Luckily the sandstone we hit that day was soft, but it was still rock instead of soil.

My uncle and cousin joined us, and we soon settled into a rotation of swinging the pickax with everything we had until we had to change out for fresh arms. Sandstone doesn't chip as much as it submits to being pulverized and loses its constitution, so to those above ground it seemed we were just shoveling fine beach sand out of the hole and adding to the particulate matter swirling in the air. When digging through stone rather than soil, dreams of a perfect hole, six feet long, by two-and-a-half feet wide, by six feet deep, become pragmatic in a hurry. Comments like, "We at least need to be four feet deep," started to emerge from the digging crew. Several of us began to periodically lie down in the grave to check for shoulder width. No reason to dig any wider than we had to. My brother had wanted to be buried "green" with no coffin; he was going to be on a burial board, a beautiful piece of walnut from a tree my uncle had milled on the farm. We had the board with us and used it as a guide to length. After a while we had the hole about five feet deep and large enough to accommodate the burial board and my brother's shoulders. We were ready.

Looking back, it was a bizarre scene: Seth's closest family members digging this hole, cursing the rock, lying down in his grave not to commune with him but to be sure we could get his body in the next day without awkwardly ping-ponging it down in front of other people—all the while laughing and telling stories about him. Dominating all of us was the blasting wind from the south. Blasting, blasting, blasting. As strange as it was, it fits our family's existence in the center of Kansas. As we dug, many of us decided we wanted the same treatment when we died. But we noted that cancer had ravaged Seth's body so his overall frame and size made digging a grave chipped by hand from rock a little easier. We looked around at several of our larger family members and said, "Nope, we'll just get a backhoe for you."

To allow for more family to attend the graveside service, we scheduled it for the next morning. We knew from the forecast that overnight the wind would shift from south to north, blowing just as hard but cold. That evening before, as more family gathered and we grieved my brother and recounted the day's adventure of digging the grave, a sudden gap between the two weather systems made it still and beautiful outside. There is no calm quite like the calm after a day of nonstop Kansas wind, and the family poured outside of my parents' house to alleviate pressure on the home and enjoy the outdoors. We knew the hell that was coming the next morning, and my family even suggested, "Should we just do it now while it's nice?"

While there is no reference to it in history books, "Should we just do it now while it's nice?" was likely the second runner-up for the Kansas founders when they chose *ad astra per aspera*—to the stars through difficulties— as our state motto in 1861. Nice days are so rare in Kansas that had we been Mayans we would have recorded them in stone calendars. We are conditioned to know to get stuff done while it is nice because that time will not last. A graveside service is different, however, and we finally decided that it might be odd to the last few family members to arrive and discover he was already in the ground twelve hours earlier, "Because the weather was better."

That next morning, we buried my brother in his Dakota sandstone tomb. The wind howled out of the north; we positioned our pickup trucks as a wind break, but it didn't help much. We couldn't hear my uncle, a Presbyterian minister, deliver beautiful remarks. Luckily the family couldn't hear my other uncle whisper to me as we carried my brother, "Watch him when you put him in. . . . I forgot he'd have shoes on, and his boots are hanging over the board, so you aren't going to have much space." To the credit of the digging crew, my brother fit perfectly into his resting place, and the family began to take turns shoveling the powdered sand and dirt on him in the bitter cold wind. While many helped, the effort I will remember most was by my uncle and cousin who had participated in the dig the day before. The shovel is ultimately a blade, and they are masters of this craft in a way most

Americans no longer are. Like artists managing the exact pitch of a palette knife as they apply oil to a canvas, my cousin and uncle worked the loose pile of rubble with a rhythm that would suggest it had been pudding. They were grieving through their work, inspired toward speed to rescue the rest of the family from standing in the miserable elements. We soon went back inside to escape the wind.

Kansas has a way of searing memories into our human brains with tools other states just don't possess. The wind during my brother's funeral was so horrible; I will always remember it. The weather at Kozicek's was so abnormally lovely that we immediately knew the day was special. For those of us creating an oral tradition in our own lives, there are obvious benefits to living in a state so inhospitable it serves as a memory aid. I also think there is more to it than that.

Kansas is a place without many physical monuments, man-made or natural. Sure, we have our prairie vistas, but those are not the front range of the Rockies, or the Sierras, or the Grand Canyon. In contrast, the nature of Kansas tends toward impermanence. Our prairie plants are designed to be burned, hailed, trampled, eaten, and frozen too early or too late, but then they come right back again. Our sentinel animal species—not just bison but also millions of birds—are nomadic. They never stayed here permanently. Imagine being a two-thousand-year-old redwood on the Kansas prairie. It would never make it! Monumental plants need stable, predictable environments to grow. Kansas is neither stable nor predictable. Our state tree, the cottonwood, specializes in regrowing quickly and throwing millions of cottony seeds to the unending Kansas wind.

As humans, encountering a harsh environment like Kansas fuels our memories, and what is the millennial tradition of humans if it is not built on tradition and shared memories? We have moved forward as a species because of remembering things and sharing those memories with our families and clans. We learn. We share. We advance. In this—a central aspect of the human condition—Kansans excel.

In an emerging era of disconnect, when it seems that memory isn't as important because we have social media feeds that can remind us what we were doing a year ago today, this deeper memory—a memory seared by weather, environment, and place—may be more important than ever.

Consider the history of the Dust Bowl in Kansas. Soil conservation efforts emerged following the harrowing decade of the 1930s, and while those efforts were adopted and then incentivized by the US Department of Agriculture across the country, the conservation efforts of the farmers in this state far exceeded that of their neighbors to the north and east. It could be said that those efforts continue because of necessity, rather than deep, learned memory, but one cannot exist without the other. Kansans know to keep cover on the soil. Kansans know to use terraces in their fields. Kansans know to have a house with a basement despite most of us never having been in an actual tornado. This is deep, learned memory.

Or consider my personal memory of the Progress School. Through oral tradition I know that Helen Sekavec asked my grandfather and his classmates to sing "Whispering Hope" in 1918—an altogether absurd fact for me to remember. But in that same oral tradition I know that she went on to marry Adolph "Hat" Barofsky, and they had two children, Pauline and Robert (Bob). Bob was so bright they were able to send him to Purdue University, which was a real achievement for Ellsworth County Bohemians in the 1940s. Bob was a year away from finishing college when the United States, in a panic about one last push from the Germans, called up yet more American youths, and Bob was among them. These boys weren't even sent to basic training—they were trained how to fire their weapons off the sides of their transport vessels headed to Europe. Bob was killed sometime between Christmas Eve and Christmas Day in the Battle of the Bulge, 1944. The through line of my own memory was as a child and knowing Helen Barofsky, in her early nineties by that point, sitting in the choir loft of our church every year on Christmas Eve silently crying.

When we think about the decision to go to war; when we think about significant policies that have broad impacts—in short, when we govern ourselves, as we in this nation claim to do—we need the long, seared memory of place to guide us. Maybe that is why Kansas has always been a state where the government was vibrant and responsive but also centered. Maybe that is why those of us who live here feel that this is a place that manages to escape the absurd one-sidedness of politics rampant around the rest of the country. We simply remember too much. Our landscape has taught us more than residents of other places.

We had one more laugh about my brother's burial. The whole point of a green burial is to allow the unembalmed body to return to the earth from where it came. Let the body disappear and extend the memory of the living person only through oral and written tradition, as we have done for thousands of years. This natural process can happen quickly in rich soils teeming with active microbiomes. Seth ended up in a natural stone sarcophagus, piled high with inert sand in a landscape so dry his body may be found largely unchanged hundreds of years from now.

I hope that's not the case. But I also know that while humans are obsessed with monuments, the prairie knows how to extend our memories in a less physical fashion, and the prairie also knows how to preserve us in a manner less destructive to our environment. Another little secret of the Dakota formation in central Kansas is the prevalence of leaf fossils in the stone. Perfect imprints, left around sixty-five million years ago, of one of nature's most ephemeral features—seasonal deciduous leaves. Ash, willow, oak, and even sassafras imprints can be found in a spot on my farm, allowing me to ponder the brief lives of these leaves. The prairie remembers, and the prairie helps us remember. We learn. We share. We advance.

Resurgence: Milk Jugs and Duct Tape in the Strip Pits

Al Ortolani

I.

C. T. pounded on the wheel well of his Ford pickup. The hammering carried through the night across the dumps where we were sitting. We considered fishing. It felt like a good night for it, the pit water still, crisp with autumn. We laughed at the thought of C. T. and his impulse for truck repair. A few hours earlier he'd roared into our campsite with a case of cheap beer and a complete campfire burning in the truck bed. He and Steve were grinning like Cheshires through the windshield. They'd gone in search of firewood to last us the night and had returned in a column of smoke. Steve said they'd come upon a bulldozed tree fall; a farmer had set it ablaze and had left it to burn down through the night. They had filled the truck bed with wood, obviously some already burning, stopped for beer at Kirby's and driven back to Crawford State Park. It was a fortuitous find.

At some point after transferring the fire to a clearing on the ground, C. T. decided his oversized tires were rubbing his wheel wells. The tires were valuable, maybe more than the truck. He jacked up the front end, removed the wheel and began hammering out the well. The noise would continue for hours, but it was *his* truck, and *his* sledgehammer. We left him for the big pit near the highway, sat under the stars, and listened to the coyotes, yelping deep in the woods.

At age seventeen the years stretched out endlessly ahead of us. That night we were untroubled. There wasn't anything we couldn't accomplish if given the time. None of us had money, but our families were respected and hard working. Our fathers expected the same of us. If given the choice, they might have joined us in the middle of the night with the coyotes and the last bullfrogs of the season. Our fathers would have brought tackle boxes. They would have fished from john boats with trolling motors. There would have been expectations for their sons.

We loved our fathers as heroes, but we didn't want to become them. Their lives were colored by the Greatest Generation—the Great Depression, World War II, Betsy Ross. If we'd been serious about fishing, we would have pulled a pole from the back of my truck. We couldn't compete with history. It was enough to drink beer and talk about girls. We knew we were young, and, if pressed, would admit that we were naïve. Woodsmoke hung on the edge of the air. C. T. was still feeding the fire. A more serious life was lurking in the months to come. At some point soon, we'd begin to make the transition to become men—college, Vietnam, marriage, and jobs that offered enough money to live on, but not much more. The strip pits were mostly abandoned at night. We liked to believe no one could find us.

Boxed In

Inside the cardboard
beside the patio fence,
the small, wire-necked
turtle, rescued

from the passing lane
on US 69, scratches
and claws against
the fibers of the box.

I hear him clearly
above the hedge clippers
that whir among
the manicured shrubs.

After dark, I drive
the roadside down Drywood Creek.
Stopping among the cattails,
I lift him from his

beer-box, moonlit nails
clawing the night air,
straining for the freedom
of wild onion and sage.

For a moment,
after he has pushed
between the reeds and grasses,
I listen for some

tumbling of the stream,
the owl call, the deer
that jumps the fence
downstream.

II.

One afternoon my mother gave me a copy of Thomas Paine's *Age of Reason*.
I had no idea if she knew what she was handing me, but it rocked the vase
on my nightstand: new thoughts, like no revelation except through natural
creation; the Bible rife with contradictions; church doctrines written by fal-
lible men. The summer before my senior year of high school Thoreau had
begun the quake that cracked the foundation of my worldview. Thomas
Paine kicked down the basement wall. On Sundays I began to skip mass, a
secret I'd keep for months. On Sundays I rode my motorcycle toward the
Newman Center but would veer into the countryside and Oldham's Pits. I
visited a muskrat who'd become a regular acquaintance. We were not close
like a person and a dog are close, but I was growing fond of the Vs he cut
through the water. It's true that I felt closer to the muskrat than to the judg-
mental priest. I never gave the muskrat a name. No one christens a rodent
in the wild, but over time, the strip pits would become my church.

Oldham's Pits were just across the bypass. I could be there in minutes
from my parents' front door. They were mule-dug pits, stripped with a drag-
line, shallow by later giant-shovel standards. The slag piles were overgrown
with sumac, poplars, and new-growth hardwoods. The dirt turnoff from the
highway was unassuming, as quiet as an afterthought. Within fifty yards the
highway noise was muffled as the road became trails. I shut down my bike
and set the kickstand. Oldham's consisted of only a few acres woven with
fishing paths and rabbit runs. Some days I'd walk, other days I'd sit on a log
and listen to the voice in my head, to the leaves on the poplar. I imagined
Thoreau in Concord. On occasion I'd bring a book to read or a notebook
and Bic pen. Nothing would come from my scribblings, but I kept them
near like a secret, like a love poem. One Sunday, inspired by a hawk, I took
off my clothes and swam out to muskrat depth. The hawk beat his wings so

close to my face that I could hear his feathers rustling. Swimming was an attempt for complete immersion. Somewhere a semi was jake-braking around the curve to Fourth Street, but I wasn't listening to the big noise, more to the small twittering of the woods.

My friend Brock Morton had introduced me to Oldham's Pits. He'd gone there for his Junior Academy of Science research, which had something to do with finding balance after artificial imbalance in a Crawford County strip pit. Science baffled me, but I liked the thought of his small boat, the quiet water. He was one of my first friends to keep his own counsel in an age of peer pressure. Once while walking along a railroad track toward Broadway, we found a spill of boxcar grain between the rails. Beans or oats, I don't recall. The dull winter sun shone flatly on the grain. Brock announced as if the entire town were listening that he could live on this for a long time. I didn't say anything. I preferred cheeseburgers.

The irony of "finding nature" on mined land was not lost on me. It would become a growing theme that gave me pause. Whereas Oldham's Pits were west of town and old enough for ash and oak to take root, east of town the steam- and gas-powered shovels were ripping south across the pastures, heaping tall mounds of dirt and clay along half-mile trenches. Here, little growth had found purchase. Access roads ran between the dumps for a mile section. In America, the Vietnam War was at the height of escalation, Martin Luther King and Bobby Kennedy had recently been assassinated. Young men's lives hung on the chance of a lottery system. I did not fear military induction as much as I feared being forced to leave home. I had begun to realize that I'd put down family and community roots, which as a wannabe free spirit embarrassed me. I was working construction to pay my college tuition. My 2-S student deferment was important to me, but mostly I lived in denial. I kept the dark bitumen of war in my chest. After work, I'd shower and eat a light supper. Our house was busy. My parents liked keeping their children at home. Our bones of contention over politics or hair length or religious outlook percolated below the surface. We maintained a fragile détente. I was fortunate in this regard. I was left alone to think what I wanted if I didn't vocalize my thoughts.

Religiously, I drove my Honda east rather than west and rode the new dumps, exploring the striations of the pits, watching them fill with water, alkaline or acid, I never knew which. Some evenings I sat on a mountain of fresh dirt and watched the sun set, the only sound being that of a few distant crows. There was beauty in the colors of desolation. One evening I rode into a tangle of trees and found an early cemetery of ten to fifteen graves. The stones were weathered and etched in nineteenth-century German. Many of the local farmers were of German descent, but I didn't recognize any names. Somewhere nearby there'd been a farm, a community. The shovel's bucket turned the earth in a semi-circle around them.

Muskrat Dump

The afternoon sunlight
warms my back
while woodpeckers drum
hollow limbs in the tree
tangled dumps. A few
remaining persimmons
darken. Wind rustles
the brown undergrowth.
Leaves clatter and snag
on bunch berry vines.
I lie among them like
a branch, fallen
and comfortable with decay.

The pit's green water
crests a canoe, red keel
creasing the surface
like the snout of a muskrat
stretching for the coal slag
shoreline. Overhead
the blue sky is interrupted
only by thoughts
of sleep,
and amazingly, out

of the scrub oak
a December butterfly,
as fragile and temporary as daylight.

III.
In junior high school we were fortunate to have a scoutmaster who was less concerned with rank and scouting etiquette than he was with being

outdoors. Frequently, we set up our canvas tents and camped in the pits. The state of Kansas owned several bison, which were kept fenced at the state park north of Pittsburg. The buffalo (as we called them) grazed a large pasture. Our scoutmaster owned a restaurant in town and had found a way to purchase one of the bison. He brought the troop to the state park, planted us on a hillside, and drove his truck into the pasture. Calmly, he stepped out of the cab, rested his rifle against the door, and shot the bison in the forehead. The animal dropped to his knees and then crumpled to the ground. I knew what was coming, but the animal's collapse startled me; too sudden, like a lightning bolt striking a tree. The bison was winched onto a trailer, carted up to our hillside, and hung with a chain from a thick-limbed elm. He was field dressed at the edge of the road. The experience was visceral. I'd never hunted. I'd never seen an animal butchered in the wild. I was amazed by the bison's sheer size, its immense death and smelly rendering. After the initial shock, I grew surprisingly enthusiastic, maybe because of peer pressure, or the testosterone of the kill, the matter-of-fact rendering of the animal into quarters. A few weeks later, we ate "buffalo burgers" while camping in the same pits. The bison was excellent. A circle that led life into death was completed. I better understood not just our food supply, but the violence of survival. There wasn't a merit badge I could sew on my sash, but the lesson was more real than the embroidery on a cloth patch.

We learned to identify animals by their scat, and by the tracks they left during the night. We mixed plaster of Paris in cans and poured it into the most well-formed tracks. After drying, we lifted them from the dirt with our pocketknives and polished the plaster to a shine with our spit-wet thumbs. Mostly, we found small game, rabbits, opossums, and raccoons. But there were deer and coyotes as well. Coyote casts were especially valuable to us. They were the most allusive, most mysterious, and most compelling. We found a print we were certain was a wolf's, due to its similarity to the coyote and its immense size. Our scoutmaster laughed and said it was just a big dog. The older boys disagreed, and we went along with them, even though wolves had been eradicated from Kansas for years. We believed what we wanted regardless of unwanted facts. At our campsite we added wood to the fire. The smoke bit our noses. We sat in small groups comparing casts, arranging them like playing cards, imagining the muskrats, the dogs that were wolves. As the sun set, the cold seeped into our clothes. We piled straw on the ground in our canvas tents. We heated them with hobo stoves made from cardboard curled inside a No. 10 can and smothered in paraffin. When lit, the stoves burned with a languid yellow flame. An unwatched

stove could set the tents on fire, and the heavy fumes could put us to sleep
forever. Some nights the cold sparked as it hung in the air. We burrowed
into our sleeping bags.

After Graduation Brock and I Rummage in the Strip Pits

where we find bonfires and bedsprings,
Windowpane and chains,
peas and carrots, cans opened, dumped
with lids awry. Rabbit fur and wind,
a cat on a trailer hitch. Lost

love, found love, love unopened. Dumped:
redemption, exemption, conscription, lawful dodging,
pectorals and biceps, anarchy, and demagogues,
high spirits and rebar. Vietnam. *Crime*

and Punishment, War and Peace, Playboy,
war paint, lacquered fruit, poetry, cabinet drawers stripped
of hardware, gutted for the kitchen of dreams. Nothing
and everything sewn in a coat lining. Flying
monkeys stoned on poppies, a scarecrow, a tin man,
a lion, monopolized. Dorothy clicking her heels.

A prayer rug frayed and threadbare, legs tucked,
twisted in half lotus: sweat socks, jungle boots,
pits of alkaline, fishing line, chicken bones,
stink bait, jailbait and maidenhead,
draft card, milkweed, and thistles. Kingfishers swinging
figure eights in an open sky. Kite string. Boots
without strings, tampons with strings, walking
on a string, promises with strings. Dragonflies
on wing. Flight. No strings attached.
The lottery: number 69.

Oily rainbows, old dogs without collars, work
without play. The beginning and the end fixed
like a fish knife, a bayonet. St. Christopher,
St. Anthony, St. Jude. (Every home

has a forwarding address.) St. Francis,
Sister Clare. A weekend with Buddhists.
Plywood, cattails, and rust,
herons and cranes and cactus spines.

Boys peering through bullet holes in a stop sign.

IV.

Deep shaft mining was the first technique used for extracting coal in southeast Kansas. Shafts and tipples dotted the county. The mines' financial success depended on employing a strong workforce. Thousands of immigrants arrived from across Europe to fill the need. They rode the trains from Ellis Island. Arriving in Kansas with little in their pockets, they settled among others who spoke their language. They worked cheap. It was said that if you wanted to walk across the southeast Kansas town of Pittsburg at the turn of the twentieth century and carry on a conversation with residents, you would need to be fluent in as many as five languages: Slovenian, French, German, Polish, and Italian. On the corner of Second and Broadway next to the Europa Hotel and the Frisco Train Depot stood a small building that was once a steamship line office. Tickets could be purchased for direct transatlantic voyages. Many immigrants stepped off the trains from New York and were received by friends and family at this spot. From there they either settled in Pittsburg or were driven to many of the small mining camps sprouting across Crawford and Cherokee Counties. Camps with names like Breezy Hill, Capaldo, and Chicopee; Litchfield, Camp 50, and Ringo; Dunkirk, Radley, and Croweburg. Each camp was clustered around a deep shaft mine with a company store. Today, long after the mines played out, the settlements have survived as unincorporated towns, hamlets clustered along county roads.

Pittsburg is heavily undermined. The location of the shafts were sometimes lost in mining records. There were maps, but I'd never seen them. One morning my grandmother walked out of her backdoor to the garage and discovered her Buick standing on its front bumper, a mine passage having collapsed into a sinkhole. As a boy, I was visibly excited. I wanted to clamber down over the hood and poke my fingers into one of the holes of the "Three Hole Buick." Surely, I could lift it free.

Grandmother lived next to the railroad tracks on Joplin Street, one of Pittsburg's busiest streets on the east side of town. She took me on walks through the train yards, usually at my insistence. I found the clatter of boxcars irresistible. The tracks were interspersed with ragged pastures, fenced for a few equally ragged cows. Sagging barbed fences attempted to keep the cattle contained. Along the eastern border of the rail lines, a series of pits had been dug. These were shallow, dug for clay, rather than coal, kiln-heated for sewer and drainage lines. Long abandoned, the dumps were overgrown with second-growth trees, thickets of vines and briar. At one vantage point the trees opened on a dell; a shadowy clearing showed remnants of a campfire, littered with cook cans and empty whiskey bottles. Grandmother called it a hobo jungle, and she refused to move more than a few feet from the railroad berm. The tone of her voice evoked fear, the wariness of a woman with a boy in tow. This was a different world for a boy whose father worked at the university. I was drawn to the men who built the fire and ate from cans. I liked the colorful labels on their whiskey bottles. I wanted to pick through their campsite like an archeologist or a junkman. The dumps ached with history.

Another string of pits ran north of the Kansas City Southern shops beyond the round house, a good spot to catch a boxcar or to jump free to avoid the railroad yard. These were the Twenty-Third Street dumps. They were more extensive than the ones near my grandmother's. Like those near her Park Street home, they had provided shelter for tramps and hobos, but they were seldom used after World War II. Twenty-Third Street was criss-crossed with bicycle and motorcycle trails. Our parents told us not to talk to the bums on the tracks. Although a few still walked the rails, we didn't pay much attention to them. Mostly, we were too busy learning to ride motorcycles on the dirt trails. The occasional lone man walking the edge of the jungle kept his distance. He meant little to us.

Toward the Missouri state line, a motocross track was bulldozed out of the dumps. A local businessman was trying to turn a buck out of the strip pits. The track was well made, and for a brief period it brought in cyclists from across the four-state area. A house trailer was moved onto the property. An older friend had taken up residence to keep an eye on things. As a senior in high school, I had worked out that I wasn't a motocross racer. I didn't have the right bike or the fearless racing temperament. My interests had grown more literary and philosophical. Books were safer than motorcycles. Thoreau wouldn't be caught dead riding a knobby-tired dirt bike. Besides, I didn't know the difference between a carburetor and a crankshaft.

One evening I was riding around town with Brock Morton, who was famous among us for his mechanical skill and his asthma. We decided to ride out to the new dirt track to visit Sam, the older friend who was "keeping his eye on the property." We drove the dirt road across the low-water bridge at Rocky Ledge and through the ruins of Litchfield. The trailer's interior design was a blend between a storage garage and a college apartment. Motor parts lay on the kitchen counter next to boxes of Frosted Flakes. Sam's bed consisted of a sleeping bag on a mattress. It may have been mildew, but something in the air kick-started Brock into a full-throttle asthma attack. He reached for his inhaler only to find that the rubber ball was missing. It must have been lost on the road. "Old school" nebulizers consisted of basically two parts, one that held the medicine, the other a rubber squeeze ball on a small hose. It took both parts to work. I volunteered to drive back through the dark to hunt for the rubber ball. My best guess was that it had dropped out of his jacket pocket when we bounced across the iron bridge that spanned Cow Creek. Brock insisted there wasn't time. I drummed my fingers on the table, waiting for him to pass out. He asked Sam if he had any plastic milk jugs. Sam stepped outside the trailer and dug through the trash. He returned with a gallon container. Puzzled, I rinsed out the old milk and then partially filled the jug with tap water. Sam found a roll of duct tape, and Brock taped the inhaler to the open end of the jug. His face was beginning to pale. His breath grew shorter. He lowered his head and put his mouth over the inhaler. As instructed, I hit the sides of the jug as hard as I could. The trapped air, now with increased pressure, passed through the inhaler, forcing the medicine into his lungs. Harder, Brock said. I hit the jug once, twice, harder each time. Brock stood up and untapped the inhaler. That's better, he said. Sam cheered. Brock Morton lived. Sam praised his quick thinking. If there was a metaphor that fit living in the strip pits, it had something to do with milk jugs and duct tape.

A Strip Mine Resurgence

In her charcoal a catfish
wallows in the shallows,
curved like a Gurkha
and knifed between arrowhead plant
and water lilies.
The afternoon sunlight flattens
a warm plastic sky
stippled with dragonflies.
The artist sits on a shoal of slag,
Tevas splattered with grainy muck,

notebook on her knees.
Each sketch is young with contradiction,
heron wings and beer cans,
glittering glass, a fishing line,
kingfishers
darting against the pit water.

A wand of cane, a cattail
caught by a blackbird, the chocolate
shine of the water turtle's shell
shimmers like a window of wavy glass
and she is pulled by the heat
into a languor, her charcoal
fading along the edges of the paper
into a sort of haze, the heat
smoothing sharp lines and softening
the morning's muscle. Suddenly,

she is lifting her Peruvian skirt
and wading into
the reflection of cottonwoods
cool against her thighs.

V.

After college, I traded my motorcycle for a Volkswagen bus, a Westphalia
camper with a pop-up roof. It was old, but I felt confident in its ability to
keep running. The camper had a folding table and a bench seat, an ice box,
and a sink that hadn't worked for years. A dome light lit up above the table.
The strip mines had always been my Walden woods, the pits like a poor
man's version of Melville's ocean. I retreated to them when full-catastrophe
living became overwhelming. By this time, I was reading Edward Abbey
and Loren Eisley. Abbey wrote of monkey-wrenching industry's machine,
draining the oil from earth movers, chainsawing billboards into kindling.
Eisley wrote with a calm melancholia about kicking puffballs into the wind
and discovering the little wildernesses that existed along roadsides and for-
gotten hedgerows. If he found a starfish on the beach, he tossed it back into
the ocean. It was possible to embrace both writers as environmentalists.
Tree huggers. In his later years, Eisley wrote that he'd begun to sleep at night
with his arms folded across his chest, as if practicing for what was to come.

On his death, Abbey's body was spirited away in secret to some unknown burial in the desert to be forgotten to time like the German graves in the pits.

One summer night, I was sitting in my Volkswagen west of Pittsburg, not far from Rocky Ledge. I was feeling very alone. I had been writing for so long that I'd lost my sense of place and time. My dome light created a wallow-like shelter, a respite of solitude. Suddenly, I was startled by a loud snorting noise. A chill ran down my spine. Something unknown but large by its sound had discovered the bus. I was unnerved by the sudden incursion into my privacy, the thought of not being alone, of being swallowed by the woods, as if I were a specimen of cricket or muskrat. At the edge of the trees a wide pasture joined the rest of Kansas, wild and open to the wind. The lights of Arma and Girard glowed on the horizon. For a moment, I wanted to start the motor and drive away. Within the pits there was a sentience I couldn't place. Maybe that of a raccoon thumped by a truck bumper. Maybe a deer clearing its nostrils of mushrooms. My neck muscles tensed. I felt if I kept writing, I'd disappear. When I parted the bus curtains, all I could see was the reflection of my face in the window glass.

Where a Deer Fell

my daughter uncovers bones,
overgrown with briar, glued to soil
by leaf meal and frost.
The forest floor clings as
we lift the skull into light, examining the
little spirit that remains,
the brittle nostrils opened to wind, the eyes filled
with the shadows of small ponds.

Shoots of honeysuckle, green briar, and grape,
a tendril of ivy and finger of mandrake
push through the spinal canal, separate
vertebrae, disjoin knee from shank and hip from thigh,
encircle a bleached jaw, tie the toothy
mandible like stone to earth, lacing the caved ribs
with vine, pulling the whitened
bones into flesh.

VI.

Brock Morton moved to Europe and helped with research on the alpine tundra. He would learn to ski. He traveled to Africa and climbed Kilimanjaro alone. He never saw Hemingway's leopard. I stayed in the strip pits, began publishing a few poems, and raised children. I sold my Volkswagen at an estate auction and bought a used Jeep CJ-7. I kept a small tent and a sleeping bag behind the back seat. I would drive into the strip pits to sit beside the water. As the darkness drew close, fish breeched the pit's surface. The occasional owl hooted across the water. I found it amusing, ironic, that I could regain my composure on land broken by machines and stripped of its resources by eastern corporations. Little was kept of the countryside's original shape, but a beauty remained. For the most part, there was little economy to be had in its ragged timber, except that derived by coyotes and fox. Personally, that was fine by me. I was reminded of the early miners who, in the heat of summer, company homes too stifling for rest, carried their blankets out to Breezy Hill to sleep where the wind blew cooler.

Today, it appears that I have followed the rail lines north to Kansas City. My children have children of their own. We live near each other. It's a good life, but I miss the easy access to the strip pits. Mining in southeast Kansas has virtually shut down. Land is being reclaimed. The dumps graded into rolling countryside, the pits turned into neighborhood ponds or sloped into watering holes for cattle. My friend Brock has returned from his travels and lives in a small house in Pittsburg. He owns a car but prefers to walk. I suppose he's still looking for another boxcar to spill a load of grain, one that he can live on for years.

Summer Storm among the Strip Pits

I have parked on a dump that overlooks
the water. Kingfishers slap surface,
dip and cut wide figure eights, lifting

like flapping hands into the sky.
Rain comes, peppering the surface
like thousands of winged insects, tapping

light fingers against the roof of my van.
Curtains blow. From the tops of poplars
I hear the wind moan, turning the alkali

over upon itself, the clay mixing
with gray shale, trickling
down from the tailings. The small soil

that runs between roots of a willow
clouds the vacant water
and spreads like the spawn of fish.

Refugia

Traci Brimhall

I didn't know I loved Kansas, with its wind skirling
through the arms of windmills, its fields gravid
with lavender, its subscriptions for sunflowers.

I thought I was pollen complaint and water hunger.
I didn't know I loved the hopeful ugliness of cygnets,

or that a group of vultures is called a wake, or that
a skull oxbows with a signature unique as a fingerprint.
I thought I loved to verb through the days, but spring

annulled that marriage, giving me to stillness. I didn't
know I would also love the discourse of chickadees

in the redbud and insects at rest on my books, their legs
testing the strength of n's and o's before flitting off.
I didn't know I would also love the sundial's secretarial

shadow. I'd forgotten I loved the blue of afternoon—
bold, bare, the white of ecstasy at its edges, the lyric

bending me over its knees. I'd forgotten how to
recite the rosary long distance, but I knew I loved
Latin in the shower. I didn't know I loved using

my breath to make a page of the mirror and draw
vines of vanishing roses with my ring finger. I didn't

know I loved wasps when I set the nest on fire. I only
meant to protect my son from his rushed in and out
through the door, but I watched them pull pearled eggs

from muddy tunnels, and I knew. I didn't know I loved
raccoons raiding day-old cheeseburgers from trash cans.

I once loved brass bands and free boat rides, but now
I love hammers for hanging pictures and telescopes
for imagining a future with mix tapes of denim and

rhinestone rodeos, my face unmasked, my arm brushing
a stranger's. Even now I love the stout pulses of magicians

and the salads my son makes from the wild in our yard—
the bitter dandelion greens, chickweed, henbit. I'd forgotten
I'm good at survival, too, that I've taught my son the uses

of the earth. Each day we walk one block further, our own
sympathetic magic, a ritual to ask the world to let us return.

I know I will love tomorrow's moon as it coats its smell
on mint. I'll love the drip torch bathing last year's grasses in fire.
I know hope is a discipline but so is the dark heat falling

toward me, a citation of grief, a joy ready to welcome a late
continue, to fly open the door for my son, already running.

Let Kansas Be Kansas

Jeffrey Ann Goudie

Eating dinner out with friends a while back, my pal Marcia asked us sister transplants from other states how we felt when we first moved to Kansas. Except for me, all expressed negatives, although each had made peace with her adopted state. I had moved from Texas.

"I felt like I took a step up," I said.

"What did you like about Kansas?" my friend Harriet pursued.

"Deciduous trees," I said, borrowing a quip a friend made on returning to the Midwest from Miami.

I was a transplant connected to Kansas through my late maternal grandmother. I loved the trees that shed their leaves, but also the green rolling hills around my grandmother's farmhouse. Mind you, my grandma was not a landowner. She rented the bottom floor of a farmhouse off Lackman Road in Lenexa, then a tiny town, now a sprawling Johnson County suburb.

My love of northeast Kansas is braided with my affection for my spunky grandmother. At that time Hollie worked at the old Rexall Drug in the Mission Shopping Center. In a crisp waitress uniform, my five-foot-tall grandmother presided as assistant manager of the lunch counter, alongside her young friend Ronnie, the "soda jerk." Hollie dyed her hair henna under the influence of her best friend at the drug store, Willie, the beauty and makeup department manager.

My mother took us to see her mother on summer trips from our West Texas home of Midland, where my father worked as a geologist. Midland saw sparse rainfall, and although my father, a Kansas City, Missouri, native, planted fir trees and a water-hungry willow in our yard, Midland was flat, dry, and dusty, scraped by tumbleweeds. In the Land of the High Sky, few trees interrupted the wide view.

For many folks who live on the coasts, Kansas and Texas appear much the same: retrogressive politically and uninteresting geographically. We residents know our states at the granular level. Southwest from the oil capital of Midland is Marfa, the hip artist mecca. Texas has the exurban sprawl of Dallas and Houston, but also the more striking vastness of Big Bend

National Park. The state capitol in Austin has been overseen by one of the most conservative governors in the United States. But Austin and Houston are among the most racially diverse, politically liberal populations in the nation.

Kansas also defies stereotyping. The state is not uniformly flat. Gentle hills surround Topeka, where I live, and steeper hills surround and intersect Lawrence. West of Topeka, the Flint Hills contain the country's largest remaining tallgrass prairie ecosystem. Our Smoky Hills sport rugged sandstone and limestone bluffs. Spare, beautiful chalk formations rise up in western Kansas, remnants of an inland sea.

Nor is Kansas bland. Lawrence, Topeka, Kansas City, and Wichita have storied traditions in barbecue and Mexican food. Garden City and other southwestern Kansas towns are enriched by immigrants working in the meatpacking and service industries. Dozens of languages are spoken in Garden City public schools. Topeka is home to the National Historical Park site celebrating the landmark *Brown v. Board of Education* decision that outlawed segregated schools. As for racial diversity, both of my widely spaced children attended Topeka High School, which has a majority minority population.

The geographies of my native state and my adopted state influence our politics. The sheer size of Texas spawns a bigger-and-better swagger. Kansas, a rectangle in the center of the country, radiates a common-sense, level-headed attitude.

A month after the dinner with my transplanted pals, I asked a friend who grew up in the Dallas area what she saw as the difference between Texas and Kansas.

"I used to think Kansas was progressive," said this Texas native. "Now, not so much."

I understand her sentiment. Just as Kansas is subtly beautiful, its politics have historically been nuanced. Founded by Abolitionists, Kansas has so far mostly resisted the fringes of the extreme far right. In line with a progressive tradition of women in politics, Laura Kelly became our third female governor in 2019. Kansas boasts a history of leadership in public health (think Dr. Samuel J. Crumbine of "Don't Spit on the Sidewalk" fame) and mental health (the Menninger Clinic was founded in 1925 in Topeka). The Kansas Supreme Court in 2019 ruled that the state's constitution protected a woman's right to abortion. That right to women's bodily autonomy was resoundingly reinforced in the first post-Roe statewide referendum in 2022. After the August 2 victory, I heard from far-flung friends. My high school best friend, living in Dallas, emailed to say the victory gave her hope. A college roommate who grew up in Kansas, now residing in New Mexico, expressed awe and gratitude.

But if Kansas has historically been complicated, subtle, and nuanced, it, like much of the rest of the country, faces forces who dislike nuance, forces who want to turn back the clock, ignoring science, diversity, and women's right to reproductive autonomy, which the anti-choice forces continue to push against, despite the 2022 landslide victory.

Texas can be Texas—bigger, badder. But I don't want Kansas to become a crude, simplistic state, shaped by punitive, restrictive laws.

Let Kansas be Kansas in all its vaunted practicality, shaped by the muscle memory of our state's proud progressive history.

A Mexican in Kansas: Self-Portrait in Four Parts

Armando Minjárez Monárrez

Los Files—The Fields

We could hear the crackle of the tires against the asphalt as the truck slowly pulled up out front, and before he had a chance to honk we'd already be rushing the wooden steps and down the red brick path. I didn't like him honking at us; it felt rude to make such a ruckus at 6 a.m. Truth be told, most people around our block were also getting picked up for work.

Lonchera in hand, we'd jump in the back of the truck camper, greet whoever was in there today, find a comfortable spot among the shovels, and set out on our forty-five-minute journey to the fields, from Ulysses to Montezuma. That drive always felt hypnotic; I think that's why I liked it: like taking an anesthetic, a minimalist landscape lulling us to sleep. Now I understand that to be called disassociation.

In bold black letters across the water tower, I read the word *Montezuma*. "That's not how you spell that," I thought. "Moctezuma; it's spelled Moc-te-zu-ma." It was an uncanny moment, reading a word with such deep personal meaning in a place so seemingly different from where the word originated.

Did I just travel to an alternate reality? A plane of existence where the mountains are flattened, and Mexicans don't speak Spanish but have skin darker than mine, and Mennonites don't speak Spanish but still live apart from us, and Moctezuma was not a *tlahtoāni* but a town, and cowboys raised cattle for slaughter but don't eat their tongues.

The summer sun was beaming above our heads, tall, luminous, and hot.

Our task was straightforward: to clear the tall weeds from the Kansas crop fields using our hands and a peculiar little shovel. Day after day, we trudged through fields of sorghum, wheat, milo, and corn, methodically moving back and forth along the rows. The summer sun beat down relentlessly, our bodies craving some relief from the heat, and in the distance, the sight of sprinklers approaching. "Agua!" I screamed to my brother and my friend.

We didn't know the hardest part of the day had just arrived. While reaching the sprinklers offered a much-needed cooling relief, what followed was a grueling, slow-motion battle through the freshly soaked muddy trenches stretched across the square-mile fields. Each step felt like pulling your foot out of a suction cup, only to sink deeper with the next. We dug deep into the earth, mud clinging to us like a second skin. Over and over, back and forth until the sun is low and the mud is dried and the Gatorade is gone, and you can finally eat the last burrito your mamma packed for lunch at 5 a.m.

My journey with Kansas began with migration from the outset. Kansas entered my consciousness when my older brother relocated from Chihuahua to Ulysses when I was ten. By the time I turned twelve, I visited for the first time this distant land I had only seen on TV during *El Mago de Oz*, or in imaginary constructions made of fragments I gathered from letters and phone calls and conversations I was not supposed to hear. My permanent move to Kansas in 2001 marked the beginning of the latter half of my life, introducing me to some of the most formidable and fulfilling experiences so far.

Having grown up snuggled by the Sierra Madre, I was offered a more austere and erratic welcome by my new home's plains. As would be any teenager plucked from their root system, I wasn't happy about this fateful move.

But I grew and endured and explored—from the high plains in western Kansas, to the rolling hills of the Kanza prairie, and to the geological formations from ancient oceans—and I began to understand the poetic propositions in this vast prairie.

I've seen clouds of orange and violet and pink sail across the vast sky, a spectacle so generous, so inconceivable that I try to memorialize it in a photograph over and over and over again, yet I always fail in that futile exercise.

Come springtime, I love waking up to the kind touch of the Kansas sunrise, and maybe, later, be jolted to my core by the force of an angry gray storm that swirls and whirls with such ease and grace across the plains. I can only describe it like a movie set, or a play where you have front-row seats on your very own porch, safe from the storm's inescapable destruction. The Kansas storm, often distressing, always irresistible.

But you know what they say: after the storm everything is calm, or maybe it's the calm after the storm? Either way, what comes after the storm in Kansas is an invitation to explore a crisp blue sky, expressive greens, and bright filtered light, accompanied by a thunderous symphony of avian superstars.

The Kansas landscape is unequivocally volatile, but as I see it, always provides an opportunity for an ongoing meditation on humility, a daily exercise on self-reflection.

El Vaquero—The Cowboy

One year for my birthday, my brother gifted me as a joke a pair of pink cowboy boots. Despite growing up in northern Mexico, where cowboy culture still reigns supreme, I never really was a fan of wearing cowboy attire, exotic leather boots, a matching belt, and fancy felt sombreros. This fact didn't change after moving to rural Kansas, a place where the cow population is nearly double the number of people.

Despite Hollywood trying to sell us its Wild West fantasies, all cowboys are not the same. These Mexican cowboys are different. Their outfits are less about cowboying and more about catching a pretty girl's eye—much like a bird does, fluffing its colorful feathers and performing a fancy dance, and, if lucky, mate, build a nest, start a family, and get a well-paying job at the oil rigs, or at the feedlots, and eventually buy a truck that signifies you've reached the elusive American Dream. Or something like that.

Two distinct versions of a cowboy, both hyper masculine and homophobic all the same.

The few times I dared to go to a rodeo at the fairgrounds, a summer affair to show off your best western outfits and watch for impossibly tight Wranglers, I would wear my fashionable (and very flammable) shiny nylon outfits with chrome accessories and gelled hair, as if plucked from a pop music video in the early 2000s.

This feeling of sticking out like a sore thumb became a familiar one. My classmates, Mexican immigrant teens with whom I shared most mornings in the ESL classroom, loved their *música ranchera*, exotic pointy boots, and Bud Light, but that just wasn't for me. My interests were just as banal as theirs; they were just less "cowboy-ey." I wanted to perfect my spiky hairdo, spending hours in front of the mirror desperately twisting and turning and propping strands of hair with sticky goo of industrial strength, just to be defeated by the relentless natural curling of my black hair. Just like I was trying to turn these curls into spikes and failed time after time, I too wanted to fit in, but to be myself meant I didn't really have an option.

Once again, that uncanny feeling of familiarity while in a strange place.

Although I didn't indulge in their fashion expression, I did indulge in the feathery dance part—a lot. I eventually found my people, an eclectic group of weirdos who loved ditching school and driving to a nearby town for an afternoon vacation, or to the middle of a random field to listen to loud music and drink, or—my favorite—going to *bailes* on the weekends to dance for as long as we were allowed.

Quinceañeras? We were there.

Weddings? Yes please.

Grupos norteños? Uh huh.

We would routinely travel fifty, seventy, a hundred miles to dance to *música ranchera, corridos y cumbias* like there was no tomorrow. Our precarious legal status meant we didn't know what tomorrow would bring, but no one does, I guess.

For most of us, on any day, our life in this faraway land could be upended by a simple random police stop, or worse, an ICE stop. Either scenario likely set off for driving while Mexican.

To be yourself meant to stick out like a sore thumb, whether you wore gator pointy boots or black pleather pants. To be Mexican meant, for some, that we were all the same.

Make Your Own Mexican

I was driving into Dodge City, eastbound on Highway 50, looking for this really tall Mexican cowboy. I finally spotted him down Third Street.

There he was, La Salsa Man, standing tall, on his own pad, with a fresh coat of paint.

Then I saw them, the conchas, as in pan dulce conchas, the pillowy shell pan dulce with the crackly top.

I could not believe it: La Salsa Man was wearing pink gator cowboy concha boots. What?!

I took a closer look at the boots and quickly realized he was in fact wearing dress shoes, shoelaces and all, and the boots were painted over the original design.

How did La Salsa Man go from an Americana soda jerk to a Mexican cowboy waiter delivering guacamole, chips, and a cerveza?

La Salsa Man is a modified Muffler Man, that quintessential mid-century roadside fiberglass fixture that populated US highways during the heyday of car travel. Muffler Men were made up of random body parts, like a thirty-foot-tall Frankenstein GI Joe doll. Over the years, Muffler Men across the country have continued to go through many transformations, relocations, and reinventions.

Our Muffler Man, now known as La Salsa Man, started as a soda jerk at the Frosty Freeze restaurant in Malibu, California, and was known in the area as Malibu Man. In the mid-1980s, Bob "Daddy-O" Wade was commissioned by the restaurant's new owner to transform Malibu Man into El Salsero, to better fit the restaurant's very own transformation into a Mexican food establishment.

At some point, El Salsero moved from Malibu to Dodge City, Kansas, and experienced yet another transformation, albeit a less dramatic one, into La Salsa Man. After a hiatus from public view that lasted several years, La Salsa Man made a comeback to Dodge City public life after going through a restoration process.

He now stands proudly—and awkwardly—right next to a huge panoramic mural by Stan Herd that depicts the American fantasy of the Old West landscape. Much like what I experienced after arriving in Ulysses for the first time, these two expressions of "cowboyness" coexist in the same space, both projecting truth and fantasy of what we should want to be.

Both La Salsa Man and conchas share complicated and layered histories that over time, and over generations, have created what they are today. Conchas, like many things Mexican, are an amalgamation of techniques, ingredients, processes, and ideas accumulated over generations after the European colonization of American territories started.

Conchas are made of an enriched dough that possibly evolved from the French brioche bread in colonial Mexico bakeries. Indigenous cooking traditions and techniques were mixed and remixed with European ones, creating a new version made up of fragments, from here and from there.

La Salsa Man has also gone through its own transformation time and time again, holding remnants of a past life, from here and from there.

Both the concha and La Salsa Man can hold a tension many of us live with every day: that our totality is made of fragments, but the whole is something else besides the parts.

The Space Between

Ni de aqui ni de alla, roughly translated into English as "from neither here nor there," is an expression long used in Mexico to describe a personal turmoil of belonging and displacement, a type of identity crisis that simultaneously accepts and rejects one's connection to any one particular place and culture.

"Do you really not speak Spanish, or are you just pretending not to speak it because you're embarrassed of being Mexican?"

Yeah, *now* I can see how this question was loaded.

My bad.

I didn't really understand why there were so many Mexican Americans or Chicanos in Kansas. They owned restaurants, lots of restaurants, they were in elected office, they were in law enforcement, they were school principals, they worked at the bank and at the grocery store.

There were the second-generation Chicanos, the OGs from the Chicano Movement, who were often older and spoke Spanish with a heavy accent. To me it sounded like an old-school rural Mexican Spanish accent, which makes sense, I suppose.

Then there were the third- or fourth-generation Chicanos, often Gen X and millennials, many of whom no longer spoke or understood Spanish, and if they did, it was so limited they avoided it at all costs. Then there were the first-gen Chicanos—this is my generation, my contemporaries, mostly millennials. They spoke Spanish fluently, though with a discernible accent, and they actively participated in social life with us.

Us, "the illegals."

We were also stratified by our own classes: the ones who crossed with a visa, now expired; the ones who crossed illegally; the ones who got papers back in 1986; those who were deported and came back; those who had kids here; those who brought their kids along; and those who left them behind.

The ones who liked school, and the ones who dropped out to start making money. The ones who went to the Catholic church, and the ones who became Protestant. The ones who marched and demanded rights, and the ones who told us we were better off staying low and docile because "this isn't our country" and "we have to behave" and "don't make the gringos angry because they can call *la migra*."

Sensationalized as something new and threatening in the media, our transborder migration continues a long-standing pattern of peoples' movement across invented geographies, from time immemorial. Because of this, we often express a poignant sentiment: we didn't cross the border; rather, the border crossed us.

While the US heartland may outwardly appear quintessentially "American," it has in fact undergone a process of Mexicanization, or re-Mexicanization. Much of the US western territory was part of Mexico until its annexation 1846.

Today, Ulysses, as well as many other communities in western Kansas, are what we clumsily call "majority minority communities," with over 50 percent of their population self-identifying as having Latine or Hispanic heritage. The rawness of self-expression manifests in our brightly painted houses, decorated with silk flowers and elaborate altars for the Virgen de Guadalupe, and presents an aesthetic of intensity that challenges the public denial of our existence.

In this journey, I have reconciled the fact that my identity is in a constant state of flux, yielding to and resisting the pressures of an ever-changing environment. I believe that the ability to adapt defines the essence of the Kansas identity.

From when Native American tribes traversed the plains in search of sustenance during the warmer months, to the European settlers who made the plains a permanent home during westward expansion, to the Kansans of the new millennium, challenging archaic and oppressive ideologies, each chapter expands a shared Kansas legacy of resilience and self-determination.

I once read a tale of a young Toltec man seeking knowledge to become a shaman, understanding one night that although he himself is made of stars, he is not a star but rather the space between them:

He was light.

Ad astra per aspera.

De aqui y de alla.

Golden State

Becky Mandelbaum

As these things go, we left Kansas on the hottest week of the year. A red rash burned over the weather map as Alec and I shoved everything we owned Tetris-style into a U-Haul, which we then dragged across the prairie and desert, completely bypassing the pretty parts. In Denver I suggested a day hike, but Alec ruptured his Achilles tendon playing Ultimate Frisbee in college (an injury I never entirely believed), so anything athletic was strictly out of the question.

The drive carried on, all garbled talk radio and forest green mile markers and Alec listing off things we needed to do once we got to California: buy a box fan, change our mailing address, get a parking permit. Boring, boring, boring. Around Vegas I asked if he'd ever go hiking with me. He turned to look at me, revealing soft pockets of darkness under his eyes. He hadn't slept the night before—at dawn I found him sitting upright in the hotel bed reading *Les Miserables*, shoveling ranch-flavored corn nuts into his mouth.

"You're free to go hiking without me," he said.

"But I want to go together."

"We'll do other things together." He was using his lecherous voice—he reached over and squeezed my thigh. "Did I mention I'm glad you're coming with me?"

"Well, nobody wants to move alone."

He kept his eyes on the road. "That is the kind of comment I will choose to ignore."

I was not without a point. So far, he'd seen to it that the move lacked all romance. He put a deposit down on the house in California without consulting me and then fell asleep an hour into our going-away party, snoring away on the sofa as my friends and I danced to "Girls Just Want to Have Fun" on the coffee table beside him. Most of our conversations over the past few weeks had revolved around how to best pack his dishware. At one point I asked if he thought I was his assistant. "If you were my assistant," he said, "I'd be paying you."

I turned and watched the desert spit out tumbleweed. It was just like in the spaghetti westerns, all red sand and saguaros. About every other minute a semi came hurtling past us, plastic truck nuts swinging from the trailer hitch.

Already, I missed Kansas.

California was supposed to be better in every way: better food, better weather, better people. In movies, the West Coast was a utopia of beaches and liberal politics, hippies high-fiving scientists at the farmers market. Meanwhile, redwoods and cheap tacos and Yosemite! My Kansas friends feigned jealousy, although they too were heading out for other lands: Madrid, Seattle, a rustic lodge in the Rocky Mountains.

Alec had his own campaign, whose main platform was that California was not Kansas: no snowstorms or tornados or governors trying to arm children with rifles. Plus, he'd gotten a job near Sacramento, teaching French literature at a university. The job didn't pay well, but it was—back to his main point—very much not in Kansas.

The university town was not by water or mountains, but somewhere vaguely between—the Central Valley. "It's the best of both worlds!" Alec promised. He had promised many things over the course of our relationship: that he would only smoke cigarettes after sundown, that I could borrow his car without asking so long as I was sober, that he would love me ferociously. This was his word: ferociously. So far, he'd made good on everything, which I credited to his advanced age. He was twelve years older than me and had been my French teacher.

Technically he was a lecturer—he had his eyes on tenure that would likely never be his, because as much as he wanted to be French, the truth was that his real name was Alex and he came from a poor farming town in upstate New York where people ate pigs' feet and married their first cousins. That his life and career were turning into something of a failure was entirely his problem, and yet sometimes it felt like my own. I'd just graduated with a degree in linguistics and couldn't think of anything better to do than follow him. What was a young woman supposed to do with her life? The answer probably should have been: Anything! Everything! She's politically liberated! But something in my gut—perhaps fear masquerading as love—was urging me to stick with Alec. Plus, I had very little money.

"You're making a big mistake" was what my mother told me.

"But I'm in love," I said.

"Love has weak legs. You'll see."

I told her I'd prove her wrong, but I could hear the uncertainty in my voice. At this point, the doom feelings were compacted into a small kernel, located somewhere behind my belly button.

Our house in the Central Valley cost three times more than the one-bedroom we'd shared in Lawrence and was, I should mention, not really a "house." Granny cottage, they called it—whoever they were. At best, it was a room in which someone had accidentally left a sink and a toilet. At worst, it was an architectural side note to the larger, two-story mission-style home in which a history professor and a veterinarian lived with their litter of blond offspring. We were there to help pay the mortgage.

Inside, Alec's head scraped against the ceiling, where a network of cobwebs stretched from corner to corner like prayer flags. In the kitchen, I put my arms out and twirled like a ballerina, my fingers grazing the cabinets. There were two rooms, one of which was the bathroom. An image came to my mind of a mastiff and a dachshund forced into a gerbil cage.

"Cozy," Alec said, and forced a smile that read: *Do not panic or girlfriend will panic.*

I said, "As a womb. Or a very, very small, overpriced home."

We got to work unpacking and ended up making okay-but-sort of-forced love on the kitchen linoleum. This is how we discovered the cockroaches. I'd never seen one up close before. Kansas had all sorts of critters—millipedes, brown recluses, cicadas—but nothing as Kafkaesque as a cockroach. Like a rotted thumbnail with legs.

"They say when the world ends, it'll just be all cockroaches and Twinkies," Alec said. He was naked, dust on his thighs.

"Where do you want to be when the world ends?" I asked.

He stared up at the ceiling, thinking. "Maybe the ocean. Watching the waves." He turned to look at me. "What about you?"

There was only one answer I could think of, and because I didn't know better, I figured it must be the truth. "I'd want to be right here," I told him. "With you."

Alec started school, and I started researching the state of California, specifically the Central Valley. I had the time—the days had begun to stretch outward in all directions, expanding along with the cosmos. The mornings were temperate, but by noon the house was an inferno; there was no air-conditioning unit (the house being not really a house), and so I grew to worship the monstrous box fan that stood by the window, whirring like a jet engine. At night, Alec grew damp with sweat so that sleeping with him was like sleeping with a man-sized baked potato. My time in bed was spent wrestling with the sheets, dreaming of house fires and prairie burns. Most of my REM cycles came in the languid afternoons, when I'd fall into naps deep as a miner's hole. When I woke up—startled by the sound of an ambulance or the feeling of sweat gliding across my stomach—I had to crawl my way back to reality, back to the scorching surface of my new life.

My research paid off in a bad way. I learned that California was running out of water, that there were too many people compressed into too little space too far from natural water sources. Even in Kansas, I'd been complicit: the production of a single California walnut required five gallons of water, and I liked to eat my walnuts by the handful. I learned that the college town where we now lived had played host to a series of freak tragedies: stranglings, decapitations, body parts Saran-wrapped and left in dumpsters. Even nature seemed bent on retaliation. More than four people had died after driving into the same eighty-year-old magnolia tree. Further research suggested the tap water might cause organ cancer and that rabid bats roamed the treetops after sundown.

Where had Alec brought me? Better question: Why had I let him?

The first week, Alec came home before dinnertime, tired and grumpy. His office was hot, and the students were stupid.

"I thought this was supposed to be a world-class public university," I said.

He brought a tub of mint chip ice cream from the freezer and hacked at it with a fork. He was on a medicine that made him crave sugar—on more than one occasion I'd caught him in bed at dawn, a salad bowl of Lucky Charms in his lap. "They're just rich kids who want to stay rich," he said. "All they really want to do is design drugs or build robots. They just need my class for the language credit."

"You're saying not one of them actually cares about learning a new language?"

Something flickered in his eyes, a premonition of danger. "There's one girl—her father's a diplomat. She already knows Italian and Spanish. It's like teaching a fish to drink water."

"A girl?"

He shoveled more ice cream into his mouth. "Don't worry, she's probably gay. They're all gay here. And Marxist."

I grabbed the tub of ice cream, brought it to my face, and licked the surface.

"Gross," Alec said, yanking the tub from me. "What's the matter with you?"

"It's mine," I said, pointing to the ice cream. "Everything I touch is mine."

He winced. Sometimes this happened: I played baby, he played dad. "Have you thought about looking for a job?" he said. "They're hiring at the cafeteria."

"I have a degree in *linguistics*."

"And my barista has a PhD in philosophy. Get over yourself." He stood and took the ice cream to the living room, which meant he relocated it about a yard east of the kitchen table.

"I want to take a class," I called to him. "I'm wasting my potential here."

He did not look at me but instead turned on the television. "It's your life. Do what you want."

I decided that academia was stupid, and so I signed up for a woodworking class I planned to pay for with the rent money I would withhold from Alec. I'd recently read an article in *The New Yorker* about a novelist who claimed to have learned everything she needed to know about writing from her years laying brick in Indiana. Surely woodworking would open up some dusty cellar door in my soul, revealing a room of glittering treasure.

The class was held in a Presbyterian church. I thought of Santa's elves and Jesus and wooden crosses, wondering if there was something inherently spiritual about carpentry, or if Jesus just happened to be good at making stuff.

I'd expected plaid-wearing twenty-somethings, but the class was mostly old men and New Age moms. We started with introductions. When I said I was from Kansas the class let out a collective coo, as if I'd admitted to being a puppy with a serious case of kennel cough. "You're sure not in Kansas anymore," one of the old men said. An invisible puppeteer gathered his wrinkles and pulled his face into a horrifying grin.

We were starting with birdhouses. Our teacher was a middle-aged man with a red beard and hands like two T-bone steaks. He came up behind me and showed me how to sand down the edges of my wood. Inhaling his aftershave, I pressed my butt into the crotch of his blue jeans and closed my eyes, thinking about the diplomat's daughter. Was she skinny? Blonde? Could she build a birdhouse out of scrap wood? The teacher cleared his throat and went to help one of the moms beside me. After class, he handed me my tuition check and said it'd be best if I didn't return. Prude, I thought, and ripped up the check.

Outside, a boy from class was waiting near the curb. "What'd you think?" he asked. He was young, maybe my age, with a hipster mustache and a tan baseball cap that said BLUEHORN WINERY.

"Not for me. I decided to quit."

"Same. I already know half the stuff anyways—I just figured it'd be a good way to meet people. You know?" He smiled in a way that suggested I was the people. He then asked if I wanted a ride. A nearby bank sign read 104 degrees, so I followed him to his rusted Civic. A sticker on the bumper read KEEP TAHOE BLUE. Inside, something had eaten away a golf-ball-sized hole in the floor. As he drove, I watched the road go by between my feet.

"So are you digging it out here so far?" he asked.

I realized it was the first time anybody had asked me this. Even Alec had avoided the question, perhaps to avoid an answer that might require some action on his part. "Not really," I said. "I know that may be hard to imagine."

"Not at all. I understand—you're homesick."

"I'm not homesick."

"Then what are you?"

"I'm just not comfortable here. I'm not a Californian."

"Maybe you should go to the ocean," he said. "That's what all the fuss is about. Check out Point Reyes if you get the chance."

We were at the "house" already. He pulled over and let the car idle so that he could jot his name and number onto an In-N-Out napkin. Theo was his name. "I work the farmers market if you're ever around," he said. "I'm the honey man."

"Honey man," I said. "That's sweet."

He was blushing as I got out of the car. Inside, I put the In-N-Out napkin next to the toaster, so that Alec would find it.

The next day, I dropped Alec on campus and took his car to Point Reyes. The drive was all metal and tension. Aside from the traffic, the road kept curving and expanding and turning into bridges. In Kansas, you could close your eyes and take your hands off the wheel. Count to fifteen Mississippi.

I found a trailhead and walked a handful of miles until the Pacific appeared on my left. Holy shit, I thought, that doesn't end until Japan. There was blue water and wheat-colored sand and cliffs taller than the tallest building in Wichita. Land, I now saw, was like pie. Who would settle for just the middle when the crust was the whole point? I felt bad for Kansas, that everything in it was the same: land, land, land. The occasional mosquito-infested watering hole. And then me, my family, all my history, and everyone I'd ever loved. If there was a map that glowed in the places where I'd loved and been loved, it would burn bright in the center, surrounded by darkness. Perhaps a lazy squiggle would mark the route Alec and I took on I–70. Perhaps not.

I scrambled down the trail to a waterfall. This close to the water, I felt the first inkling of claustrophobia. It occurred to me that the openness of the sea was a lie: the ocean was not space, it was the opposite of space! It was a wall, a cage, a no-man's-land promising imminent death.

Nearby, a group of people had congregated around a beached seal. It took me a while to realize that something was wrong with it. It was craning its neck in a sickly way, as if trying to break itself in half. Without warning, it began to convulse. White foam streamed from its mouth as quickly and voluptuously as soft serve. It was going to die, and these people were going to watch it.

"It's having an orgasm!" a young man yelled.

Around him, the women squealed in joyful disgust. One raised her phone to take a picture.

Leave it alone! I wanted to shout, but had the ridiculous suspicion they would turn to me and know I was from Kansas. *You're not even from here,* someone, probably the kid wearing the pink bandana, would say. *This is just how we do things. It's ocean stuff. You wouldn't understand.*

Later that night, Alec laughed when I told him the story. We'd just made love and were in bed, face to face. He'd been sweet that evening, making lasagna for dinner and then massaging my feet, which were sore from the hike. After dessert, we unpacked a box of candles and lit them in the bedroom. It smelled like our apartment in Lawrence: vanilla and mint. It was easily the best night we'd had in the house yet.

"Your friends used to shoot squirrels with pellet guns," he reminded me. "You didn't find them morally bankrupt."

"That's different. These people at the beach were malicious. And anyways, those guys used to make squirrel stew."

"Squirrel stew isn't a thing."

"I'm telling you—they made stew. They weren't killing for sport."

"All right. Your friends made stew. Either way, you just hate the people here because you think you're tougher than them."

"I do not."

"You do. You think they're soft because they eat avocados and go surfing. And like you're some hardened warrior just off the Oregon Trail."

"None of that's true!" I regretted raising my voice. I wanted to stay nice, for the evening to retain its kind trajectory. The mint candle was still burning on the nightstand, casting a friendly orb of light onto the wall. *Help me, candle,* I thought. *I'm losing him.*

"Have you discussed any of this with the napkin man?" Alec asked. My stomach dropped—I'd forgotten about the napkin. About Theo. I wanted to undo it, to take it back and throw it in the trash. "I don't know anything about a napkin man."

"You don't know anything about that napkin on the counter?"

"I do not."

"Did you think I wouldn't call the number?" He looked at me hard, unblinking. "You fuck with me, I'll fuck with you back."

The words made my throat ache. "That's not a nice way to talk to the one you love."

"I'm tired," he said, turning away from me. "Some of us went to work today."

I held my tongue, pressed my fingernails into my palms, where they left little frowns of pain.

If Alec wanted me to work, I would work. For the rest of the week, I swept and mopped and ran Q-tips along the baseboards. Once everything was spotless, I started cooking elaborate meals that smelled so good Alec had no choice but to eat them. On Friday, I thought I'd try the farmers market, which blossomed in the center of town in the evening, while Alec held office hours.

I walked along the crowded produce stalls, making a point to eat as many samples as possible. I touched everything I could, running a lazy hand along phalanxes of pluots and cabbages. Like he promised, Theo was at the honey table, surrounded by plastic bears filled with golden liquid. We made a plan to meet at the ice cream stand a half-hour later, when he had a break. Before moving on to the pickle stand, I tapped the cap of every honey bear on display.

As it turned out, Theo had turned twenty-three since I last saw him. He bought me a scoop of coconut ice cream with one of the two-dollar bills his grandmother had sent him for his birthday. She lived in Oregon. Every year she sent him fifty two-dollar bills and a nickel for good luck.

"I've heard nice things about Oregon," I told him. Cone in hand, I was steering him away from the market, toward campus. Toward Alec.

He looked at me like I'd just mentioned his childhood best friend. "I *love* Oregon. My dream is to start an organic farm outside of Portland. I have loads of friends who live there. They just love it. There's so much to do, and the food's incredible." He went on like this, as if Portland were paying him to advertise.

"Why don't you just go there, then?"

It seemed the thought had never occurred to him. "I don't know. I mean, I'd need to find a place. Save some money. I guess it just doesn't seem like the right time." He glanced shyly at me and smiled. I pulled him toward the French building, where Alec happened to be walking out with a redhead. She wore a white bow in her hair, like a dove had flown into her head and died there.

Alec saw us from across the courtyard and shot me a nasty look. "This the napkin man?" he called.

"Only if that's the diplomat's daughter," I called back, and then pulled Theo back toward the market. The moment was over before it even began.

After a few minutes of silence, Theo said, "Was that your dad?"

I usually laughed at this type of question, but now it just made me sad. "Yes," I said. "That was my dad."

"I didn't know you moved here with your family."

"I did—we're very close."

"He looks like Vin Diesel in twenty years."

"I'll tell him you said that."

Before we parted, Theo asked why I'd never called him. I told him I was sorry and then gave him Alec's cell number—which technically he already had—and told him to text me if he was feeling lonely. I wanted Alec to get whatever message Theo had to send me, to understand that even though I'd followed him across the country, my loyalty was not to be taken for granted.

Alec beat me home. He was watching a French movie, all accordions and lovers rushing up to one another in brick alleyways. I hated when he did this—my French was terrible, and he refused to use subtitles.

I went into the kitchen, where I was determined to make a cheese soufflé. Soufflés were Alec's favorite—he would have to apologize if he wanted to eat any.

"I'm making a soufflé," I called to him. "Cheese, not chocolate."

Like clockwork, he appeared in the kitchen. "What was that stunt on campus?" he asked. "Who is this napkin dude?"

"He's a friend."

"You have friends now?"

"Yes. His name is Theo, and he's my friend. What about the redhead? Is she your friend?"

"She's my student," he said. "They're this weird thing you get when you're a teacher."

"I see."

"You think I'm fucking her," he said.

I looked up at him. "No, I don't. I *know* you're fucking her."

"Well, I'm not. She's my best student."

"Once upon a time, I was your best student."

This was supposed to be a joke: I'd barely done the homework in his class. One time, I turned in a receipt for a milkshake, and he handed it back to me with a bright red A+ across the top. He smiled at me, the cute smile where his green eyes went twinkle-twinkle. He may have been oafish and bald, but he was attractive in a Viking–meets–Mr. Clean sort of way.

"I'm mad at you," I said, getting the eggs from the fridge. "I don't like it here."

"I know you don't."

"So what are we going to do about it?"

He sighed, turned off the twinkle in his eyes. "What do you want to do?"

"I should probably go home, right? That would make the most sense." As soon as I said it, I knew it wasn't what I wanted. Like anyone without a backup plan, I wanted the original plan to work out.

"It's not even winter," he said half-heartedly. "Maybe you'd like the winter?"

"It doesn't even snow here. I looked it up. What kind of place doesn't snow?"

"It snows in the mountains. We can go to the mountains and see snow."

"I don't want to go see snow like it's some relic in a museum. I want it to actually snow. I want it to rain. I want the sky to do something, anything at all." I was suddenly tired. The "house" was hot, the air thick and fragrant. There were orange trees in the yard, and in the evenings they let off a sweet, sickly odor.

Alec took me into his arms. He used to smell like a thunderstorm, but they didn't have the same laundry detergent here, so now he smelled like nothing. He had always reminded me of thunderstorms, the mixture of rain and wind and power. We'd spent our first week together in bed, spring storms raging outside. During the days, I worked at the university's map library, and he'd come visit, bringing peanut butter sandwiches and sodas. We'd play the map game, in which one of us would name a town on a map and the other had thirty seconds to find it. In the evenings, we'd walk back to his apartment, where we'd watch movies and eat takeout, wait for the room to flash yellow with heat lightning.

He didn't feel the same in California. How could he be like a thunderstorm when there were no thunderstorms to compare him to? When I looked at him, it was like a layer had come off, revealing some muted version of the Alec I'd known back in Kansas. I wondered what he saw when he looked at me.

As he held me, I closed my eyes and pretended like we were back home. In the morning, we'd walk to the bakery around the corner and split an order of biscuits and gravy, share a mug of coffee. We'd go back to his apartment and make love, do a crossword, read books. I realized all of this was possible in California—there were biscuits and gravy, bakeries and crosswords. But it wouldn't be the same. It couldn't be.

"Are you tired?" he asked.

I nodded, my tears dampening his shirt. *I miss you*, I wanted to say.

"Let's go to sleep," he said. "Forget the soufflé."

We shuffled to bed, where I immediately fell asleep. At some point in the night, Alec left the bed and went to sleep on the couch—he'd done this once before, saying it was cooler there than in the bed, where I radiated heat.

In the morning, I put on a red tank top and gathered my hair into a ponytail. Wearing my hair up gave me a headache, but every time I did it, Alec complimented me. *You've got such a pretty face*, he'd tell me. The morning felt sad, and I wanted to look pretty for him.

In the kitchen, he looked up from the table and squinted at me. I waited for him to compliment my hair, but instead he said, "I got a dick pic at one in the morning. Guess from who?"

I bit my lip.

He had a piece of paper in front of him, which he slowly pushed toward me.

"What's this?" I asked, although I could read what it was: a plane ticket from Sacramento to Wichita.

"We'll get you some big suitcases so you can check a couple bags. Everything else, I'll mail you." He looked down at the ticket, ran a hand over his head.

"Is it the girl?"

"No."

"Then what is it?"

"It's everything. It's every minute since we got here."

I was trying not to cry. "Do you still love me?" I asked.

He sighed, looked again at the ticket. "It's like every day, I'm trying to take a goldfish for a walk—nobody's really enjoying it."

A moment passed in which my body floated outside of itself, bumped against the ceiling like a helium balloon. Then he said, "I thought putting your hair up gives you a headache."

The room grew dark, a tint of gray swallowing everything it touched: the table, the walls, Alec. As quickly as it came, it left, restoring the house to a mocking brightness. Closing my eyes, I imagined my first breath of air in Kansas. It would be cold already, a layer of frost twinkling on the sidewalks. My mother would collect me from the airport in her minivan, the same old lightning-bolt crack in the windshield. She would not say anything—she wouldn't have to. We would simply drive off through the saddest, ugliest city in the world, a city of Burger Kings and pawn shops and antiabortion billboards and residential streets bursting with plastic playground equipment and ratty front yards patrolled by toddlers in dirty diapers, snot dripping from their grimy little noses—noses their mothers would die to protect. Inevitably, my mother would turn to me and smile. Put a warm hand on my knee and squeeze three times. *I. Love. You.*

Section II: Elemental Landscapes

I am interested in the way that a man looks at a given landscape
and takes possession of it in his blood and brain. For this hap-
pens, I am certain, in the ordinary motion of life. None of us lives
apart from the land entirely; such an isolation is unimaginable.

—N. Scott Momaday, Kiowa, "An American Land Ethic," 1970

Earth's elements lie wide and open across most of Kansas. It's what we're
known for: soil and rock, air and sky. Depending on where you stand, wa-
ter falls from the clouds or huddles in the aquifers below. In the spring,
and sometimes fall, lines of controlled fires trace across the landscape. The
wind, tornadoes, and thunderstorms shake things up.

No wonder Kansas has awakened artistic visions in people, many un-
trained in the studio. The natural elements of this place translate beautifully
through the basic elements of art, especially line, texture, and space. Before
S. P. Dinsmoor fell in with cement narratives at the Garden of Eden, he shaped
limestone into logs to build his cabin home, complete with carved tree knots.
A few years later Inez Marshall, convalescing after a harrowing truck acci-
dent, noticed a small rock in the yard. With her father's knife, she carved
it into a squirrel. "From this point on, I felt that nothing else mattered. My
main objective was to chisel rock," she later said. The Grassroots Art Center
in Lucas, four blocks from the Garden of Eden, has many of her works,
including a large-scale covered wagon complete with horses and people.

Whereas Dinsmoor and Marshall were moved by stone, Maud Stevens
Wagner of Emporia took to the sky, flying from her prairie home to travel
with the circus as a trapeze artist. She settled back in the Flint Hills years
later as the world's first female professional tattoo artist, her own body cov-
ered in exotic images. Performative crank M. T. Liggett also harnessed air
when he answered the call to create. His funny, satirical, political, and (let's
just say it) misogynistic welded steel totems and whirligigs creak and spin
in the strong Kansas wind along Highways 400 and 54 in Kiowa County.

Of course, there have been more traditional, less eccentric artists in-
spired by the Kansas landscape: Birger Sandzén of Lindsborg, who saw vivid
pinks and glowing oranges where others saw flat land; Lisa Grossman of

Lawrence, whose love affair with the Kansas River has made all of us see anew how the sun alights the Kaw; and regionalist John Steuart Curry of rural Jefferson County, whose statehouse mural *Tragic Prelude* is aflame with a tornado, a prairie fire, a bison hunt, and our state's primary righteous indignation. So many others show us the grace of the Flint Hills, the quietude of plowed fields, the humble beauty of Arikaree Breaks.

The authors in this section likewise create connection with the elemental landscapes of Kansas. Today's environmental writing approaches the earth more holistically, intentionally giving voice to both our history and to the water, soil, air, and animals themselves.

Poet H. C. Palmer brings us through land and sea to a single night with his father long ago and the unmistakable, audible voice of prehistory underneath his feet, remnant of the Western Interior Sea. (Hold your breath at Monument Rocks, south of Oakley, and you'll feel it, an underwater formation with sea creatures the likes of which we have never seen.) Thomas Fox Averill's story of a young woman committed to the fossils of western Kansas—and the right to learn about them—is an inspirational story of scientific curiosity and fortitude.

Kansas is a strong and resilient landscape, but one also in need of kinship. Megan Kaminski defends the mighty bison, the "furred kings" of the Great Plains. My essay goes to the Kansas River in search of healing and discovers that the watershed, as immense as it is, carries heavy burdens. Jesse Nathan journeys through a landscape epic, the reader bearing witness as he reimagines a Kansas Purgatorio. The call to action comes from Rex Buchanan—our time here began when the inland sea receded but is still dictated by water. We need to take this seriously.

Say "Kansas" in a room anywhere in the world, and someone will reply, "Tornado!" Tom Averill carries us through the tornado in Kansas literature, a whirlwind of poems and scenes that show us the respect, heartbreak, and humor of these touchdowns that can last mere seconds but leave us forever changed. Robert Rebein's tornado is within: complex feelings toward home and the clarity that Oz is usually just like anyplace else.

Michael Kleber-Diggs describes the Kansas land as a softness, one that works in partnership with his grandparents as they fished with and fed two young boys who needed protection from a hard world. Indeed, versions of this softness resonate throughout Elemental Landscapes. Kansas can be soft, and it can be temperamental and tough, but it is often a place that evokes a yielding tenderness from those who walk its soil.

—Leslie VonHolten

Tide

H. C. Palmer

The earth was forcing me to not forget her.
—Jim Harrison

My father believed the bedrock beneath our ranch—
    once an immense sea—
was still alive, that natural rhythms persisted
    in its sluggish consolidation.
He taught me to listen for echoes of breaking surf,
    but I couldn't hear them—
even at night with the wind quiet and my ear pressed
    to an outcropping.
He believed the gravitational pull of a full perigee
    moon could still move
the old limestone. He called it *Land tide*. I thought
    that, too, improbable,
until one night the moon rose so full of light we could
    have counted the calves
in our pasture. Then, when its bottom edge caught
    the crest of a hill,
and just as I felt the prairie lift and inch sideways
    beneath my feet,
he said, *There. That's it.*

I have never recovered from that night, or the weight
of his hand on my shoulder.

Digging with Darwin

Thomas Fox Averill

I—Origins

Her life was dug deep, and started with the simplest forms. The hawk, wheeling in the sky, descending, pouncing, then rising with a talon-pierced rabbit, mouse, snake. The trees, stunted and leaning away from the prevailing winds, their leaves dusty. The undulant tracks of snakes in the dusty road, one of them the bull snake that kept the barn free of mice, moles, and, once, half a litter of mewling, just-born kittens.

Chalk outcrops lined every rise and hill, creating a story of another time—not the era Gillean Schensen had been born into, but an era before hawk, tree, and serpent. From the time she could walk, her father took her hand and they scoured the chalk for what he called "evidence" of the great Kansas ocean.

In Gillean's first sure memory, she is barely three years old. Walking the bluffs with her father after a thunderstorm that shook her sleep, she bends for a triangle in the chalk and pulls out a shark tooth. "You have an eye," her father declares. He carries her all the way home on his shoulders, where she presents the tooth to her mother, who fixes her pancakes cooked in the shapes of clam shells, fishes, and shark teeth.

"You were named for a fish," her father tells her. "One that swam in the Kansas Ocean." The Gillicus lived during the Cretaceous period and was as native to Ogallah as Gillean was now.

After the shark tooth, her father dubs her "Thunderwalker." Not for the great dinosaurs that fascinate him, but because erosion created by thunderstorms reveals new discoveries. A night of lightning and thunder will always be followed by a scouring of the bluffs.

At age five she takes the bus to school, two full hours a day when she cannot be outdoors, her sharp eyes to the earth. She memorizes the landscape to and from, determines someday to hunt for fossils in every bluff she sees. Over the next two years she scours that ground with her father, when they can spare the time.

Her second-grade teacher is a man. He wants to get to know them, he says, as though he were their own father. He has come to Ogallah to do *more* than teach, to make a difference in their lives. One day, he announces *Show and Tell*. Gillean runs from the bus up the long drive to her house eager to pick and label her best thunder-walking specimens.

II—*Show and Tell*

"What about the turtle you found?" asks her mother. "*Claw-Toes* might require less explanation. Everybody loves animals."

"Some of my fossils are animals," Gillean says.

"*Were* animals."

"Of course she'll take her fossils," says her father when he comes in from baling the last of the fall hay.

"And say what about them?" asks her mother.

"What they are. Where she found them. Their age. She knows these things," insists her father. "Gillean, when was the Cretaceous Period?"

"Sixty-five to one hundred million years ago."

"Turtles can live to be over one hundred years old," says her mother.

"What's wrong with my fossils?" asks Gillean.

"I love every one of your bones and every bone you've ever collected," says her mother, and hugs her. "I just wonder about the other kids."

"I wonder about them, too," says her father.

He helps her choose her best specimens. They create small placards. *Gastropod*, they write. *Brachiopod. Fern. Ammonite. Clam. Shark tooth. Laurel leaf. Fish vertebrae.* They wrap each hard-won fossil in thick wads of toilet tissue and pack them in a shoebox for a safe ride on the bus.

Gillean has trouble sleeping the night before, dreams she is swimming among the chalky bluffs of her farm when something tears at her foot. Before she can turn to see what has bitten her, she wakes. Her feet are cold. She puts them under her blanket. Outside, an owl complains about the wind, a barn window slaps open and shut, trying to loosen its hinges.

The other children bring turtles, snakes, Lego creations, barbed wire, postcards from summer trips, embroidery just-stitched, cross stitches of alphabets done by their grandmothers when they were in second grade. When Mr. Luke calls Gillean to the front, she carefully unwraps her specimens from the tissue and places them on a table. She sets each placard beside what it names. Hands behind her back, she begins the short speech she practiced the night before while waiting for sleep. "All around here, in the rocks, I find fossils. These specimens are all that's left of the plants and animals that lived here a long time ago. Back then Kansas was covered by an ocean." She holds each fossil up and pronounces its name.

"I can't see them," says a boy from the back of the class.

"They're just stupid rocks," says another.

Gillean wants everyone to see, but she can't pass them around. The chalk is porous, breakable. She has ruined fossils when she forced the rocks too quickly from where they rested in a bluff. She hands out the shark teeth.

"I've seen millions of those." Billy sometimes pulls Gillean's hair on the bus.

"Me, too," says someone.

Mr. Luke comes forward. "Children. We need to show Gillean the same respect she showed for what you brought to share. Gillean, did you find these yourself?"

"With my father mostly," Gillean says.

"Who created these?" asks Mr. Luke.

"My father says they were created by time." Gillean explains, her seven-year-old voice quavering, about Kansas being an ocean, and sea creatures in the sea, ones that are now extinct, and the earth shifting, and Kansas drying up and all of it taking millions of years. "Maybe even billions, my father told me," she says excitedly.

"Who is your father?" asks Mr. Luke.

"Charles Schensen," says Gillean.

"And what does he do?"

"He's a farmer."

Mr. Luke goes to the blackboard. With a piece of chalk he scratches, *We have fathers and our fathers have fathers, but all of us have one Father, a Heavenly Father.* "The Heavenly Father created the heavens and the earth," says Mr. Luke. "And in six days. And though he rested on the seventh day, those of us who believe in Him never rest in our work to glorify his name. Do you go to church, young lady?" His voice has grown loud as thunder.

"No." Gillean picks up her fossils and begins to wrap them in the toilet tissue.

"They're poop," shouts Billy.

"Quiet, class," says Mr. Luke. He helps Gillean wrap the remainder of her specimens, his fingers already chalky from the dust of the blackboard. He is careful with her treasures, his voice now gentle. "Maybe you should go to church," he whispers. "Learn even more about Creation." He puts the shoebox on the shelf for safe-keeping. "For the long ride home," he says, as though he knows what will happen.

The boys taunt her, trying to snatch her box. A fourth-grade girl has heard about *Show and Tell* and knows Gillean is going to hell. Others chant, "Gillean's going to hell. Gillean's going to hell." The driver stops the bus and quiets them, but the hour home moves with the deliberate speed of geologic time. Her parents ask about the *Show and Tell*.

"Fine," she says.

The next spring, on a morning after a thunderstorm, she and her father hunt fossils. She unearths her terrible day of *Show and Tell*, the chastisement and taunting.

"Don't worry about it," says her father. "If you live right, it won't be your last *Show and Hell*."

III—Class Trip

Gillean's fifth-grade class is greeted by an old woman, a volunteer at the Fick Fossil Museum. Margie points out the portrait of Vi Fick and brags about how she made her "painted sculpture paintings" using "fossilized fossils."

"Mrs. Fick made arrangements from the shark teeth she and her husband found on their land, over eleven thousand of them," explains Margie. "She was an artist. Of course, she didn't have children. She would love seeing all of you who come to visit her artwork."

Gillean tours the large room. Everywhere, she sees fossils, but sometimes she has to look closely. The sharks' teeth are arranged on a painting of the American flag, tooth points marching right on the red stripes, left on the white, and diagonally as stars against the blue. Other shark teeth are arranged in kaleidoscopic patterns inside oval frames. Tiny clams become the bark of trees, or berries, or rock formations, depending on the color of the paint and their placement on the picture. Fossils are shaped as animals being named by Adam in the Garden of Eden in Vi Fick's fossilized Creation. Gillean thinks the fossils might be more interesting if they were unpainted, close enough to study. She has seen pictures like this Creation in her grandmother's illustrated Bible.

An American eagle is fashioned entirely of unpainted rattlesnake rattles. Mrs. Fick has also created a wax painting, over five feet tall, of her husband, only he is naked and hairy. "A replica," Margie says, "of a Cro-Magnon man, carrying a piece of wood."

All of the art, like the Cro-Magnon man, is a caricature of art. "Pay attention to the display cases," her father told her the night before. "To anything unadorned. They *did* make some good finds."

Among these is Margie's pride and joy. "Come," she says, after Gillean tells her the story of how she got her name. "We have our own specimen of the fish that's inside the fish." In Hays, Gillean knows, at the Sternberg Museum, is the Xiphactinus that swallowed the Gillicus, the larger killed by something, and the two of them fossilized together in a diorama of the fish-eat-fish world of the Great Inland Sea.

The Gillicus is an almost perfect specimen, and Gillean likes to see the fossil she was named for displayed outside the stomach of the huge Xiphactinus that Charles Sternberg found. "He lived around here for a time, Sternberg did," says Margie, "and the best things here are the things he found." She stands closer to Gillean, and whispers, "Don't tell that to the Ficks."

"I like to collect fossils," says Gillean.

"They are a complete mystery to me. The tip of an iceberg I can't imagine."

"Don't you believe in evolution?" Gillean thinks of the glass cases full of fossilized plant and animal specimens.

"Not really." Margie moves away to tell her stories to other children.

Fossil fish heads peer at her from the walls. They have ravaging teeth, vicious, and their expressions are grumpy. Maybe because they are out of their element, Gillean thinks. On display, the tip of the iceberg of fossils, they are curiosities instead of real examples of lives lived in a time nobody tries hard enough to understand.

"Tip of the iceberg?" her father says when Gillean recounts the class trip over the dinner table. "More like the tip of the Sternberg around here."

IV—Ogallah Walking

As she grows into adolescence, Gillean intensifies her search for fossils. When she is fourteen, her parents encourage her to attend a university fossil camp. She is too old to call herself Thunderwalker, but she no longer has to think of herself as different, for all the kids at the camp are enthusiasts. They've read their Darwin, they've visited museums, they've been on digs. They think her name is cool. "I wish my folks had named me Rex," says a boy who befriends her in their two weeks in Scott County.

In high school, she takes as many science courses as she can. Some teachers stick to the facts, while others ask questions like, "At what rotational angle did God tilt the earth?" When she's run through all that Ogallah High has to offer, her mother drives her to Fort Hays State. Gillean knows, "As you've known all along," her father tells her, what she wants to be when she grows up.

She enrolls at the University of Kansas, becomes familiar with the fossil collections there. She gives herself over to science, to fieldwork, to the

discoveries of small fragments that, together, might tell a larger, more co-
herent story. She feels part of an evolution: the evolution of Evolution as a
theory, as evidenced in the fossil record, as better and better understood.
Like a fossil, she is a tiny part of something larger. She is no missing link,
but she might discover some link. Her own life is linked to the earth, she
who was born into a land that her classmates always called "The Middle of
Nowhere." In this nowhere Gillean has found the exact and specific world
of science, a world at the center of an evolution of billions of years in which
her life is one second, but as important as every other second in the time
that has led up to her life and will also lead away from it. She will not be a
missing link.

Whenever she is home, she goes thunder-walking after the rain—for
who else will? She finds fossils—for who else has eyes better trained for the
curve of bone, the hint of brown, the crumbling fissure under which the
past will expose itself? She knows these fossils will not likely be remarkable,
but walking is a meditation. Eyes on the ground, she names geologic time
like a mantra. *Graneros* with its ashy shale, ninety-two million years old;
Greenhorn with its yellowing limestone, eighty-nine million years old; and
so on, through the Cretaceous that is her home.

Walking is seeing. Walking is purpose. Walking is the cultivation of
attention.

V—Fossil Stations

Each summer, Gillean travels Kansas, each place fossils are found, searching
for the remnants of evolution, those signs that sustain the theory of natural
selection. She thinks of these places as her true homes. She travels from the
University of Kansas to Echo Cliffs, those three-hundred-million-year-old
sandstone bluffs that echo *time, time, time.* She knows Moline and Ottawa,
Kansas, where seashells and coral have permanent fossil homes. In Western
Kansas, Cretaceous layers spit out petrified fish into air and sun.

Some of Kansas is named for fossils. Miocene, which geologically means
recent, was a town in Leavenworth County. Sponges and seashells are com-
monly exposed in Greenwood County rock, called shell-rock, also the name
of a township and Shell Rock Falls. Large lizards from Phillips County still
rear their heads, teeth bared. When Professor Benjamin Franklin Mudge
collected fossils there, he suggested the stream where he found these riches
be named Silurian Creek. Only Saurian Creek exists there today. A stream
in Russell is known as Fossil Creek. An early stage-line stop was named Fos-
sil Creek Station and kept its name when it serviced the new railroad. But

local residents dropped the *station*, and then the *creek*, and simplified the name to Fossil, then changed it to Russell, leaving only Fossil Street—which is also US Highway 81—as the fossilized, nearly forgotten namesake of early Kansas fossil enthusiasm.

Oh, and Fossil Lake, and the oil fields formed by the compression of ancient organic materials from the lush environment that once existed during the time of the inland sea. *All* of Kansas, oil rich, gas rich, fossil rich, Gillean knows, *IS* Fossil Station, for she has made herself at home at each site, has dug and learned, has experienced Fossil Station, Kansas, for herself.

VI—Digging at the Keystone Gallery

Gillean is certain she can find a mosasaur, has found fragments near her Ogallah home. The summer before she starts graduate school at KU, she apprentices herself to Charles Grant at the Keystone Gallery near Scott City. He and previous generations of his family have made significant finds. He leads tours and welcomes her help. The Keystone Gallery is made from native rock that contains fossils. Once a schoolhouse, it is filled with fossils.

After a month of leading people on digs, she is discouraged. "I used to have a sharp eye," she complains.

"You've made some nice finds," he tells her.

"Not the one I want to make," she says.

"We are not in control," he says. "Just like what we discover was not in control."

The summer is dry, the land dusty. Their jeep tracks disappear immediately—after all, the Kansa tribe are the People of the South Wind. Each day, Gillean feels as though it is the day before, the land exactly the same, as it will be the next day. She longs for rain, for change, just as in her life she longs to make a difference.

She has graduated at the top of her class, but wants to *prove* she is at the top. She hunts every day, whether or not Keystone has a tour. Grant tells her to rest, but she needs to find a mosasaur, and maybe a slightly different mosasaur than has been discovered before. She will study it, perhaps as her graduate thesis. Like all humans, she needs to discover, to explain, to understand. "We have to look," she tells Grant, "for no other creature will. We are the only ones who can understand."

"Do you understand the world you search for?" asks Grant. "Do you believe the universe can only be understood by human beings?" He wonders how she is any different from those who deny evolution, saying it can only be understood by God. "You're just substituting human beings for God.

You're not giving up the idea of a superior being, you just think the superior being is you. I don't like that brand of evolution."

"What's your brand?" asks Gillean.

"We're complex, but we're only one of thousands of species. We're having our day. Mosasaurs had theirs. Do you expect anything different for Homo sapiens?"

"While I'm here," says Gillean, "While Homo sapiens are, I'll do what we do—understand and explain what got us where we are."

"We can agree on that," says Grant.

Grant has not been able to secure permission to hunt fossils on the Johnson place. "The sign says no hunting, and that goes for fossils as much as antelope," old Matthew says. Gillean is certain that is where her discovery lies. Two months pass as she rationalizes what will be her trespass: *Why should one man be able to stop the progress of all humankind? Can someone really own a fossil, a section of land, the minerals below it, the air above it? If eminent domain can take someone's property for the public good, shouldn't the same concept hold for the public good of finding something that will increase human understanding of the past?*

Gillean tells Grant she needs a week away. Family business, she explains. She has scouted a promising washout on Johnson's land, so secluded that her tent site will be within ten feet of an abandoned coyote den, and coyotes always know where human eyes are least likely to venture. She has what she can carry on her back, and when her friend Will drops her that night, holding the barbed wire strands apart for her to slip through, and hops back in his car to drive away, she is exhilarated. She does not feel alone; she feels surrounded by the presence of her next discovery.

She spends her first night in the open, the shimmering stars pressing her to the earth. They move in waves when she squints her eyes. She sleeps, finally. A rumble of thunder makes her wish she'd tried to pitch her tent in the dark. Rumble turns to clap, turns to the artillery of summer storms in Western Kansas. Soon, the wind lashes rain in nearly horizontal sheets. Gillean rolls out her tent and crawls inside, her head the only pole. Pea-size hail invades the small opening she has left for air. The wind lifts her tent, and she wonders if she'll go flying across the Plains, never to be seen again.

The storm finally walks past her on its giant legs, brushing her a couple of times with its awkward tail before swooshing into silence. Dawn presents itself as a gray sheet.

Her backpack is a sponge, barely afloat in the opening of the washout. She drags it to higher ground, a crotch of exposed rock still below the horizon of buffalo grass and swelling hills. She is too tired to search her backpack for granola bars and water. She lies down, waiting for the sun. Usually, she is patient, enjoying the gradation of light, the rock, roots, and soil coming into focus like a Polaroid photograph, but today she is as trapped as a fossil in rock—she can't walk out, across the Johnson place, back to the Keystone Gallery, without giving away her deception.

The sun nudges her awake. Her cheeks glow. The water has washed away, and though her tent is a sopping deflated balloon, she can imagine it as home. She shifts to level ground. She opens her pack for food and sits in the sun warming herself like a lizard on a rock, like *the* lizard on *the* rock across the small cutaway. The thin creature runs under a shelf of rock. Where it has vanished a small brown half-moon appears, perhaps a fossil. *Her* fossil. She fills her small bucket with water, grabs a brush, and begins her day.

The shelf runs deep. Gillean wets the chalk rock and brushes it from fossilized bone. That bone is connected to another, and that to another, until Gillean cannot reach farther. She squeezes herself into the gap and works quickly. As bone follows bone she knows she has found a sizeable creature, longer than she is tall. She crawls from the small space.

The declivity in the rock is narrowing to nothing, so she spends the rest of the afternoon and evening throwing water into the space below the fossil and scraping out chalk rock—not to expose fossil, but to create a bed for her to lie in as she works the next day. She will burrow, work until she exposes the entire fossil, then get help when she knows what she suspects is true: she has found a huge mosasaur, perhaps the biggest ever for Western Kansas.

Days pass slowly. Gillean has not brought enough water, and though she trusts the water Johnson's windmill pumps into a nearby livestock tank, the brackish water is threaded with algae and is almost too thick to swallow. After three days, her food supply is low. She eats granola, an apple, and some nuts in the morning, nothing at night. She can sleep hungry better than she can work hungry. And work she does, both exhausted and excited. The fossil above her is taking the shape she expected. The real work is in scraping out the work bed she lies on, deeper and deeper each day, until she works by feel alone, it is so dark. She is skin and bones, but is nearing the mosasaur's head—the creature's ribs have narrowed to the size of fingers, then disappeared. She is eager for the appearance of that powerful jaw bone. She scrunches against the rock for power, scraping forward, wetting rock, brushing and troweling with redoubled effort. Until she can hardly breathe.

She pushes herself backward, toward the entrance to her small burrow. She must rest. Her backside brushes against the ceiling that holds her fossil.

The mosasaur pushes back, pinning her from foot to pelvis. She is trapped, pressed in a rubble of fossil and rock as though she is the specimen.

She tries to kick away the debris, but her legs will not move. The pressure intensifies, begins to hurt. From her stomach up, she is free in the small space she dug for herself. She gulps air in her panic. How will she survive the two days before Will's car sails down the road to wait for her at the fence line of the Johnson place? She is certain that she will die.

Gillean tries to calm herself, breathes slowly. She must conserve her air, her energy. She is a scientist. She must think logically. But she cannot. She sleeps and wakes in darkness, slowly suffocating as the oxygen in her air is replaced by the carbon dioxide she herself exhales. She can move her arms, and she reaches up to gently feel the vertebrae of the mosasaur, her mosasaur. She *must* have a head. If anyone should find her, says her morbid reasoning, let them at least find a complete fossil.

She sleeps, wakes, sleeps with no consciousness of the passage of time. An hour might be millennium, for death is a joke that continues long past the punch line.

She wakes to blue sky, air. Cool water trickles down her throat. She tries to move but dizziness forces her to hug the earth. Grant is there. Will, too. And a man who says, "She ain't the first to trespass. But I thought, she's cute and I'll give her a chance. She's a tough one, too. Survived a gully washer. Worked like a dog." He spit. "You folks worked cattle like you hunt for fossils, you'd have something to show for it."

Gillean sits up, dizzy and nauseous. She retches. The burrow where she was trapped is now clear of the rubble, fossilized bone mixed with chunks of chalk rock. Her mosasaur, ruined. Will squeezes her hand. Tears squeeze from her eyes. She sits up again, then stands.

"Do you need to go to the hospital in Scott City?" asks Grant.

"How long . . . ?" She looks at Johnson.

"I saw you in there around noon. Come by at four and saw the rubble."

"I must have passed out," she says. She breathes deep, blesses the miracle of air. "I was almost to the head, I'm sure of it, and now. . . . " She points to the crumbling rock, to the fragments of fossil, destroyed beyond sightly repair. "Damn it," she says.

"Your life is more important than your discoveries," says Grant.

"I'm a fisherman, honey," says Johnson. "The stories I love best, well, they're about the ones that got away. That's always your best one, the one you dream about."

She begins to cry, tears with the same saline concentration as ocean water.

As she has the thought, she feels both elation and despair. "I'm starving," she says. After more water, then food, after she watches the others break her camp, after she stares at the bluff, the cut away of the creek, the distant windmill, the blue sky, after she memorizes her fixed position, she leans on Will and they walk toward his car. Her dig is done.

Later, she writes to Mr. Johnson: "Dear Fisherman: Thanks for catching me." She remembers her Darwin, one passage in Chapter X speaking to her summer with Grant: "There has been much discussion whether recent forms are more highly developed than ancient. I will not here enter on this subject, for naturalists have not as yet defined to each other's satisfaction what is meant by high and low forms." She no longer has the satisfaction she once felt in being the higher form.

She receives a holiday greeting from Grant, a picture of a fossilized mosasaur nearly covered in snow. *Because of you, we now hunt on the Johnson place. Glad we are not finding you—the human within the fish. See our latest find, two weeks ago. Thanks. Paleontologically yours, C. G.*

VII—Hearing
Gillean attends the State Board of Education science standard hearings on the teaching of evolution, but, like all the scientists, only as an observer. The Creationists and the Intelligent Designers will have their say, make their attempts to question and refute the 140 years of science corroborating Darwin's Theory. Ah, *theory*, Gillean thinks, what a misunderstood word. So many people have mistaken *scientific theory* for mere speculation, even ignorant guessing.

She has been ridiculed and misunderstood before: *Show and Hell*, when she was chastised by her teacher. In ninth-grade science class, when they learned natural facts like "How tall did God make the sequoia tree?" Still, she is unprepared for what she hears in the Memorial Building in Topeka, in 2005. She writes down the words, hoping someday to read them like fossil evidence. The ID witnesses and the conservative panel of the Kansas State Board of Education leave their record. Gillean attends to these words, to her "hearings":

Evolution is, she transcribes, "Atheistic, Godless, Naturalistic, Materialistic, Brainwashing, Immoral, Dogmatic, Blind Chance, a Ridiculous Notion, a Bizarre Fantasy Tale, something that Could Not Have Happened This Way, Not True, Basically a Theory, Rigged, Utterly Preposterous, Profane, Vulgar, Obnoxious, Alienating, Takes Away the Idea We Were Born for a Purpose, Purposeless, Counter to Most People's Mindset and Beliefs; it Takes Away Hope, Undercuts Belief with Blind-Chance Natural Law, Berates Students, has a Negative Impact, is Lacking in Data, Imposed on People, Cannot Create Complexity of Life, reflects a Nation Under Materialism, is Bad for Relations with the Islamic World, is Godless, Evil, Cannot Be Proven, is All Just Theory, is Science as Religion, is Inadequate Exploration, is Misspelling—as though Typographical Errors Followed Blindly Could Eventually Create Something as Complex as Human Beings—is Religious Discrimination, Completely Materialistic, Poisonous Ideology as Undisputed Fact, Hedonism, says Nature Is All There Is, is a Secular Humanist World View with No Scientific Justification."

Evolutionists are "Related to Monkeys and Come from Apes, Conspiring, Secular Humanistic, Microphone Hogs with Unopposed Access Through Teaching and PBS, Fussy, Boycotters, Gutless Wonders, Avoiders of the Bright Light of Modern Science, Selectively Suppressing Information, Childish, Embarrassing, Entrenched with Bias Called Naturalism—Theological Naturalism."

Someone insists that Darwin became a Christian, confessing that "I just meant it as a theory, I didn't intend for people to believe it. God is the creator of the Universe."

Gillean agrees with the Darwin who wrote that when a species goes extinct, a few remnants survive: "A few of the sufferers may often long be preserved, from being fitted to some peculiar line of life, or from inhabiting some distant and isolated station, where they have escaped severe competition." What better description of the State Board of Education hearings, this island of isolated fear on which true scientists have refused to set foot and thus compete with the suffering Intelligent Designers and the Creationists. Darwin himself wrote: *It is so easy to hide our ignorance under such expressions as the "plan of creation," "unity of design," &c.,. . . . Anyone whose disposition leads him to attach more weight to unexplained difficulties than to the explanation of a certain number of facts will certainly reject my theory.* And Kansas, focused on fear of the inexplicable, rejects evolution. The hearings turn out not to be hearings, but a tongue-lashing of evolution.

Gillean is the fish within a fish, but not the Gillicus swallowed by Xiphactinus. She is Gillean swallowed by the dinosauric Kansas State Board. She cannot know that within a few years those who called the hearings will be voted from office and the science standards restored.

VIII—Listening

After the hearings, Gillean needs air, needs space. She drives to one of her fossil stations, the country roads around Monument Rocks. She loads a CD, her favorite chapters of *On the Origin of Species*, eager to hear the voice read Darwin's words about gratuitous mysteries, about his vain endeavor to grapple with eternity, about wonder and impressions and marvels.

The night sky is gorgeous above her, and the ocean floor holds her up. Soon, in the light of a slender moon, the Kansas pyramids rise before her. They are monuments, but not built to honor a king, nor built to house the dead. In these formations, the mighty and the dead rise toward the night sky, where the stars are made up of the same elements, the same stuff as the air, the earth, even her own body, and the voice reading Darwin tells her, *The consideration of these facts impresses my mind almost in the same manner as does the vain endeavour to grapple with the idea of eternity.*

How she admires Darwin. Most people, she thinks, are so humbled by what they do not understand, cannot understand, that they turn it to miracle. In doing so, they do not worship miracles, they worship their own ignorance. She will be like Darwin, content with mystery, humbled by ignorance, but humbled even more by what she *does* understand. Darwin's words float in her mind as fossil creatures once floated in the ocean of Kansas: *When I view all beings not as special creations, but as the lineal descendants of some few beings which lived long before the first bed of the Silurian system was deposited, they seem to me to become ennobled.* With such words, such thoughts lifting to the heavens, Gillean walks under brilliant stars. She stands beneath the towering rocks. They are both remnant of, and monument to, the fossil sea of Kansas.

They say

Megan Kaminski

buffalo buffalo buffalo, but these are
bison named false by settlers who
dusted the prairie dry, dealt death to
furred kings. Returned un-ghosted with
the red-haze of sunset, guided by stars that
even in absence never stopped singing them;
they call us into place. What's lost cannot be restored,
but what of repair? Suturing seeds into prairie,
tall grasses call with bison and us into night,
into dreaming together beneath this Kansas sky.

A Prairie Channel

Leslie VonHolten

I am floating a mile west of the Bowersock Dam, trying to quiet my mind. I keep my ears below the surface of the water and pull my thoughts inward: I tell myself there is no undercurrent below me, no croaking catfish the size of dinosaurs, no water-buried mysteries reaching up to grab my leg. Slow, deep breath. This is silly. I open my eyes. The towering cottonwood trees along the bank shimmer in the moonlight.

This close to the hydropower plant, the river is often as still as glass. It flows underneath, but here on top it is like a lake. I hold onto a clump of spikerush and focus my gaze on the depth of stars above. Suspended, my body-self is not claimed by earth or sky, but held in place by the forces of both. I picture the shovelnose sturgeon scraping the bottom below me, mudwater propelled through their mouths and pushed out their gills, their whisker barbels seeing their way in the dark around old tree trunks, antique washing machines, and so many tires that were meant to preserve the integrity of the riverbanks but slid to the center, as all things do.

This is the Kansas River, the longest prairie river in the world. People who live near it call it the Kaw, a nod to the Kanza peoples who lived at its confluence and hunted across these grasslands. The magnetic pull of the river's immense watershed is within my arms. I imagine it this way, anyway—gravity gathering all the water runoff and debris to this central artery. Water and debris—dead plants, ag chemicals, dog and cow shit, motor oil, anything that we drop within the fifty-three thousand square miles around us. The watershed cleanses the land. It's a lot of work carrying what me and this river are trying to hold during this dark night.

I bought an illustrated book, *Kansas Fishes*, and I delight in the joy ichthyologists bring to naming these creatures. Descriptive, memorable names break my heart a little bit: the pugnose minnow, the Iowa darter, the central stoneroller. Many are endangered or have been extirpated from this region. My heart loosens at the thought of them unable to survive in our waste, the dregs of economic prosperity as we build our lives on the lie of linearity, disregarding cycles and connections. This river life could be better—purified, clean, home to schools of hornyhead chubs cheering us in their skittish surprise, their goofy names: "We're hornyhead chubs!"

We ask this river to carry everything: our economy and industry, our curiosity, our history, our sins and secrets. Our bodies and boats and buoys. We want the river to flow, but to stay within its banks. We want to use the soil clear to the river's edge. The river is not allowed to bloat and spill over. We sandbag and work hard to keep its water from our farmland and our homes. We want the river to behave predictably, according to our desires, against rules we know are set by larger forces.

Prairie grasslands are significant for their wide spaces empty of trees. But tall cottonwoods celebrate water on the prairie, gathering at the banks of rivers and streams, bursting up from low areas and springs like a cheerleader, like a hype man: "Here! Water! I found it for you!" When I paddle the Kaw, cottonwoods flank me the entire way. The prairie has a different vibe along the river: shaded, quiet. Great blue herons glide along the banks, their long bare legs and knobby knees trailing straight behind them. Once they settle near the water's edge, they stop and eye me silently.

This summer, I am learning to find the channel. I paddle my discount kayak back and forth across the breadth of the river to stay in the continual, meandering flow that remains as constant as possible. Sandbars form in the water and wait patiently to ground my boat. Beached, my first reaction is to use my paddle to push off. The blade sinks into the soft sand. Then I dramatically lunge my body from the waist, back and forth, to move the kayak inches forward or backward. This sometimes works. Sometimes I sink deeper into the sand.

Beaching myself on a sandbar is such a lazy metaphor, but here we are. It is best to save some dignity and just get out of my kayak. This is not easy in running water. It takes a fortitude of the thighs and a graceful choreography that is not me. My heavy body and challenged muscles and torn and unrepaired knee fight me. Often I will free the boat and fall back into it, only to have my added weight ground me again, but in a few more inches of water.

But when I find the channel, bliss! Is this not the goal of all of our days, to flow in all that we do, mind and body? On the river, in creative work, on the basketball court. Flow is good. To achieve flow, I must achieve the channel. Connect with it.

Channel water does not flow linearly. I follow my friend, a trained river guide, and she can see what I don't: how the water ripples certain ways over sandbars and gnarled, submerged trees. We paddle to the north side, and then immediately work our way to the south edge. Then back over again, and finally a short bit quietly, smoothly, down the middle. My kayak, as a cheaper-end model, does the job, but even in calm waters I must continue to paddle to keep the nose facing forward. I have to earn my flow. My shoulder muscles burn.

As fatigue sets in, I nurture my envy of channel-instinct. I envision the shovelnose sturgeon gliding easily along the riverbed under us, their long faces Hoovering midges and mayflies as they go. I know they have their problems, that this river is not an easy one to live in. But they know the channel. The true course of this river is their home.

Shovelnose sturgeons are a hardy fish, but they too are declining in numbers. Dams are the primary culprit, but so is overfishing. Their roe is sold as caviar, although they are now protected under the Endangered Species Act. It takes a female seven years to reach sexual maturity, and even then she will only spawn once every few years. A clear channel upstream, deep water, and high turbulence are necessary for successful mating. All of these factors are threatened. I ruminate on the sturgeon and take a new appreciation of my tired arms paddling above. Envy is a low emotion. I cast it away from us as we continue downstream.

I'm pulled to the Kaw this summer like never before. Work and misplaced ambition have disconnected me from myself, this land, my home. When the pandemic began, I was already bruised, depressed, and anxious. Losing my job gave me a clarity I desperately needed: these dark feelings were not the battle scars of hard work. They were the markers of a life that strayed from its natural course.

My teenage daughter and I started walking along the river in the evenings. Something to do. We collected driftwood and shared it with fellow hikers along the trail. We met families also collecting driftwood and compared our finds from a distance. I read Jim Harrison's *The Theory and Practice of Rivers* and felt a correction flow within me. I would no longer work to be someone I am not, contorting my body into clothes I hated, or smiling through conversations about misunderstood billionaires and the good they do for the world.

And so I decided: if all of this land comes to the river, then I will too. My summer is kayaking, swimming, camping, reading, exploring, and hiking this life-vein of our watershed. It is time to be humbled by the sandbars. To delight in the flow of the channel. To send gratitude down to the shovelnose sturgeon, that funny-faced beauty, for giving life, for being the steward of this center of everything.

One February during an odd 60-degree Saturday, I loaded my kayak and gear and went to the river. Frisbee golfers were playing along the river park with their dogs and microbrews, all of us infected with a false spring fever. The warm air was joyful. With a jaunt in my stride, I carried my boat down the ramp, smiling at two Labradors chasing each other along the lower bank, mouths agape. A smaller, scruffier dog ran higher up near the parking lot, barking at top volume, feeling the freedom of being outside.

It was not until I set my kayak down that I discovered my rookie mistake: the river was frozen. My brain paused a beat. Frozen water, in this warm sunshine on this open-sky day. Then I remembered the frigid temperatures earlier in the week, the nights in the teens, the morning commutes in the low 20s. I had worn my heaviest coat just three days earlier. Of course the river is frozen. It remembers better than we do.

River memory. I think more about what this river holds. Like all American rivers, the social history of the Kaw is grim. Near where I stood dumbfounded at the melting ice, a sign commemorates the murder of three Black men who were hanged from the bridge in 1882. Isaac King, George Robertson, and Peter Vinegar had defended Peter's fourteen-year-old daughter from sexual assault by a white man. The man was later found dead in the river. A mob of over a hundred white men pulled King, Robertson, and Vinegar from the jail, placed ropes around their necks, and threw them over the bridge one by one, where they hung through the night and into the next day. The white-owned newspaper bragged about the event, called it vigilante justice. Margaret Vinegar, Peter's fourteen-year-old daughter, barely escaped the mob. She died in prison from tuberculosis six years later.

The men were buried in a potter's field at Oak Hill Cemetery, unmarked. As local remembrance activities began to organize nearly 140 years later, the story of the lynching was a surprise to many. Racial terror did not happen here, in Kansas, the "Free State" established by Massachusetts abolitionists. This was not the South. Yet when the truth set in, we still corrupted the narrative, saying the lynching was "forgotten to history." Later we were corrected again: the trauma lived in the homes of Black residents over all these decades, in stories shared from generation to generation. Details of the story faded over time but still echoed through families. There were parts of town to be avoided, or a knowing respect paid to the potter's field. Behavior was baked into the community's culture so deeply as to not be seen.

There is other quiet damage here in the water. In beef and farm country—wheat, corn, sorghum, soybeans—the watershed carries nitrogen, phosphorus, herbicides, and pesticides, as well as plowed topsoil, to the Kaw. Confined animal feeding operations (CAFOs), loosely called feedlots, impair waterways because of their concentration of waste. PFAS, per- and polyfluoroalkyl substances called "forever chemicals" because of their slow breakdown in the river, flow here. Today, PFAS are also in our bodies, so pervasive is their forever-ness, and in this way again the river and I are the same.

"Don't drink it," a young ecologist said to me as our canoes coasted near one another. We had been chatting about our love of the water, the beauty of the river, the incredible night and day we were spending with other women who had dedicated their careers to learning and saving this prairie watershed. Her warning—"don't drink it"—came like a mantra, almost flat and unfelt. I could tell she ended many conversations about the Kaw with that blithe but firm warning. My place of peace and healing is also damaged, in need of care.

On the water, I sometimes think about the one river baptism I attended during my late childhood. I was raised in a Pentecostal home: speaking in tongues and tambourines were Sunday-night rotation. Hours-long alter calls saved the souls of our damaged and hurt flock. I left the church decades ago, but looking back I see my religious upbringing as a somatic engagement with faith. Physical and exuberant.

In my church, baptism was performed in the sanctuary, in a large jacuzzi-like tub behind the pulpit. Baptism by full submersion was our sacrament to cleanse sins from the body. I was full of complex emotions as I stood shaking in the water. Our minister was a fiery sort, dramatic and kind. "Your old self will be buried with Jesus. You will rise from this water like Christ!" He squeezed my nose and plunged me backward. I was a teenager, and my baptism was spontaneous. My faith had begun to slip and erode; this was likely an attempt to feel rekindled. Yet here I was in a large tub filled with tap water that went down the drain and through the municipal wastewater system.

Once my sins made it to the river, they had been properly treated, I guess; sanitized and swept away like dishwater. But my aunt's congregation in southern Missouri was a little more wild, more old-fashioned. They lived closer to history, closer to the seasons and the earth. Their services had an emotional vitality that was frightening. The river baptism I attended was a strange and beautiful experience, full of loud hollering and old diction, a cleansing of sin and rebirth of self in the flowing water. Locusts buzzed, and green was everywhere: in the trees, along the wild bank, on the woody brush that pulled at our skirt hems. As the pastor prayed and dunked his believers, their sins were carried by the watershed to be something other than us, something strong enough to carve granite and gentle enough to hold ducklings. The river could carry our deep screwups and dilute them to a grain of sand.

I am no longer of this faith; I left the church at eighteen and would not talk about it for years. Eventually a spiritualism began flickering in me again, one common to all of us who are drawn outdoors. A connected knowingness among the trees and grasses, a delight and wonder in unexpected encounters with an indigo bunting or wild tom turkey on the hiking trail. I wonder if my church had maintained its sense of awe, had held a sacred appreciation of the natural world, that maybe I would have stayed. But my experience there was a taming of the heart that goes against everything I see around me.

Religion has been wielded by industry and governments for centuries as an excuse to tame the natural world. Rivers and prairies may be the biggest victims of this. European settlers plowed the Great Plains beyond recognition, and whole agencies work to divert and move rivers. I am not so naïve as to say none of this needs to be done, at least to some degree. But it could be done better. Like me, the prairie and this Kansas River watershed need nurture and healing.

Given a natural existence, rivers can and do self-purify. This requires the right balance of natural elements like oxygen, the right pace of movement, the right bacteria, and time. A large dose of time. Floodplains around our river need to be reclaimed, and dams removed. Imagining change on this scale seems impossible. But when the hornyhead chubs and pugnose minnow are gone, we will lose our ability to repurify—not just the river repurifying, but our own culture and selves. We cannot apologize when there are no pugnose minnows present to flourish again, to take back their place in the tributary.

I despair, but affirming change does happen.

Near the sign that commemorates the deaths of King, Robertson, and Vinegar sits a small pocket park where Iⁿzhúje'waxóbe, a massive, twenty-eight-ton Siouxan quartzite boulder, stood for nearly a hundred years. It was moved to Lawrence in 1929, and a plaque was drilled into it to commemorate white settlers from the New England Emigrant Aid Society—Free Staters who had moved here from Massachusetts in 1854 to establish Kansas as a state free of slavery.

Iⁿ'zhúje'waxóbe (pronounced EE(n) ZHOO-jay wah-HO-bay) is a sacred item of prayer for the Kaw Nation. For millennia it lived miles upstream at the confluence of Shunganunga Creek and the Kansas River. History was again "forgotten" until, generations later, members of the Kaw Nation reminded the community. They had not forgotten. Today Iⁿ'zhúje'waxóbe has been rematriated to the Kaw Nation and stands proudly at Allegawaho Memorial Heritage Park in Morris County. There has been no controversy.

This is good news and has been embraced by everyone I know. We should right past wrongs. But as I float in the water, I wonder if sins are ever corrected within our lifetimes. The people who stole Iⁿ'zhúje'waxóbe are all gone now. The mob who killed King, Robertson, and Vinegar never paid for their murder. If this river re-purifies, it will not be in my lifetime. I float and worry. Corrections come too late. What can I do with my healed self, with my relationship with this river? I float and ask: what does the river need from me?

I watch the sun set and turn the river gold against the darkening sky. A tenderness comes over me that I can only describe as love. I want to call it a oneness, that the river and I are the same. That seems arrogant, and overwhelming, as the river is so much, so big and deep and complex. But I do love this river, this expansive channel that gives and holds water and accepts all. Love for the lost souls who surely remain within its depths, and their families who persevere through mysterious loss. Love for men like Peter Vinegar and his daughter Margaret, who should never have known the horrors they faced. Love for the Kanza who believe in an enduring sacredness and will fight for what was taken.

If this is a sentimental reaction, I'll own it. I have learned and experienced the hard act of love, for people and pets, for place and community. If there had been more love to counter the white supremacy that hung men from bridges in 1882, and to counter the equally toxic supremacy to bury the history for 140 years, we would be better citizens today. If there had been love in the board rooms and planning meetings of industry, our children would not be born with forever chemicals in their bloodstreams.

Love acknowledged that Iⁿ'zhúje'waxóbe did not belong to this town. This is good news. I reflect on this shimmer of hope as I send love out to the darts and shiners and chubs. And so much love for the silly-faced, channel-gliding shovelnose sturgeon. My guide. They have no idea the emotion and grief they have carried from me these past three years.

Between States

Jesse Nathan

[Walking the creek. Springtime.]

I'm remembering it took twenty minutes
for the local firefighters to reach us the night the lightning
   got the attic blazing. Long enough to take a bath. I'm remembering
as the road-grader growls by somewhere, its unremitting blade
      leveling the sand of a road,
         bunched and rutted,
         stopping the land from taking it back—

stopping it in the language of a straight line.
And I'm remembering how someone used to toss
   Busch Lite empties down our crushed-limestone drive,
thrown from a passing pickup, cans silver-glossed
      azure and partially crushed.
         Imagining the hush
      of the creek bed in winter's crust,

ice sounding off. But it's April, and April is stinging nettles,
sneezeweed and terse breezes, wide-awake skies, vein-blue tulips—
   I'm remembering a rainstorm mudding the road even as I pedaled
home, left the bike, ran soaking through fields following the lips
      of the waterway that appeared
         articulate, weirdly
      lit-up in lightning. Imagining Romani my grandmother heard

in that pasture as a child, they would canvass the farmhouse,
barter for milk. At dusk the calls of their children. Imagining
   people before that who tracked this route, maybe camped
on these banks, fished, called out to a friend
   a strategy or result. Could eat what they caught

without second thought. I'm remembering
            the placard in the half-ring
            of fading pines off Old 81

describing a people who must've had scores of words for
zephyr, people who (say the translators) could sing, "My children,
    when at first I liked the whites, my children, when at first
I liked the whites I gave them fruits, my children,"
    a people whom the white government
sent surveyors to to establish a trail's way
            through these parts (my aunt used to sing
            "When the prince wants an apple, he takes the tree . . . ")

and the envoy arrived in that grass sea
    to wheedle the Osage and the Kaw,
    offering $800 and a few saddles
for a promise of permanent free passage. Local trapper
        as translator. He the best
    they could scare up, his Kaw sketchy at best, and I'm imagining
        my relatives soon flooding in
            with cabinet and poppyseed,
bonnet and springtooth, hope chest and hedgerow,
    their book full of martyrs, dear as a mirror
    and quilts made in the drunkard's path
    by hands that wouldn't hold a drink, obsessed and kind
selectively, women and men enough of whom
            must've believed when they were told to
            hallucinate a past to quell a present, told
"These are the Gardens of the Desert, these / The unshorn
            fields, boundless," in blank
        verse it was home to "a race, that long has
passed away" "in a forgotten language, and old tunes," "all is
        gone" though the actual act of emptying
            was actually still happening
        even as they set to plowing (that first time like plowing
            a doormat, the sod rent open
            with a sound like a zipper)

harrowing, reaping, shocking, threshing,
                which is to say by 1846 the Kaw
were penned in reserves, by 1873 pushed out of state, and by 1876
        ("Boundaries. Forced marches. Monoculture . . . ")
my foreparents by the powers
    are granted swaths of so-called open land
            to open up, and I'm imagining, first of all, much water
    under no bridges, the streams like this they would've seen
            foaming with fish, peppered with turtle, an opus of birdsong
                    they'd have heard, and maybe heard also of two men
            who set out from the northeast border
killing 800 wolves before they reached the Smoky Hill River,
                and I'm seeing buffalo
        (10,000 killed in one hunt in 1882 by men with Sharps)
            as I watch a black bull corral the herd
in the paddock I'm threading through,
    whose hump is a massif, whose head is
        low so his body's like a road grader,
    the droves rambunctious and nervous as they quick-march,
            they must've heard me in the underbrush
    or they've heard and seen that Gleaner,
road-bound dust comet
    traversing one of these little concrete (lime and clay) bridges
            that's all the speaking these roads and creeks
    are wont to do with one another.

And when it's gone, and the cattle gone, and the air cleaner,
    the quietude I think not "strange and empty," the creek
            not foaming with dace, but cocoa-brown
            with topsoil, the ground
            greened over by recent rain, a clown-

    faced cloud somersaulting slowly as a contrail
punctures her nose, plane proving a scratch
    that dissolves on the cosmic glass, frail
trace of cities, I'm down here imagining the chaff
            in the air of olden times
                and a people, my
            mother's, who must've believed the line

that these contours were theirs to grid, grounds theirs "years /
before" they landed this "gift outright" blank "still unstoried, artless,
   unenhanced" for the taking
      like a creeper takes that cottonwood
   by the ears, takes what it wants, while still giving
an impression of peace to a poet
   having a sit before he blunders on with his eclogue,
passing not through a prairie, not
through a woodland, but through a *prairie woodland*
      (technical term for this band of life, woods along streams
                  surrounded by oceans of grass,
         I'm remembering the way, flying in, the creeks seem to cross
      the gridded roads like veins drawn over graph paper)
which natives and settlers relied on, spotted afar, to locate
         what water there was
      among networks of vines and tough shrubs
that clinch these muddy lips,
   this mustache of canopied verdure running a few feet on either
bank, a curt succession
      from lovegrass, dropseed, bluestem, to great big trees
      rising from "abominable desolation"
   where "nothing points" though it happens to be home
to lady's slipper and pheasant and kingfisher and windmill-grass
   and what are states to them? What are states
      to bobcat and nitrogen-eating bacteria and dung beetle
   and racerunner and sunflower, to carpets of sorghum, beans,
      cornfields replete with large centipedish machines, woodland
   a slender band of betweenness, whose meandering logic
seems but is not whimsy through the subsoil.   Of course
   this state already had a song. Had "revery," had "chants going forth"
like how the Pawnee would sing before battle,
   "Let us see, is this real,
let us see, is this real,
   let us see, is this real,
this life that I am living?"

I'm looking where a log points, a slippery log
that makes its point over the real froth
    as I waver between real banks to the real knob
the trunk lands on, this land of lightning bug and common gray moth,
                of the misnamed prairie dog
                    not canine but squirrel, the meadowlark not
                    any kind of lark, the horntoad not

            toad but spiked lizard, the jack rabbit truly a hare,
                the prairie chicken truly a grouse, the locust
            a false acacia, even the buffalo were
                really a species of bison, but in their crush
                    to have and sow the place
                        I can picture the settlers' pinkish faces
                    and sometime glee as they attach their names

to things like *catlinite*, pipestone, maroon erratic
    tracked in on the feet of glaciers crushing spruce forests,
        used (and called what?) by First Peoples
    for carving pipes, fine-grained, soft,
        picked up by my loner grandma
            who'd pick over roadsides, scour the gravel drive
            for wheat-sized one-celled fusulinids, searching them out
        as if divinities slept in minerals, in chips
    of meteorite and shark teeth,
and I'm remembering that it wasn't the land that carved me apart,
    but a system of culture, a school of
flak from an elder if you couldn't pull a straight furrow,
    whose term for the leftover corners
    of wheat left standing at the cambered angle
of a turning combine's path
    was *jews*. I'm remembering someone saying he hadn't
    done his jews yet. And I'm imagining the neighbor in a CASE hat
sweating as he forces the waterway in his field
to flow straight, trenches out the curves, tautens the meander
    to get a few more acres of arable land. *Plow
    the dew under*, went the old saying. Meaning
get out there early and turn the soil, a culture

of extraction displacing itself, its sports teams
   called the Pipeliners and the Threshers,
 the wells failing, the farms drying up, the schools
   consolidating, and I'm remembering mine was a school of
milk all over my locker, of laying tacks on an outcast's chair,
 the usual cruelty with a rural edge,
   remembering that I, who got kicked in the spine,
   had my own complicities
in the unstated contract of "freaks for export only"—

 all that projected emptiness. Only the land was always a solace.
     I recall it as I cross now under a bridge at the bend
       in the road that was Empire, cattle town, "erased," felt one
       newcomer to the prairie, "blotted out"—I've always loved
   that unroomed vertigo, a sky that swallows you—
and I hear again the grader hacking
   somewhere back around the section, his angled blade
   a balm to the quadrangle's party,
    which gave us passable roads and the persistence of windmills,
   he's following the latticework his ancestors laid
over branchings of stream and river
   (which look from above like leafless trees
     or paint peeling, or like cracks in a wall)
   "Eternal prairie and grass, with occasional groups of trees,
Frémont prefers this
 to every other landscape," Charles Preuss
   wrote on their way to taking California, "To me
it's as if someone would prefer a book
   of blank pages," and always
I want to linger in those pages
   but I'm imagining the "tension

   between singing and the journey," remembering
 people I knew who worked red-eyes
at the hatchery in the nearby town, who'd brag
 of killing runts in creative ways, knocking them to slime,
       Candace, Carmen, and the Hacker boys,
         figures grown up with
         who don't know what figures they seem

for whiteness and sex and bored destruction, I'm remembering
          some uncle saying, *Best not to marry*
  on the other side of the creek—
                but I say a border is also a world,
  zone of cottonwood hackberry luxurious weeds towering
      and scarcely a human presence, a golden haze
          where monarchs lunge and bounce
      in private liberated gloom
that must from above look like giant

interlocking hooks, I'm imagining the bobolink's view
    who flies with the aid of the stars,
      how a month ago the stream was ice,
  how an hour ago a mare was stretching her neck
      over barbed-wire fences
        for the sweeter grass, and I'm imagining
      these stinging nettles in my path

    electrify my shins, imagining my stanza standing
for the grid within me, while my lines run on
    like creeks across pastures, beneath a huge sun
of remembering, already halved by the line of the land,
    land half imagined, half vanished
      as a fog comes
      not upon the earth but out of it.

Notes

Material quoted but not attributed comes from an Arapaho Ghost-Dance song translated by James Mooney in 1896 ("My children . . . ."); William Cullen Bryant's poem "The Prairies" ("These are . . . ," "a race . . . ," "in a forgotten . . . ," and "All is gone"); Amy Clampitt's poem "The Prairie" ("Boundaries . . . "), Laura Ingalls Wilder's novel *Little House on the Prairie* ("strange and empty"); Robert Frost's "The Gift Outright" ("years . . . ," "gift outright," "still unstoried . . . "); W. H. Auden's "Bucolics," specifically the "Plains" section ("abominable desolation," "nothing points"); Emily Dickinson's "To make a prairie . . . " ("revery"); Walt Whitman's "Starting from Paumanok" ("chants . . . "), a Pawnee war song translated by Daniel Garrison Brinton in 1890 ("Let us see . . . "), Carl Becker's essay "Kansas" (in this case the line has been abridged from "There is a saying here that freaks are raised for export only."); Willa Cather's *My Ántonia* ("erased," "blotted out"); and Raymond Williams's *The Country and the City* ("tension . . . "). Books by William Least Heat-Moon (*PrairyErth*) and Wes Jackson (*Altars of Unhewn Stone*) were invaluable resources in the making of this poem, as were the circulars published by the Kansas Geological Survey. The "large centipedish machines" are irrigation systems. A farmer—"the neighbor in the CASE hat"—who forces a stream in his field to flow straight does so because he figures it'll give him a few more bushels at harvest time. Straight lines he deems more efficient, and more suited to his machinery, than the meandering line the waterway makes. Turkey Creek was a dividing line in the community, separating two groups of Mennonites who, despite their many similarities, came from two different communities in Europe, communities that represented two different traditions, and who did not forget this fact in their new land.

It All Comes Back to Water

Rex Buchanan

About thirty years ago I was in Kiowa County in south-central Kansas working with a couple of other folks to measure the flow from a spring along Thompson Creek. We were inventorying springs in the state. It was a Friday afternoon in late October, unseasonably warm and sunny. A good day to be out.

We spent Friday night in Ashland, then went back up to the Thompson Creek drainage the next morning to finish what we had started. Overnight the weather changed: a cold front came through, and the temperature dropped into the upper 30s. The wind was blowing from the north, and a slight mist filled the air.

As we hiked down the creekbank toward the spring, we saw something incredible: all the nearby cedar trees were covered with butterflies. Monarchs. They'd obviously been migrating south, gotten caught in the sudden shift of weather, and settled into the cedars to wait for the sun to warm things up so they could resume flight.

The trees were dripping butterflies. The landscape reminded me of those photos of the location in Mexico where the monarchs spend the winter. I'd never thought I'd see such a sight, especially in Kansas. But here the butterflies were.

And the butterflies were here because of the trees, the protective vegetation. And the vegetation was here because of water. The trees were drawing on stream flow and spring flow, sheltered by the break in the landscape that the creek had eroded into the hills.

Like much that goes on here in Kansas, most everything we saw that day came back to water.

For eons, plants and animals have been drawn to water sources in the state, the springs and rivers. That's especially true in western Kansas, where precipitation is scant and sources of surface water like lakes, rivers, and springs are more rare and thus more precious. One species of aquatic insect, a riffle beetle, is found only in a spring run at Lake Scott in Scott County, and nowhere else in the world.

When Indigenous people came to Kansas, they were also drawn to the water sources. Many archeological sites are in stream bottoms. When I was working with coauthors on a book about Native rock carvings in Kansas, we quickly saw that many petroglyph sites are close to water sources, especially springs. Those springs were, I believe, perceived to be an entrée to other underground worlds that we cannot ordinarily see.

When white settlers began to show up on the plains, water was central to their explorations and routes. They often traveled along rivers, the way the old Santa Fe Trail parallels the Arkansas River in central and western Kansas. Sometimes the trails went from spring to spring to spring, as they did in eastern Kansas, where a reliable, clean water source was critical. Alcove Spring in Marshall County, along the Oregon Trail, and Diamond Spring in Morris County, along the Santa Fe Trail, are good examples.

As white Americans began to build towns, they often did so with water in mind. Think of the locations of the state's biggest cities: Topeka, Lawrence, Manhattan, and Kansas City, all hard on the banks of the Kansas (known locally as the Kaw). Junction City, where the Republican and the Smoky Hill Rivers come together; Salina along the Smoky; Wichita at the confluence of the Arkansas and Little Arkansas Rivers (and before we go any further, please know that Arkansas, in reference to the river in Kansas, is pronounced AR-*kansas*, not Ar-kan-*saw*, the way the state name is pronounced). Even out west, Garden City and Dodge City are along the Ark, and Liberal is not far from the Cimarron.

Think of how many places in the state have incorporated "spring" into their names: towns like Bonner Springs, Baxter Springs, Lost Springs, Crystal Springs. That's in part because many of them were also sites for spring water resorts, places where people came to "take the waters," drinking and soaking in spring water to cure what ailed them. Probably the best known of them all, and one of the most historic, was Waconda Spring in Mitchell County, considered sacred by Native people, and later operated as a spa until the 1960s, when it was inundated by the waters of Glen Elder Reservoir, one of several dams built in the Kansas River watershed in response to the 1951 flood.

But water did not just determine where people settled. It often determined what they did. As early as the 1600s, Plains Apache and Pueblo villagers in El Cuertelejo (at today's Lake Scott) used a trench system that funneled water to crops in one of the state's earliest examples of irrigation. In Lawrence, a dam built across the Kansas River in 1874 first provided the power to grind grain, then powered buildings in the town, and eventually produced electricity, which it continues to do today. Only a decade later, water from the Arkansas River was diverted for irrigation in southwestern Kansas. Miles of irrigation canals were built—some now abandoned, others still in use. Today the underground Ogallala Aquifer provides much of the water that is sprinkled from center pivot systems, each of which generally irrigates about 160 acres (or one-quarter of a section), though some are larger. Those sprinklers put water onto corn that is grown to feed cattle, which are then butchered in packing plants in southwestern Kansas, plants that have attracted workers from across the world to Liberal, Dodge, and Garden.

It all comes back to water.

In many ways, water is central to who we are as a people. It determines where we live, how we live, and much of what we do.

And that poses issues in a state like Kansas, where the water situation is so different from one end of the state to the other. Because it rains a lot in eastern Kansas, surface water is plentiful. Lakes and rivers provide the water for places like Johnson County, the county with the biggest population in the state. Significant amounts of groundwater (water found under the ground in aquifers; aquifers are rocks, sands, and gravels that are saturated with water the way that water can saturate a wet sponge) are rare in eastern Kansas, except along big rivers like the Kaw, the Neosho, and the Cottonwood.

Western Kansas is another story. Precipitation and surface water are rare, but groundwater is plentiful. The water-saturated sands and gravels that make up the Ogallala Aquifer in the subsurface hold a huge supply of high-quality, easily pumped groundwater, water that took millions of years to accumulate.

In the 1900s, irrigators used big mechanical pumps to pull the water up from the Ogallala. Yet as early as the 1940s, scientists recognized that pumping was lowering water levels in the Ogallala. A resource that was once thought to be infinite, people saw, could be used up. In the 1950s and 1960s, that "using up" began in earnest. Center pivot systems allowed farmers to irrigate rolling land that could not previously be irrigated. Those systems sprinkled the water evenly onto crops, applying it more effectively and efficiently than in the past.

The result was an explosion of irrigation across the western third of the state, irrigation in places like the sand hills along the south edge of the Arkansas River, places that could not raise much before. Prior to irrigation, dryland farming focused mainly on traditional crops like wheat. But with irrigation, farmers could grow more profitable, thirsty crops like corn. That attracted feedlots, some that fed up to 100,000 head of cattle. And those feedlots attracted packing plants that had once been in urban areas like Wichita, Omaha, and Kansas City. Instead of hauling cattle to the packing plants, the packing plants came to the towns and cattle in southwestern Kansas.

Water levels dropped. Across much of western Kansas, water levels in aquifers now decline a foot or two every year. That may not sound like much, but multiply each year by the fifty or sixty years since irrigation boomed, and the declines add up. Keep in mind that the Ogallala is highly variable from place to place across the state—in some areas it holds hundreds of feet of water, and in other areas far less. In some locations, a substantial amount remains. In other parts of western Kansas, large-scale irrigation is no longer feasible.

Every January, teams from the Kansas Geological Survey and the Kansas Department of Agriculture's Division of Water Resources (the state entity that regulates water rights) fan out across western Kansas to measure water levels in about fourteen hundred wells, many of them irrigation wells that take water from the Ogallala Aquifer. I've been helping with that effort for twenty or twenty-five years. I do this partly because I get to see things in western Kansas, like the canyons of the Arikaree Breaks in northwestern Kansas, herds of antelope and mule deer, a dusting of snow on the sand sage prairie south of Meade. Incredible sunrises and sunsets and nighttime sky.

It's not all fun and games. Some wells harbor dead animals, the kind that put off a smell so strong you can taste it, and it doesn't taste good. Some-times you have to wade through mud and snow or change a flat tire. One year, on the Cimarron National Grassland of southwestern Kansas, I lost my bearings in a fog worthy of London, and I'd probably still be out there if it weren't for my GPS.

But I mainly help measure wells because it's important and because I learn so much, especially about irrigated agriculture, since I grew up on a dryland farm. Measuring those wells each January has helped me under-stand the complexity of water-level declines, which are made complicated by culture, economics, hydrology, and, like many things in modern life, the law.

In Kansas, people must obtain a legal right—a water right—in order to pump large amounts of water, whether for irrigation or manufacturing or municipalities. By Kansas law (and in much of the American West), the person with the oldest water right has priority over their neighbors. That is, when there is not enough water to go around, the person with the oldest water right is entitled to their water before people with more recent (or junior) water rights can get theirs. This practice is called "first in time, first in right." It is a somewhat self-policing system, one that depends on water-right holders to enforce their rights. For example, a person with a junior water right may pump their allotment of water, unless they impair the ability of their neighbor with an older right to pump their allotment. To stop the junior right holder from impairing the older right, the senior water right holder must file a complaint with the state—which they seldom do. Complaining about water is not a good way to get along with your neighbors here.

So pumping continues in spite of the declines. It's not hard to see where we are headed. In parts of the state, large-scale pumping is already difficult or impossible. In other places, the lifespan of large-scale irrigation is projected to be twenty-five to fifty years, assuming pumping continues at the levels it has in the past.

This path is not sustainable. But what to do? There's the rub. Over time, irrigators have become more efficient, figuring out ways to put just about every drop of water to use. But that doesn't translate into less water being used. Water conserved in one place is often used to grow more water-thirsty crops. Some voluntary cutbacks have begun. In Sheridan County in northwestern Kansas, farmers voluntarily came together in 2012 to cut back pumping by 20 percent. These measures had to begin as voluntary agreements; remember, the state in general will not curtail a water right unless somebody complains. The result of these agreements has been more careful irrigation and different cropping practices. Even so, farmers have made about as much money as before.

Places where those voluntary cuts have occurred are like George H. W. Bush's thousand points of light. One or two locations won't make a huge difference; they must be widespread to really matter. These voluntary water-use agreements do show a way, but only if widely adopted. And in southwestern Kansas, where the Ogallala is the thickest in the state, they have not gotten much traction. Instead, ideas like importing water from northeastern Kansas are more appealing, although the cost of energy to move that water, construct the infrastructure, and fight any legal battles to move that water probably makes that idea a non-starter.

In the meantime, water levels decline—more in dry years, when irrigators pump more water, than in wet years, when they pump less.

Lest you think that water issues are confined to western Kansas, let's talk about surface water. Beginning in the 1940s and 1950s, Kansas saw the construction of big reservoirs, mostly in eastern and central Kansas. Today they supply water for much of the population, but those lakes are silting in, filling up with the soil that erodes mostly from farm ground and is carried by rivers into the lakes. Everyone knew this would happen. But because we're so dependent on these lakes for drinking water and flood control and recreation, we cannot let them fill up with silt. Getting rid of that sediment (by dredging, say) and keeping those lakes as viable water sources is hugely expensive.

At the same time, water in rivers has become more dear. In central Kansas, streamflow provides water to places like Cheyenne Bottoms and Quivira National Wildlife Refuge; migrating waterfowl rely on these sites, especially because other water sources in the Great Plains have been plowed up or have dried up. Much of that streamflow has been swallowed up by irrigators who pull water from wells near the creeks and rivers that supply the Bottoms and Quivira. (Those wells are drilled into alluvial aquifers, the shallow sands and gravels that neighbor the streams and leak water into their channels, keeping streams flowing during dry times. But as irrigation lowers water levels in the alluvial aquifers, those aquifers no longer supply water to the streams.) A series of delicate legal negotiations in the 1990s helped get more water into the streams that feed Cheyenne Bottoms, but no such deal has been worked out at Quivira, where the marsh often fails to get the water it needs, even though the wildlife refuge has a water right that predates those of most of the upstream irrigators.

If the refuge were to file a successful impairment complaint, it would cost those upstream irrigators (the ones with junior water-rights) money.

In western Kansas, surface water is even more rare today than a few decades ago. Since the late 1980s, the Arkansas River has been largely dry from Garden City to Great Bend. For a time, that was because irrigators in Colorado used more than their share. But after a lawsuit that dragged on twenty years (*Kansas v. Colorado* makes Charles Dickens's *Bleak House* look like an open-and-shut case), Colorado now delivers water to the Ark. But by Garden City, the water is gone, diverted directly onto fields or sucked up by alluvial wells. Today's Arkansas streambed is sandy. People run four-wheelers down the Ark. In places the riverbed has grown up in vegetation.

Every once in a while, not often, when it rains a lot, a little water flows in stretches of the Ark. People go down to see it, expressing surprise: surprise at the sight of water in one of the biggest rivers in the state.

What does that say about Kansans?

Sometimes people ask me, What'll things look like out West a hundred years from now? I don't claim to know. But I'd guess there will be less irrigation and more dryland farming. Less corn, more wheat. Maybe more cattle grazing on shortgrass prairie. I don't think the High Plains will just dry up and blow away. But our options will be considerably more limited because there will be less water. With less water and probably less economic activity, there will probably be fewer people. We already know about the emptying out of many of the counties out west. Less water will just mean more of that.

I also begin to think about the people a hundred years from now, and what they will think about us. As much as we would like to think of ourselves as enlightened, I'm not sure that is how they will see us. I wonder if they'll look back on us and say, "What were you thinking? You dried up rivers. You used billions of gallons of water, high-quality water that took eons to accumulate. You used it to grow corn, and more than a quarter of that crop generally goes to make ethanol. Now we can't make a living out here. What were you thinking?"

But maybe I'm wrong. In the past few years there's been a renewed interest in water issues. More funding, and a greater understanding of what kind of cuts would be necessary to reach sustainable levels of pumping. Those voluntary efforts seem to be gaining traction in the Ogallala. Is that enough to change the course we are on significantly, or are they too little too late, just delaying the inevitable?

I wish I knew. But I know this. It all comes back to water.

A few years ago, I was helping with a field trip that involved a stop in far southwestern Kansas at Point of Rocks in the Cimarron National Grassland, land that was taken out of crop production in the 1930s because of the Dust Bowl drought. It was spring, and western Kansas had enjoyed lots of rain. From the top of Point of Rocks, the grassland was covered by blooming wildflowers, mostly the hazy orange of *Gaillardia*, or blanket flower. I grew up in central Kansas in the 1950s, and I'd read early accounts of the plains that describe the prairie as a "carpet of wildflowers." I never thought I'd see that. But I did that day, in arid southwestern Kansas, in the most unlikely place, a place defined by water scarcity.

And I saw those flowers because of water.

Tornado!

Thomas Fox Averill

Tornados may be as common in Kansas literature as they are in reality, with noteworthy poetical and fictional touchdowns at least as frequent as the famous ones all Kansans know: Irving, Udall, Topeka, Andover, and Greensburg, for example. A tornado launched the broadcasting career of Bill Kurtis, who, while finishing his law degree at Washburn University of Topeka, was working for WIBW television. When the 1966 Topeka tornado ripped across the city, from Burnett's Mound, through downtown—even tearing copper from the dome of the State Capitol—and beyond, he was the voice of reality, imploring people with his famous line: "For God's sake, take cover." He said in a speech fifty years later: "Until those seconds after 7:00 p.m. on June 8, 1966, I had made the decision to practice law in Wichita. For months I had been agonizing between law and a career in television, even though television journalism was just a toddler, inventing itself as it went along. Now, the potential showed itself. It could save lives. If it could do that in 1966, what potential did it have for the future? From a cauldron of tragedy, I was given the privilege of seeing inside the future and it changed my life. The law would have to wait." Indeed, the law has waited all through Kurtis's brilliant and accomplished career.

The first and classic Kansas fictional tornado comes at the beginning of *The Wonderful Wizard of Oz* (1900). Some speculate that author L. Frank Baum—because he was fascinated with cyclones and had included news of the nationally famous Irving, Kansas, tornado in his *Aberdeen Saturday Pioneer* when he was editor—was inspired to use Kansas as his setting because of the fame of that particular twister.

Uncle Henry sat upon the doorstep and looked anxiously at the sky, which was even grayer than usual. Dorothy stood in the door with Toto in her arms, and looked at the sky too. Aunt Em was washing the dishes.

From the far north they heard a low wail of the wind, and Uncle Henry and Dorothy could see where the long grass bowed in waves before the coming storm. There now came a sharp whistling in the air from the south, and as they turned their eyes that way they saw ripples in the grass coming from that direction also.

Suddenly Uncle Henry stood up.

"There's a cyclone coming, Em," he called to his wife. "I'll go look after the stock." Then he ran toward the sheds where the cows and horses were kept.

Aunt Em dropped her work and came to the door. One glance told her of the danger close at hand.

"Quick, Dorothy!" she screamed. "Run for the cellar!"

Toto jumped out of Dorothy's arms and hid under the bed, and the girl started to get him. Aunt Em, badly frightened, threw open the trap door in the floor and climbed down the ladder into the small, dark hole. Dorothy caught Toto at last and started to follow her aunt. When she was halfway across the room there came a great shriek from the wind, and the house shook so hard that she lost her footing and sat down suddenly upon the floor.

Then a strange thing happened.

The house whirled around two or three times and rose slowly through the air. Dorothy felt as if she were going up in a balloon.

The north and south winds met where the house stood, and made it the exact center of the cyclone. In the middle of a cyclone the air is generally still, but the great pressure of the wind on every side of the house raised it up higher and higher, until it was at the very top of the cyclone; and there it remained and was carried miles and miles away as easily as you could carry a feather. . . .

In spite of the swaying of the house and the wailing of the wind, Dorothy soon closed her eyes and fell fast asleep.

Like *The Wonderful Wizard of Oz*, many Kansas novels begin with a tornado. Langston Hughes uses one in *Not Without Laughter* (1930) to introduce readers to his characters and his place, the fictional Stanton, Kansas. Aunt Hager Williams stands in her doorway examining a "sulphurous yellow" sky, and then sees "a black cloud twisting like a ribbon in the western sky." She and her grandson Sandy try to leave for next door, where a Mis' Carter has a cellar, but as they open the front door, they hear "a deafening division of wood from wood," and see "the front porch rise into the air . . . sailing high in the gathering darkness, . . . soon lost to sight." Then comes rain, roaring "on the roof of the house," pounding the windows, and then "only the lashing noise of the water, coupled with the feeling that something terrible was happening, or had already happened."

John Ise researched and wrote a fictionalized account of his parents' experiences homesteading in Osborne County, near Downs, Kansas. He creates a connection to Irving and that famous (Oz) tornado in his 1936 novel *Sod and Stubble*:

> The great black cloud masses in the background were moving forward heavily but rapidly, sending out intermittent flashes of lightning that made the background only darker. Fleecy clouds beneath raced along madly, dipping low and rising again, twisting and whirling and scurrying this way and that, as if in a veritable panic. . . . The rain curtain beneath the scurrying clouds presently turned a luminous green, against which the trees and the stable stood out in spectral silhouette; a deathly quiet intervened, the leaves on the trees stirring tremulously, in weird contrast to the vast commotion overhead; then the clouds over to the northwest circled and rushed together, and a black funnel dropped toward the ground—the dreaded cyclone!
>
> A few great hailstones came hurtling down and bounced along the ground, vivid streaks of lightning flashed from the outlying clouds, while the great, black cloud stalactite moved relentlessly forward, writhing and bending sinuously, reaching down menacingly toward the ground, then rising again, as if loathe to begin its work of desolation.
>
> Rosie was calling insistently from the cellar, and Henry closed the door and went down to join her. . . . Then the wind suddenly struck, the cellar door creaked, and the cabin shook above them. . . . For a few minutes the wind raged, and then slowly died down. Henry climbed up the steps, lifted the cellar door and looked out. The sun was shining bright and serene! . . . The stone house was still standing, and the stable, and the chicken house. The storm had missed them! . . .
>
> Anxious about the fate of neighbors up north, Henry hitched the horses to the wagon and took Rosie and the children up to Bartsch's. . . . Chris Bartsch's promising wheat was completely ruined by the hail, dead chickens lay scattered about the yard, and the backs of some of his horses and cattle were covered with blood; but Chris's smile was unchanged. He was thankful it was no worse. The next day came news that the cyclone had left a ghastly path of ruin eastward. Irving, a hundred miles away, had been torn to kindling.

A poem, in its brevity, can still capture the drama and intensity of a twister. Witness the following, by May Williams Ward, published in *Kansas Magazine* in 1939:

Tornado
Leaves stood still and our hearts stood still
But the sky was a-boil with clouds,
A coppery wrack and the greenish black
Of shrouds.
We dove for shelter and none too soon.
The universe swayed and swirled.
The monstrous horn of a unicorn
Gored the world.

At the beginning of his 1963 novel *The Learning Tree*, Gordon Parks describes not only a tornado but also another storm as his main character is introduced to his sexuality. Newt is examining an ant hill when an extraordinary wind chills the air, destroying the hill and jolting Newt from his reverie: "A great swirling black cloud was moving toward him from the southwest, . . . broad at the top, gradually narrowing to a point at the bottom near the earth—looking every bit like a spinning top." He starts to run, looking like "a small, wiry broad-shouldered scarecrow, his tattered shirt and bib overalls flapping from the wind."

The sixteen-year-old Mabel has been sent to find twelve-year-old Newt, and she reaches him just as the storm strikes Cherokee Flats (Parks's fictional name for Fort Scott). She picks him up to carry him to shelter, but they fall, and Newt cuts his leg on a plow edge. They finally struggle toward a nearby smokehouse, while the "high winds, rotating counter-clockwise, pushed, snatched and twisted them over the violent countryside." Newt falls yet again: "His head struck first. Pain jolted through his neck to his belly and shimmied out to his toes."

Mabel tears a strip from her dress to tourniquet Newt's bleeding leg, then tears more and begins cleaning him up. The half-conscious Newt wakes up hurting and cold, and Mabel finds a blanket. She reassures him: "'Be warmin' you up in a minute. We's lucky to be inside. We's smack in the middle of a cyclone. Everything's gonna blow away if this keeps up.'"

She orders him to take off his wet clothes, and she yanks off the remains of her dress and they shelter under the blanket together. She pulls "Newt hard against her naked body. 'Come closer, boy, if you want to git warm.' . . . And

soon the warmth of Big Mabel brought a glow to his own body, and a hard-
ness to his groin—one he had never felt before." Newt experiences a differ-
ent kind of storm: "The killing house shook all over and the shingles kept
flying away, but Newt felt even warmer. . . . And though the storm blew on,
it was not long before Newt completely forgot its blowing."

In Robert Day's iconic novel *The Last Cattle Drive* (1977), narrator Leo,
along with his boss Spangler and crew, are exposed to every possible ele-
ment Kansas can serve up, including, of course, a tornado.

At sunset the light turned green against the clouds. It was still. We kept
looking over our shoulders. Opal turned on the lights. Jed spotted a
funnel dropping out of the clouds to the southwest.

It was high in the air and pulsed down, then up, then down. It seemed
to float, as though in a news film, far away and not real. . . . I looked
ahead. There was no place to hide, I thought. Then I thought: Is there a
place to hide with two hundred and fifty steers and four horses, a truck,
three men, Opal, a cat, and one bingy heifer? The funnel sucked itself
back up into the clouds. . . . Jed whistled and slapped his hat against his
leg, then pointed the hat to the northwest, where a funnel had come out
of the clouds about ten miles away and was surging toward the ground.
It was growing thick toward the top like a weightlifter's thigh, but as it
touched the ground, the bottom two-thirds was thin and lithe. We could
not see the ground it touched. . . .

Jed pushed down the broken window to get a better look. "She is coming
up the hill," he said evenly. "She is tossing wood in front of her." . . .

"Step on it," I said, looking out the back window. We jumped ahead.
Tree branches and sheet metal sailed onto the road in front of us. . . .

"It's coming down the road! I yelled. "On the right side—it's coming
down the road!" Spangler looked in the mirror.

. . . Jed opened his door and looked back.

"You turn right at the next road," Jed said. . . .

"Keep going," I said, looking out the window.

"You swing the truck wide," said Jed.

Spangler yelled. We could hardly hear him. He rolled down his
window, and we could hear the hissing turning to a roar. . . . And clear
as could be, I could see fenceposts and a water tank being sucked in
at the base. Trees along a ridge were bending in toward the pasture. In
the failing light that funnel was visible darkness. We made the turn, the

trailer whipping behind us but staying upright. The funnel cut back of us. . . . We drove a mile south and stopped and got out.

"Now we've got a fucking mess," Spangler said. "Cattle all over this country and it's dark." We stood . . . watching the funnel plow over a hill and then float in the air for a time, before blending in with the dark clouds in a dark sky.

The sun was down, and a string of trailing clouds was beginning to cover the horizon. It got dark quickly and then began to rain.

Dallas Wiebe, poet, novelist, and longtime editor of the *Cincinnati Poetry Review*, was a Mennonite from central Kansas, and on every page of his 1987 *The Kansas Poems* he writes a tornado snippet as a running "footer." Some of the pithiest:

Tornado

The birds get awfully quiet.

There goes the barn.

Do me a favor
And wipe out
    the rich.

I hope it hits the church.
I'm tired of sermons.

The southwest corner
    of the basement
Was covered
    with our green sweat.

Did anyone remember
to turn off
the gas?

It's funny
How a low pressure system
Can give you
    high blood pressure.

Once I was milking a cow.
My dad yelled, "Run."
I said, "What's the matter?'
As the water in a field spun up into the air,
Billboards flew across the highway
And a house turned on its foundation.
The cow's name was Daisy.

In the debris
The skull of a pig.

It's one way
  of getting the family
  together.

Come again.

In May 2007 an EF5 tornado destroyed 95 percent of Greensburg, Kansas, which was rebuilt over the next several years as a "green" town. Playwright Marcia Cebulska was commissioned by the William Inge Center for the Arts to write a play honoring the struggle, survival, and rebuilding of the town. She interviewed citizens of Greensburg for much of her material, and local residents were actors in the 2012 premiere of *Rooted: The Greensburg Odyssey.*

Voices of the Community

The sky started to look dark.
The sky looked green.

Huge drops of rain began to fall.
The lightning was wicked, just wicked.
We felt the strong wind.
The wind drove gravel right into our skin.
The storm siren went off.
We head for the basement.
The house begins to make an odd creaking noise.
We hear things banging around.
I hear a screaming wind. A high pitched screaming wind.

The windows bust out.
The doors start slamming.
Banging and crashing.
This can't be happening!

Yul

Have you seen it out there? Have you seen our town? Cattle feeders tangled up in power lines. Trees lopped off like they was toothpicks. Houses picked up and smashed to bits. Everything gone. The whole town is gone.

Tamara

This is our town after the tornado. Grass torn out of the ground. Car parts up in trees. A house completely flattened except for a closet standing with a wedding dress left hanging inside. People lost their loved ones, their homes, their baby pictures. We had ourselves a tornado, but we sure didn't land in no Oz.

A fascination with weather, the "vertical geography" of Kansas, led Caryn Mirriam-Goldberg to collaborate with photographer Stephen Locke to capture "tornadoes, tempests and thunderous skies" in *Chasing Weather* (2014).

Respect the Storm of the Storm

Watch like your life depends on it.
The first wave pushes the blackbirds
over the seam of the darkening west.
Uplifting wind multiplies and divides the world.
Flags tatter themselves in its speed. Then sirens.

From the overhang of your porch, wait
for the imprint of lightning to open your eyes.
Surrender to the wide yawning of thunder, the tendrils
trailing the supercell, and the one sweet songbird
at once unaware and aware. Follow
the storm of the storm, not the storm you expect.

When the rotation makes landfall, go inside swiftly.
Rush the stairs to the basement, grabbing the small cat

and photo albums on the way. Call the neighbors
from the crawl space. Press the anxious dog to your chest.
Turn up the weather radio and let the tone of danger
vibrate through your beating heart.

Obey the hunter you once were thousands of years ago.

In Kate McIntyre's "Culvert Rising," from *Mad Prairie* (2021), an ideal-istic young teacher, making it her mission to educate the young in a rural western Kansas town, discovers too many of their dark secrets. About to be burned at the Maypole her students built to celebrate spring, she must also endure the insult of a Kansas tornado.

The sky had sickened to the green-yellow hue of twisters. The siren atop the school roared over the keen of the wind. The clouds streamed forward, punctured by dashes of lightning. Miriam tried to pick out shapes in the vaporous mass, to spot the beginnings of the end. A few feathery nubbins of fog plucked delicately down for mere seconds only to suck back into the main mass, which roiled purple-black. At last, the world hurts like I do, Miriam thought. A pathetic fallacy, her literary training reminded her. The clouds didn't care a whit for her sorrows.

"Hurry, hurry," urged Mr. Kalt. The teachers stuffed pages of *Teaching is Learning* all around Miriam and Mrs. Winkler—under their knees, in their armpits.

"What should I do with these?" a teacher asked, holding up the three knotty pine boxes containing Miriam's family's ashes.

"Keep them with me," Miriam said.

The teacher shrugged and wedged them between Miriam's legs. Mr. Kalt struck a match. Jericho would get his wish. The Maypole would burn. Mr. Kalt stabbed the match around the crumpled paper and threw it right in the center of the pile. The wind thundered like a fully laden Mack truck. Everyone except Miriam and Mrs. Winkler clapped their hands over their ears.

"Look!" Mrs. Sheldrake said. Behind the school, a thin finger of cloud reached down toward the earth. Teachers and students all paused to gape as the finger grew into a thumb, then a whole arm.

Mr. Kalt grabbed a thick handful of matches, scraped the heads against the box, and threw the lit matches at Miriam. He turned tail and sprinted for the shelter of the school. He easily outpaced the teachers, who didn't pause a moment for Miriam's students, trailing at the back of the pack.

Most of the matches blew out, but a lit match ignited a wad of paper right at Miriam's armpit. A tickle turned to a prickle. The prickle turned to a sting. Wind fanned the flame. The axis mundi broke the back of the world. The May Pole at her spine formed a divining rod that would guide her to the bosoms of her dead beloveds. Miriam accepted the void's gifts. The tornado split in two. Each funnel widened, dancing with its twin. The turbid air bellowed and charged the women on the pole, a bee-stung bull unfathomably big and strong.

"Nothing ever perfect. Have u noticed that?" Miriam asked Mrs. Winkler, who was beyond response. That had been one of her mother's sayings, infuriating for all its truth. Miriam never did tell her mother how much the saying annoyed her. It doesn't mean anything! Miriam would have liked to have shouted right in her dead mother's face. Of course nothing's perfect! Or maybe everything is! Have you ever thought of that? Miriam knew one thing: between the wind and the flame, there was nowhere for her to go but up.

Why I Hate *The Wizard of Oz*
Robert Rebein

Imagine having the land of your birth, a place about which you harbor complex and wildly ambivalent feelings, reduced to a banal cartoon. Someone asks you where you're from, and when you reply "Kansas," the well-meaning stranger grins and blurts out, "Where's Toto? Oh, that's right. We're not in Kansas anymore!"

You get this in New York, Indiana, California. Even as far afield as Paris, you get it. "Kansoz! Ah, oui. Les munchkins!"

How to say you hail from a place uninhabited by tinmen and sweet little girls in pinafores, a demanding, starkly beautiful place with twenty-mile views, sunflowers as big as your head, and night skies so clear you might believe yourself to have been born among stars? Where the wind blows without cease and flies bite like vampires and the stink of the slaughterhouse overhangs everything like a toxic cloud. Where it's not unusual for a kid like you to receive his first shotgun at age ten, drive a wheat truck at twelve, and solo in a Beechcraft Debonair at fourteen or fifteen.

"Does that sound like Oz?" you want to ask.

You don't, though. Why bother?

When the tornado came and swept you away, as you knew all along it would, it was not to drop you into some Technicolor fantasy, but rather into the same world of Applebee's and Best Buy the jokesters inhabit. That's the context here. That's the reason you refuse to join Dorothy's fan club.

There Was a Tremendous Softness

Michael Kleber-Diggs

First, the hard thing: about a month before my twin brother, Martin, and I turned nine, our father was shot and killed at the dental office he owned.

That was about forty-four years ago now. It isn't unusual for people to know me for years without knowing that my father died or how. When I speak about it, I feel a need to soften the news, to comfort the listener, to protect them from my hardest loss.

When my father died, I was not yet old enough to consider the possibility that such a thing might happen. I knew people died, maybe even that children died sometimes, and I'm pretty sure my thinking on it stopped there.

Which is my way of saying all of it was shocking, a real disruption, a re-ordering, a shift in my thinking and in my connection to people and places, a shift so large that I did not notice it until decades later.

Now, as I look back on it, I imagine the day differently. I see it a bit more from my mother's perspective: the call that came to her, who she called in response, the team she assembled, all the people leaving their day to help us, everyone thinking *what to do about the boys*, the plan to come to our school, to pick us up, the decision on where to take us to deliver the news.

And, after that, what to do *with* the boys, what to do *for* the boys.

All the decisions that had to be made; all the tasks that had to be completed.

I'm too ashamed to tell you how old I was when I first considered how lonely that time must have been for my mother, how devastating and exhausting and sad.

Eventually—after a few weeks, I think—it was decided that my brother and I should leave Kansas City and go to Wichita to live with our maternal grandparents, Arthur and Grace, while our mother did all the things she had to do associated with her hard loss. Arthur and Grace, who every single grandchild called Granddaddy and Grandmommy, even when we were all well into our adulthood.

They had a small home on a standard lot—a buttercream-yellow house on East Eighth Street, in the northeast quadrant of Wichita, but barely northeast, more central (eight blocks off Central, in fact). Grandmommy's Oldsmobile, a gift from the family she worked for as a housekeeper and nanny, was always in their one-car garage, and Granddaddy's green-and-white older Chevy truck was always in the driveway, off to the side on a parking pad he'd added himself. Company entered through the front door, but in the many years they lived there, I don't think I ever did. We entered through the garage or the side door. From there, the basement stairs were straight ahead, the garage was to the left, and the kitchen was to the right. As you entered the kitchen, up a stair or two from the side entry, there was a small pedestal ashtray with one of those push-button trays that would sink and spin to send spent ashes into a container below. The ashtray usually held three or four tobacco pipes, plus yesterday's ashes and that day's too. Atop the pedestal there always rested a can of Prince Albert tobacco.

Their house was a fragrant house: pipe tobacco and smoke, Folgers in the morning and Sanka in the afternoon, bacon and brandy, cocoa butter and inexpensive aftershave, Polident and Fixodent. Mothballs in the basement, detergent on the sheets, hot food at the stovetop every morning and every night. Bacon, wheat toast, and eggs scrambled for us in the small bit of bacon grease that was not poured into a used coffee can and kept around for cooking. Red meat, some kind of potato, a green vegetable—mustard greens or collard greens (always with a ham hock), spinach or green beans—with a roll and a small dessert, homemade ice cream or cake, the best peach cobbler ever made, something sweet every night. Lunch was usually cold meat on plain bread with yellow mustard, a few chips, and a piece of fruit. Sometimes, Granddaddy would make what he called "choker sandwiches," so named because its three ingredients—bread, peanut butter, and honey— were difficult to swallow.

Beyond the kitchen, there was a small living room (to the left) and a small dining room (to the right). Through the dining room, there was a year-round porch my grandfather had also added himself. Beyond the living room and dining room, there was a bathroom and two bedrooms—theirs was off to the right a bit, and ours was off to the left. We had two twin beds with old plush mattresses and dense, durable pillows, and both beds were quite high off the ground. In the basement, there was a family room with a few recliners and a television. Past that, there was a bedroom where our mother's only brother, our grandparents' youngest child, had slept before he left for college a couple of years previous (he had a collection of *Playboy* magazines and more prurient periodical temptations in a wooden chest at the base of his bed). The rest of the basement was unfinished. There was a room where Grandmommy kept canned goods and her preserves, a small room with a shower Granddaddy had installed at some point, beyond that the washer and dryer, and, off in the far corner, things they stored—coins in coffee cans, documents in cardboard boxes, a couple of guns, my granddaddy's fishing equipment, his golf equipment, and lots of things I cannot remember, not even generally.

Perhaps now is a good time to tell you I am an unintentionally unreliable narrator. Sometimes I say, "I have a terrible memory," but I'm not sure that's right. I remember some things quite well: the smells of my grandparents' house, what I watched on television the night I learned my father was dead (*The Man from Atlantis*), who starred in that show (Patrick Duffy), what I did the morning of my father's funeral (played tetherball with Martin), and riding in a limousine for the first time.

There are lots of things I do not remember well: my father's funeral service is a blur of general images. I don't remember the interment at all. I don't remember the names of most of my grade school, junior high, or high school teachers, even those I loved and admired.

Every once in a while, things come back to me. When they do, I wonder if my memory is terrible or if I've cultivated a selective memory. I read or heard that when traumatic things happen, human beings respond in particular ways: fight, flight, freeze, fawn, forget.

I'm pretty sure I chose to forget. When I try to remember that time, I notice I can recall things that were pleasant or soft, things that kept me from falling apart. A few hard things endure: my mother's face when she came to tell us the news, my brother's face as she told us, and the first night without my father, trying to get to sleep in the bottom bunk, worried about nightmares, imagining I might disappear too.

I think my brother chose something besides *forget*. My theory is *fight*. He remembers a lot, especially in comparison to me. Because we are twins, I wonder sometimes if my ability to forget (or sequester hard things away) depends on my brother's ability to remember. Comforted in a belief that a record of that time could be kept without me, I deleted my files or hid them away and forgot where.

I don't know how long we lived with our grandparents. Sometimes I try to piece it together: we left Kansas City not long after the funeral; we enrolled in school in Wichita the following fall. There was a winter that we lived at Grandmommy and Granddaddy's. We had a birthday there the following April, I think. We moved out of the house in Kansas City the following summer, I think.

Time was a blur back then, so let it be blurry here.

I could ask Martin or my mom, and they would tell me. I could ask them to fill in the gaps for me, but I want this to be my story, and I hope something like truth will come from how I felt and how I feel. Anyway, as you read this, assume the facts are close, generally correct, true in emotion and tone.

My grandparents moved from Watonga, Oklahoma, to Wichita when my mother was quite young. I think they wanted to start a family and needed to be near work that would allow them enough income to do that. Before the house on East Eighth Street, there was another house, a bigger house. My mom mostly grew up there. I don't know why they moved to the house on Eighth. I don't know if they downsized by choice or circumstance.

The lawn at our grandparents' house was perfect. Granddaddy worked on it at least a little bit every day. There was a produce garden in their backyard. You accessed it through a chain-link fence just past the side entrance. There was a small patch of pristine grass between that garden and a small metal shed where Granddaddy kept his tools and his lawnmower. As I remember it, he worked on other people's lawns and hauled things in his truck, and, by that time in his life, primarily did odd jobs here and there. Grandmommy worked part time, which I probably imagined had more to do with her age than with the unexpected presence of two nine-year-old boys in her house.

My grandparents seemed quite old to me then. They weren't. I did the math. They were around sixty, seven years older than I am now. They both had many years of life left—my grandmommy died in 2015, almost forty years after I lived with her. Granddaddy died in 1997.

My grandparents moved at a precious pace, never watched television back then, mostly drank decaf, and listened to Paul Harvey and the Kansas City Royals on AM radio. They had dentures and rarely ate at restaurants or after 6:00 p.m. They had chifforobes and davenports. They had slipcovers. There was a small marble-topped table in the living room with one of those glass dishes on it filled with sublime ribbon candy that was so old it had gone soft.

Grace and Arthur were shaped by the Great Depression. They kept almost everything they received and oriented their lives around enough, not abundance. My grandfather whittled and got his hair cut at a place where old men got haircuts and played checkers and looked at naughty magazines we were not allowed to touch. Grandmommy was in the ladies auxiliary at her church and attended long services faithfully every Sunday. She wore spectacular hats and knew her way around the kitchen at the church too.

That's where I see her, standing in the kitchen, cooking or cleaning. Grandmommy was soft and short—5'3" or so. She had medium-brown skin and wore wigs sometimes and spectacular hats (it bears repeating). Grandmommy wore polyester pants and bright-colored shirts to work but simple, bright-colored cotton dresses besides. I think she made most of them herself. She wore sensible shoes and inexpensive eyewear. She had arthritis in her hands. She was quiet and hugged us often. She had five kids. By the time we arrived at her house, she'd mastered a balance between expectations and space. We were expected to go to school, and that was pretty much it. If we weren't acting right, at home or at school, she'd ask a calm question like *Where did you get that idea?* Or *Where did you learn to use words like that?* She was never angry or upset with us, except one time when I was rifling through the refrigerator and rested my shoe on the inside frame, appalling her to tears and prompting her to remove all the contents and scrub the interior with bleach and water. She was frustrated with Granddaddy sometimes, but she had just cause. Our grandmommy was a church lady. She made and served food at weddings and funerals. She encouraged the family's attendance every Sunday. If she had any vices, I didn't know about them.

Our grandparents didn't do many things together. As far as I know, Grandmommy found joy in society at church; I'm certain our granddaddy found joy in the society of men and games with varying ranges of skill and luck—golf, cards, dominoes. Otherwise, they worked in the house or on the yard.

They also worked their garden. Their house was on a standard city lot, not much land at all. The garden sat just behind the back porch, and, working from memory, it was just a bit longer than the porch, twelve feet or so, and eight or nine rows wide. There must have been two plantings each season. As I remember it, the garden produced lettuce, tomatoes, cucumbers, spinach, peas, beets, and watermelons. Both of our grandparents tended the garden, not often together. We helped like nine-year-old city kids would help. We learned to hoe. We moved weeds in a wheelbarrow the twenty-five feet or so to the side of the shed. We picked things that were clearly ready and left everything else alone. With my grandparents' garden, whatever could be eaten was. What could be canned or pickled was; those things were always eaten too.

I had not gardened before I gardened with my grandparents. I likely had helped my mom pot or plant a few flowers, but we did not have a vegetable garden in Kansas City.

So the summer after my father died was the first time I really gardened. I gardened a lot that summer. We watched some TV shows (*Ultraman* and *Davey and Goliath*) but not many. There weren't many kids in the neighborhood, so we didn't go outside to play very often. We took the summer off from football and baseball. I probably wasn't much of a gardener. I imagine now my dirty hands and knees. I feel like I remember watching things grow and ripen. I'm sure I carried things into the house. I know we ate things fresh off the vine. I distinctly remember hoeing and getting calluses on my hands. I know Granddaddy used his pocketknife to cut fat slices of tomato and eat them at the kitchen sink.

I'm sure I was bored at the time, but when I look back on it, I remember those days with pristine fondness; the images are hazy and soft like a dream.

My father was in the kitchen, talking on the phone. For a moment, I wondered if I should say "good morning," as was expected, or allow him to have his call without interruption, as was also expected. I don't remember what I decided or what the outcome was. I remember kissing my father's cheek. I remember his tight morning scruff and the smell of his aftershave.

From there, I fill in the moments with assumptions. The assumption is that Martin and I did what we usually did. We walked down a small hill from our house, then up a big hill, to Silver City Elementary. Other kids would have been around. Maybe I had to carry my three-quarter-size cello with me that day. We would have arrived at school. The day would have started as it usually did.

I know we were taking a standardized test. I confirmed this with Martin. I remember analogies, fish : fisherman :: pheasant : __________. Martin and I were in fourth grade because we had skipped second grade. I don't remember if it was morning or afternoon or how far into the day we were. But at some point during our school day, a man went to our father's office, where he worked as a dentist, asked for drugs, and then, when our father said he didn't have any, shot him twice.

Later, responding to a provocation I sensed beyond sight or sound, I looked up from my test to see my teacher. I saw her looking at the classroom door in a way that compelled me to look there too.

I remember seeing my mother standing in the doorway, and I remember understanding from her face—

something terrible happened
something terrible happened to our father
we would not see our father again

We walked to a home nearby. The home belonged to our parents' closest friends; their children were Martin's and my closest friends. In the master bedroom, where, a week earlier, we'd watched *Charlie's Angels*, our mother, speaking in short clear sentences, told us our father had been killed and how he'd been killed. I remember she asked if we had any questions. I remember the expression on her face and not having any questions. It was about six weeks before our ninth birthday. I remember my brother had a question, but I don't remember what it was (even though he has reminded me several times over the years). Death was more theoretical to me then than it is now. I understood only that we would not see our father again.

Then home: visitors and care packages, lots of desserts and very few rules. I remember wishing I could breathe underwater and talk to fish. Family arrived, friends. Not much else. The passage of hours and a couple of days. The passage of time beyond the clock or calendar until the day of the funeral, a day with its own specific occurrences—Martin and I dirtying our new suits playing tetherball in the front yard, how upset that made our mother, her tears. I remember the limousine ride to the service, looking out the window instead of inside at Martin or Mom, noticing familiar landmarks that also seemed brand new. I remember a somber gathering at our Presbyterian church, where they played songs my father liked: "Bridge over Troubled Water" and (I think) "A Whiter Shade of Pale." I remember the church was packed. I remember the reception, where I understood for the first time that, in the eyes of those assembled, I was both pitiable and pitied.

In Kansas City, we played outside with kids around our age, built ramps for bicycles and forts with the deepest "dungeons" we could dig. We threw dirt clods and water balloons at other kids while they threw them at us. We shot BB guns (which our parents forbade us to do) and squirt guns (also not allowed). We played wiffle ball and tried to wander past our boundaries, as far as the TG&Y, without getting caught. If we made it to the store, we'd pool our meager money for something to share, usually candy or pop. Sometimes we stole cheap things. I remember boosting a plastic compass—not a real one, but a useless spinning dial with no true north.

For the most part, time outside was scheduled time: recess, compulsory after-school playtime, Cub Scouts and then Webelos. We engaged in intentional activities, the kind of things you planned for and built in, exceptions to our largely indoor lives.

In Wichita, we played with cousins sometimes, but we were usually with our grandparents. We ran errands with Granddaddy. We sat in the truck while he did his work. At the end of each day, he'd give us some money so we could buy candy at a candy store. Many days passed before I understood that my brother purposely dragged his feet choosing his candy so Granddaddy had enough time to buy a pint bottle at the liquor store next door. We had left most of our things in Kansas City—our bicycles, board games, puzzles, and books. We didn't finish the school year. During the week, one grandparent or the other watched us or took us with them as they went about their day. After errands and work, we helped in the garden or played dominoes. The summer passed by pretty quickly. So it seemed that not long after we arrived, we started school.

Near their garden, I swung one of my granddaddy's golf clubs for the first time. Granddaddy showed me how to grip the club, how tightly—"Hold it like you would hold a bird"—how to draw it back and bring it down and through. He said things like "pure is better than hard," and "if you can par with a seven iron, hit a seven iron off the tee."

But most weekends, Granddaddy took us fishing.

I was born at 10:00 a.m., and my brother, Martin, was born at 10:07 a.m., on April 15, 1968, eleven days after Martin Luther King Jr., was assassinated, twins in twin cities. Our house was in Kansas City, Kansas—always a free state—but the hospital was in Kansas City, Missouri—formerly a slave state. I always say I was born in Kansas. There were riots in both cities, and a curfew was in effect. I know my parents drove to the hospital after curfew, when it was dark. I know they were stopped by the police. Martin Luther King Jr. was born Michael King, but he and his father changed their names to Martin when Michael King was young. I got MLK's first name, my brother got his second, and we both share a middle name with him. When we were born, we lived in what I remember as a small light-green house. We moved when my brother and I were pretty young. The only thing I remember about that green house is the black-and-white, four-slice toaster we had there.

Not long ago, I was talking to my mother and brother on the phone. I asked my mom if I could try to describe our second house in Kansas City, the house we lived in when our father died. I wanted to test my memory against my brother's, against what really was.

As I remember it, we had a wide driveway and a two-car garage leading to the basement, where there was a storage room, straight ahead; a laundry room, off to the right; and what we called our playroom across from there. Outside, a set of stairs with a wrought-iron railing led from the driveway to the front door. There was a small entryway, and, beyond that, our living room. It had a window out to the backyard. I remember we had a green couch with slipcovers on it, and a safe hidden behind a painting on one of the walls. To the left of the front door sat our kitchen, on the way to a dining area with two sliding-glass doors that led out to the backyard. To the right of the entryway, there was a hallway with two bedrooms on the right and a bathroom on the left. At the end of the hall, to the left, there was a family room where we watched TV—*Donny and Marie, Hee Haw, The Man from Atlantis, Barney Miller*, basketball, football. My parents' bathroom was along one wall, and their bedroom was at the far end, recessed a bit, down a stair or two.

In the front yard we had a weeping willow tree and a tetherball pole. Along the side of the house, leading to the backyard, there was a small hill that supported a little sledding. Just as you entered the backyard, we had a Sears swing, where wasps took up residence in each end of the top pole. Then, the backyard itself: a concrete area where once there was a swimming pool. A generous stretch of grass, and, beyond all that, along the back and side, a wooded spot all the neighborhood kids called the Okefenokee forest.

When I finish describing the house as I remember it, my mom explains that I have the rooms in the hallway a little bit wrong, and that I forgot a room. Beyond the master bedroom, behind accordion doors that were held closed with a magnet, there was another room—our father's den. My brother remembers not only the room and the order of all the rooms in the hallway, but other things, like a woman standing next to our mom in our classroom doorway when she came to school that day, and what the woman's name was (Georgia), and what her nickname was ("the ice cream lady") too.

I remember general things: our father was busy getting his dental practice going. He also had an ownership share or a majority share or was the sole owner of a new restaurant that wasn't doing well. He was taciturn and mercurial. I remember fearing him sometimes and trying to stay out of his way.

General things: like our mother was the wife of a hectic man, raising young twins while working herself. Our parents had desirable obligations in the small, tight-knit social circle of Black medical professionals in Kansas City. Our mom was a registered nurse, and she was social too (still is). She was also in The Links, an organization for Black women professionals; our father was active in the Missouri chapter of the American Dental Association and another national association, for Black dentists. Busy. We seemed to be concerned with appearance and appearances. All our friends and their parents seemed to be too.

General things: sometimes we played baseball or wiffle ball with our dad in the backyard or went jogging on a 440-yard track nearby. Our dad was fit and trim. He usually ran in khaki pants and pristine sneakers. We watched football on Sundays sometimes. My dad grew up in Boston and liked the Celtics and JFK. A few specific things: he also loved the TV show *Barney Miller*—it made him laugh. I remember his laugh. I remember he liked ice cream and had it almost every day, usually vanilla. He liked blueberry pie too. He wore a small mustache, cut low, like his hair. Both were impeccably maintained. He had a five o'clock shadow every night when he came home. I still remember how it felt to kiss his cheek—sharp and rough. He tended to his appearance with care. He was fond of Hickey Freeman suits and stylish loafers. His shirts were thick cotton and expensive. He favored French cuffs, held fast by ornate cufflinks. He wore Aramis aftershave, the brand I've worn my entire life. He had a black Volvo coupe with leather seats; our mom had a Volvo sedan with cloth seats. He liked music, but I don't think he danced. We went out to eat at places like Red Lobster, and we were always allowed to order whatever we wanted (at Red Lobster, we always added hush puppies). Our dad drank whiskey from crystal decanters he kept in the family room. I remember how it smelled on his breath. As far as I know, he did not drink to excess.

There are things I've been told many times over the years, what I call the mythology of my father, all of it true. He was an outstanding student his entire academic career. He spoke French fluently and knew Latin. He was a talented baseball player. He was fastidious. He never wore jeans and rarely wore sweatpants. It's a silly memory, but I remember once he bought me and my brother each a small toy boat for the bathtub. They came from the Avon catalog and were little barges big enough to hold a bar of soap. They had paddles you could wind up with a rubber band so the boat would travel across the tub. They were a spontaneous gift, which was unusual. As I look back on it, the distance between him giving us those boats and his death was very short, a week or two.

I vaguely remember playing checkers sometimes and learning a bit about chess from him. One year, for Christmas, our parents gave us an expensive and elaborate knowledge system for use in learning math and geography, history and science. I knew our father wanted good things for us: good schools, good outcomes there, and good lives. I know he cared a lot about what and how we were doing, and I know we were loved.

We had an edgy house, an eggshells house. Order was maintained with abundant rules: rules for breakfast and rules for dinner, rules for outdoor play and for returning indoors, for homework and housework, for clothes, for bedtime, for how to act when our dad was on the phone, for how to act when he came home from work, for when we had company, for when football was on. When liver and onions were served, you ate liver and onions or else. You ate whatever was served, and you would not be excused until your plate was cleared. When the streetlights came on, as you hurried home, you made sure not to leave your sweater underneath the weeping willow tree in the front yard again. It was wise not to ask to stay up a little later. Fibbing was a felony. All consequences were certain and swift, unless they needed to wait until our dad got home. Punishments were furious, fueled by frustration, fatigue, and fear. We had Black parents in the '70s; spankings were forceful and common. People were trying to keep their kids safe, alive, and out of the unjust criminal justice system.

Kansas is blessed with sky, not water. We usually fished in creeks or large ponds. Most of the time we drove away from town a bit, east toward El Dorado or west toward Goddard, to fish at Works Progress Administration lakes. The quiet and pace of the house prevailed at the edge of each body of water. Not much happened, and what happened took its time. We had rods that were just the right size for our bodies, simple reels, and blunt sturdy lines. We fished with lead weights and bobbers. My brother and I had lures; Granddaddy usually fished with bait. We mostly practiced casting and reeling. Granddaddy fished. Every so often, he'd point out that one of our bobbers had gone under. If our catch was too big, he'd help us bring it in.

Granddaddy was about my father's size—5'8" or so. He had medium-brown skin and a thin, straight-ish afro, mostly gray. He was wiry and strong. His hands were huge. His fingers were huge too, and his knuckles were angled and amplified by arthritis. I never saw him run or move above a saunter. I rarely saw him sit down until the day was done. As far as I know, he never ate margarine or drank skim milk. He was a protein man, though he wouldn't say it in that way. He worked at a packing house for most of his career. Dinner, as I've said, was usually red meat. We had poultry sometimes. Pork accompanied breakfast. We ate fish on weekends after fishing. Granddaddy never held a gym membership or lifted weights, but he moved without stopping from when he got up until he laid himself down, from when he was born until he died.

Like my father, he had a mustache and shaved around it every day. He wore inexpensive aftershave—Aqua Velva or Skin Bracer—and almost always wore a hat or cap if he was outdoors. He had simple, generously sized wire-frame eyeglasses, with visible bifocals or trifocals. Grandaddy usually wore jeans or overalls, and he was fond of patterned shirts. He smoked tobacco from a pipe throughout the day but not all the time—Prince Albert from a pouch when we were out and about and from a tin can when we were home. Brandy was an issue; I remember that. It accompanied every afternoon and affected the evening sometimes. There was a point when he needed to stop, so he did. That was years after we lived with our grandparents, when Martin and I were in high school or maybe even after that. Granddaddy was kind to me and my brother. He wasn't slow to anger; as far as I know, he never angered. Whenever I was around him, he was unfailingly quiet and patient and kind. If we were doing something we weren't supposed to do, he would shake his head disapprovingly. If we were not doing some chore we were supposed to do, he usually did it—the task needed to be done. In both cases, I'd feel terrible.

Sometimes, when we fished, Granddaddy let us take a sip of his beer. He drank Coors from cans. He kept the come-away pull tops, crushed each can with his hand or foot, and, when he had a bag full, took them, along with any other cans he found, to sell for scrap. I remember the beer as carbonated and a bit warm. It was the first thing I drank that wasn't milk or water or sweet. I never had enough Coors to feel any way in particular, and I didn't like it as much as my brother seemed to.

I don't remember specific fishing trips, except one. I'll tell you about it later. I remember general things: the summer heat, very long outings that were probably quite short, the sound of a transistor radio at a low volume, usually playing a Royals game. I remember his small cooler, filled with beers, a little juice, and a little ice. I remember an ellipsoid red-and-white bobber he had; a round orange-and-yellow bobber; old, dented lead weights of various sizes and amounts; a chain we hooked our catches to; and a rectangular cuboid ruler with a scale at one end, used for weighing and measuring fish. All of it was kept in a small metal tackle box that had bounced around the truck bed a bit and was in line with Granddaddy's general tendency to favor function over form.

I recall the joy of casting out and reeling in, even when nothing was on my line. I remember my grandfather's skill and wondering how it was

I could stand ten feet away from him while he thrived and I starved. I remember waiting. I remember waiting punctuated—rarely for me—by the shock of a sudden pull against my line, the dramatic down arch of my rod, the fast clicking sound of my reel rushing out, the work to bring the line the other way in.

At some point during the time that my brother and I lived with our grandparents (or perhaps a few years after), I learned about Verna Mae. My mother was the oldest sibling her entire life, but Verna Mae was my grandparents' first child. She died when she was two, I think, of the flu; I vaguely recall a medical error associated with her death. There was a small plaque in her honor in our grandparents' basement. When I talked to Grandmommy about it, Verna Mae had died thirty-nine years before. Around the same amount of time between my father's death and the writing of this essay.

grief : people :: water : rock

So, by the time each of us told our story, we had acquired an ability to speak about our losses without losing our voice, without a tremble. And yet, for reasons that are mysterious to me and will remain mysterious, I feel like my relationship with loss was shaped over time, while my grandmommy's relationship with loss was shaped by the times.

It's a theory I have. Losing a child was more common back then, I think. Women's loss was. Black loss. Black families' losses.

Please don't understand me to say that what my grandmommy carried was small or light or unsurprising. I know it was shocking and heavy. I was a child when we talked about it. A child with his own loss; a child who needed sheltering and received it.

With the benefit of time, experience, and perspective, I wonder now if the love and care our grandparents offered us was shaped by their loss, if they extended to us in our grief what they would have wanted in theirs. It is possible they had been supported and sustained by a loving community. I was too young to ask. So I am left to wonder what or who—if anything, if anyone—was, for them, salvation.

At the time, I don't think I thought about it, but as an adult, I have come to understand that my mom stayed in Kansas City for a lot of reasons. She sold our dad's dental practice and his stake in the restaurant. She likely dealt with insurance companies and lawyers. I think she attended the criminal trial and met with police officers and prosecutors. She grieved. She got back on her feet. She got the house ready for sale and sold it. Martin and I went up with our grandparents to "help" load the moving van. I have come to understand that my mom spent the time when we lived with our grand-parents getting ready—administratively, physically, mentally, and emotion-ally—to join us in Wichita.

Our mom. She is short like her mom was: 5'4" or so back then, shorter now, at eighty-two. She had short, straight dark-brown hair back then and has a short carob-and-gray-colored afro now. When we were young, she was fond of patterned dresses, and I've always known her to care about her appearance too. I think of my mom as many things. She could be stern or playful. She has a broad emotional range and an expansive willingness to share how she feels even when how she feels is hard to consider. Related to that moment in time, here's how I think of it now. After an excruciating loss, our mom reunited with us in Wichita. We got an apartment, then a condo, then another. My mom went back to school and got a master's in psychiat-ric nursing, then taught at Wichita State University. She sent us to summer camp, took us on modest but wonderful vacations, exposed us to art and ideas, invested in our projects, encouraged us, and scolded us. My mom is a woman of uncommon endurance. She is among the more vulnerable people I've ever met and among the strongest.

At some point after we lived with our grandparents, my brother and I got Ronco Pocket Fisherman rods and reels for our birthday or Christmas. We lived by then in a condominium community called Country Lake, "lake" being a generous term for what it was. It was more like a pretty-good-sized pond. There was a creek nearby where we grabbed crawdads only to let them go, but the lake of Country Lake was stocked with catfish and small-mouth bass. Martin and I fished there several times a week—catch and re-lease unless we grabbed something grand. We took big fish home for our mom to scale and gut and cook.

In high school, we lived in a condominium community called Chisholm Creek, which had a real creek that was wide enough and deep enough to fish in. We fished there too. We usually fished alone, but I sometimes fished with a Vietnam vet who lived nearby and told me stories about the war.

We were moderately skilled by then—not Grandaddy good, but good. We affixed our own night crawlers. We graduated from the Pocket Fisher-mans to full rods and reels. We had tackle boxes full of equipment, lots of lures, thoughts about test lines, and ideas for fishing in different kinds of wa-ter. We didn't use bobbers. We could sense when a fish was nibbling, could tell what was on the line by how it fought, and knew when we were snagged or encountered a catfish. We knew when to fight and when to let the fish run. Sometimes, we woke early to go fishing. We went fishing after school plenty of times and most weekends. We knew how to fish. We knew where to fish. We had grown more patient. We had learned how to be still and wait.

A specific memory from when we lived with our grandparents: Granddaddy took me and Martin fishing at a catfish farm outside of town, a rectangular pond overstocked with hungry catfish. There weren't many trees. We checked in at a shed without air conditioning, and the man who worked there sold us a few things—bait, etc. He was an older man, at least Granddaddy's age. He had white hair and a medium-length white beard. He was a mostly outdoors man, and his skin was rough and red. I don't remember specific conversation, but in my memory the man was Kansas kind: colloquially conversational, social regarding the business we were there to transact.

There were no clouds around, and there was no shade to seek. It was summer in southern Kansas, and the sun worked on us real hard. When I think back on that day two things stand out, and the first was the almost unbearable heat.

It seemed not to affect Granddaddy at all. This wasn't fishing, really. Our cast-to-catch ratio was comical. Almost no technical skill was required. The things it's helpful to have when you're fishing—smart equipment, sensitive hands, knowledge of the water, a feeling for where the fish are biting (connected to time, season, temperature, weather, and knowledge or experience), patience, a solid hook game, and a sense for how to bring the catch in—these things were not needed at this catfish farm. I'm sure our excitement was purchased by Granddaddy's boredom.

Catfish stay low in the water, down near the muddy bottom, where it's cool. They don't move around a lot. When you catch on one, it feels more like a stop than a fight. I used to think I'd hooked a log or a boot or got tangled in a mess of weeds.

And so it was that day, catching my first catfish. I'd been reeling my line in slowly, then everything stopped. I thought I was snagged, and in the effort to get unstuck, I realized I'd landed a fish.

I brought it in gradually, like you would work a wrench in a tight space: turn a bit, reset your hand, turn a bit, reset your hand. It took a while. I remember Granddaddy watching me, but only a little—if this one got away, there'd be another one soon. There was a sudden silvery thrash near the pond's surface, and there it was, an ugly whiskery thing, probably both bigger and smaller in reality than it appeared to me back then.

Not my first fish, by the way, even if it was my first catfish. I'd caught fish on other trips with Granddaddy. And there'd been fishing of a sort back in Kansas City, through Cub Scouts—little guys, crappies and sunnies and such. I remember reaching for the catfish, wanting to do it on my own, to be a fisherman, and getting whipped and stung by its barbels, and feeling hot and hurt and elated. I know Granddaddy set his rod and reel down, came over to me, took hold of the fish like a person would hold a bird, unhooked it with casual ease, and put it in our bucket. I imagine he said something affirming.

I know Martin caught fish that day too. I remember that, but I don't remember whether he unhooked his own. If I had to guess, I'd say he did.

I don't know how long we stayed—a very long time that was actually not long at all. We put our bobbers and weights and bait back in the tackle box. We hooked our hooks on one of the eyes on our fishing poles and tightened the line to hold them in place, then carried our catch back to the shed, where we paid by the pound.

The second thing that stands out: pouring the fish into a metal pan that sat atop a scale. The men somehow accounting for the weight of the water. The fish thrashing about wildly, beating against each other and the sides of the pan, trying to flip out and get away. The proprietor reaching up to a light switch I had not seen, connected to the pan and the scale, flipping it on—then off—with a single finger. I will never forget how suddenly the fish stopped moving at all, how still they were, how calm.

After our mom joined us in Wichita, we visited our grandparents occasionally, not a lot. In the summers we'd visit the family farm in Oklahoma. It had a pond too. We would leave at night. Granddaddy would put a mattress in the back of his truck, and we would drive about four hours (back then) to our land in Watonga, a bit northwest of Oklahoma City. I don't remember doing much at the farm—a few light chores. By the time I was old enough to remember going there, it was primarily a space for family reunions. We'd gather with Kansas cousins and Oklahoma cousins and Florida cousins— outdoors, playing and working.

My mother and her siblings still own the property, and someone checks on it from time to time. We rent it to a farmer nearby, mostly for grazing. The land we own sits atop the Anadarko Basin, a massive field of oil and natural gas. Once a month, the family gets modest compensation from an oil company that leases the mineral rights. Dividends for the land paid for

Grandmommy's last years, when she lived in an expensive memory care unit.

I live in Saint Paul, Minnesota, now. My wife is a horticulturist, and we live near a park about a four-minute walk from a city lake about 1.3 miles in circumference. It has two docks, one for launching canoes, kayaks, and paddleboards, and one mostly for fishing. The lake is home to channel catfish, Northerns, bluegill, largemouth bass, walleye, and a few other kinds of fish. Quite often, even in winter, I see people fishing there, from the dock or shore or on top of the ice. I am not among them. I don't own a rod or reel or tackle box anymore. Sometimes, if I'm up at a friend's cabin, I'll cast a few unlicensed lines, but even counting that, I haven't gone fishing in years.

I'm a writer, and large parts of my life are spent indoors, hunched over a Moleskine or laptop. I read a lot, and I'm more likely to go to a poetry reading than a pond or a creek. I love the outdoors though. I took up one of my granddaddy's other passions—golf. It's a rare round that I don't consult his wisdom. Quite a few of his golf clubs are in my basement; a cousin in Texas has some too. I also have all but one of the golf balls he gave me. They're hard, like rocks, and have a wide red stripe around them. The one I don't have, I placed near Granddaddy's hand as he lay in his casket.

I don't have any of his fishing equipment. My aunt Joyce has it at her home near Dallas. She told me his tackle box was passed down to him by his own daddy.

I enjoy cycling and try to go camping with my wife and her sister and her husband at least once a year. I love scenic hikes by day and sleeping on the ground. I love the ritual of looking for flat land, putting a tarp down, raising a tent, looking for wood and kindling, building a fire, making meals in a Dutch oven, never hurrying, never running but never resting, moving all day from one joyful task to the next, quiet and calm.

Often, when I'm outdoors, I think of my grandparents and how connected they were to the land. Their connection was organic and unscheduled. They began their married life in Oklahoma. My mom was born in a small town called Geary. My grandparents grew up Black at a time when being Black was even more difficult than it is today, when acquiring and keeping land was more difficult, so you cherished it. You mowed and planted flowers. They lived at a time when you made use of everything you had to help you survive. You farmed the acres your parents fought to get and keep; you grew enough food in your backyard. Except for my granddaddy's passion for golf and clubhouse games of chance, my grandparents didn't seem to have hobbies. They didn't watch television until later in life, and for vacation they went to the farm—and worked.

But I think of them when I'm outside. When I'm golfing or camping or on the rare occasion when I go fishing. I think of them when I watch my wife work in the garden or when I'm hiking along a quiet trail.

Black people alive today can see their parents and their parents' parents and all of their ancestors in almost every blessing they have. It's true for me, as well, and so are these facts that persist beyond memory, that maybe even obscure my memory: just before I turned nine, something happened that was very hard. The kind of hard that reshapes a life immediately and gradually, over time; the kind of hard some people never overcome.

And soon after that hard thing happened, there was a tremendous softness:

Arthur and Grace . . .

in their fragrant home, in their home with its purposeful cadences—constant and calm. We were parented there by grandparents with grandchildren who needed abundant care.

If I close my eyes, I can comb my grandfather's thin, gray afro between my fingers or feel again my grandmommy's pillowy bosom against my face. I smell Sanka brewing on their stovetop and hear a radio, mostly catching the AM station they wanted, cracking and humming in the background.

If I close my eyes, I can travel back in time to when I traveled back in time and lived for a certain number of days in what will always be my favorite home, the home of my salvation—a buttercream-yellow house on East Eighth Street, not far at all from the center of Wichita, Kansas.

Notes

I am thankful for my grandparents, Grace and Arthur Glass; my mother, Lequetta Diggs; my father, Dr. James A. Diggs, D.D.S.; my brother, Martin Diggs; my aunt Joyce Smith; my aunt Laura Ross; my cousin Karla Smith; my cousin Bettye Sabree; and all my family members, on both sides, for their support, encouragement, grace, and space. My family is loving and rich with people who value, cherish, and maintain our memories and artifacts. Together we remember and carry forward the stories of those who came before us.

Section III:
Deep Roots: Family & Community

. . . This son of hers, my grandfather,
still walks the streets with me.

Some twist of blood and heat still spark
across the time bridge. Here, listen:

Air draws through these lungs made from his.
His blood still pulses through this hand.
—*Denise Low,* "Walking with My Delaware Grandfather"

Prairie ecosystems are known for their deep roots; some grasses stretch as far as fifteen feet into the earth. Ecologists once believed that this helped grasses compete for low groundwater, but today they know that deep roots aid plants in growing within community with neighboring species. In trees, fungi systems within and among tree roots appear even to speak to one another, sharing resources and warning other trees that danger is present, protecting and serving the greater species.

We humans also live in personal ecosystems as complex and mysterious as the mycorrhizal networks below us. When healthy, we thrive in reciprocity within the relationships of family and community, although defining what that is can be as complex and slippery as the language of scientists exploring these new underground frontiers.

"Where're you from?" is a common question in Kansas. It's a loaded question, of course, but hopefully asked in good faith. What if we asked it straight—*Who are your people?* You could start with naming one of our 105 counties or 627 incorporated cities and towns. But think of all the communities of people within those spheres: the schools and neighborhoods, churches and civic groups, workplaces. Tight-knit families and families scattered to the winds. The quilt guilds and library committees, rotary clubs and café philosophers. The boozers at the tavern on Main. The LGBTQ+ Pride club and the extension PRIDE members (now renamed the Kansas Community Empowerment program). Gamers and hunters, lowriders and activists, shade tree mechanics and HOA boards, festival committees and historical societies. Folks new to town and others here temporarily.

It's a lot of microculture to fathom. Immeasurable kindnesses and generosities, slights and harms, visions and aspirations. For community to thrive, it must be translated, handed off to new generations, adaptable. This section explores the many ways community holds—or doesn't—across Kansas.

Rachel Seth Coleman's essay bridges faraway lands through cooking and shows us how adults can strengthen a child's sense of self and show her the powerful beauty that blooms from transplanted roots. Raylene Hinz-Penner demonstrates the fortitude of young girls on the Great Plains and the communities that depend on them. And Rachel C. Jackson shows us the way generational stories reverberate through the blood and bone of our descendants, transferring knowledge through our roots.

But community isn't easy; our current loneliness epidemic tells us that. Yet it's a part of our social DNA and describes us to others when we venture toward new horizons. B. H. Fairchild's poetic opener addresses these complex feelings from the perspective of the son who does not have the heart, brains, or courage to return to family or community. C. J. Janovy's deep dive into the origin story of Gilbert Baker, creator of the Pride Flag, and the community that wished to welcome him back shows us the need to leave and the pull of returning.

Like the roots of plants, community requires tending. Valerie Mendoza tells the story of her parents and their friends who, when faced with prejudice, built intentional community to care for their Latinx elders. Megan Kaminski's poem pays homage to the brave women of the Amazon Army who fought for labor rights in the mines of southeast Kansas. And Davis Hammet shows us that the work continues today—and that the place you have put down roots can do better.

When the storms come—or the wildfires—it's the folks you neighbor with who will save you. Ian Frazier explores the aftermath of Great Plains wildfires in 2017, showing us that often rescue and safety come from close by, and then often from afar. Matt Perrier's essay about raising cattle in the Flint Hills demonstrates how this neighboring can inspire the next generation to strengthen their root systems and carry on family traditions.

Perhaps our communities and families (given and chosen) can be directly inspired by the root systems of this grassland. We are just as complex and fascinating. What if we did not compete, but rather collaborated and held firm in the storms and protected the riverbanks together? Happily seeding in the spring and resting in the fall. Communicating secretly underneath the soil, warning of dangers, and, when healthy, celebrating the wins.

—Leslie VonHolten

The Second Annual *Wizard of Oz* Reunion in Liberal, Kansas

B. H. Fairchild

They have come once more, the small ones.
They crowd around my mother and her friends
at the F. Nightingale Retirement Home
and sing *Wizard of Oz* songs like hymns

and let themselves be called "munchkins"
by the palsied, ancient ones who cling
to that memory and Dorothy taken
through the Kansas air but cannot recall

the green city or the yellow road that leads there.
Mrs. Beaudry, who owned the coffee shop,
cannot find her hands, and Mr. MacIntyre
is searching for his long-dead wife and is happy,

finally, when she calls. For these the actors
sing their tunes, and for the wheelchair aged
and the ones on metal walkers that clump
like awkward giants through the halls.

For these the rayon flowers, and the Bible
opened to a text they cannot read. For these
a trip to Oz Land, and a photo sent
with a letter in which my mother writes,

Some children came today. They seemed so grown
and fine and reminded me of you back when.
This, to a man with neither courage, brain,
nor heart to find his way back home again.

Local Flavor

Rachel Seth Coleman

The air inside our avocado-green Chevy Nova had begun to cool, afternoon light melting from gold to gray, but my little brother and I didn't notice the time or the surroundings. Rapt, we leaned as close as we could to the front seat where our father spun the tale of a hero's quest in faraway, long-ago India. Never mind that our car sat in a supermarket parking lot in Dodge City, Kansas. This regular stop on the twenty-mile trip that combined grocery shopping with piano lessons felt full of faraway wonders. While Mom took advantage of weekly sales, Dad entertained us with stories about a prince's three challenges to win the hand of a Rajput princess or reclaim a stolen throne. Sometimes, the prince recovered the magnificent Koh-I-Noor diamond, capitalized on mistaken identity, or rode elephants as he outsmarted those who would betray him. Whatever the plot, the story traversed the subcontinent, from jungles to the Rajasthani Desert to the snowy Himalayan Mountains. It was the place Dad had called home the first fourteen years of his life, and his descriptions of the food, the colors, and the smells fizzed with authenticity.

Meanwhile, our mother worked her own kind of magic. The mission? To feed her family with love and care. On a budget. A small-town pastor's wife and homemaker, she never had to buy beef or produce: folks from our church filled the drawer at McInteer's Meat Locker on Main Street and shared their gardening know-how and bounty. But Mom had also set out to reclaim the foods of her husband's youth, a task requiring ingenuity worthy of a fairytale heroine.

For my father, real Indian food was as far out of reach as a lost fortune. Dad had catalogued a treasure map of long-lost delights: *chana dal*, the crunchy, peppery roasted chickpea snack sold by street vendors; *jalebi*, shiny orange sweets, shapes dripping with sugar syrup; *aloo gobi*, the dry, addictive combination of cauliflower and cubed potato, dotted with mustard and cumin seed, whole green chilis gleaming in the steam.

Perhaps his stories served as inoculation against forgetting. He couldn't allow the early years of his life to fade like the handwritten notices in the window of our modest hometown grocery store. R&M's IGA stocked apples, bananas, Idaho potatoes, celery, and the like. My childhood eyes snagged on Cracker Jacks and candy, but I imagine the spice shelf offered a similar farm-kitchen array: salt, pepper, seasoned salt, cinnamon, probably parsley. Chain supermarkets—like the one outside the car where we sat enthralled—offered a slightly wider, often less expensive variety of staples. Still, this was 1970s Kansas, where "Oriental" food meant adding a can of cubed pineapple and some Kikkoman soy sauce to a casserole dish.

The town that welcomed our little family in 1974 was as simple and straightforward as the landscape where it perched on a flat circle of horizon. Most houses looked like the ones next to them, white, beige, a few trimmed in gray or green, all with neatly kept yards. When my parents first visited as candidates, my mother told me she had watched with growing unease as the trees dwindled in size and number the farther they traveled. As a girl in Minnesota and Pennsylvania, she anticipated the transformation of the landscape every autumn as leaves turned from green to gold to red. This country looked desolate to her, barren. Please, God, don't send us to this place, she prayed.

Of course, the story told to me as a child was past tense, with a self-evident conclusion. Here we were, in a speck of a place in a corner of the state that looked nearly empty on a map, settlements spaced like spilled seeds on a kitchen floor. My father was Indian by birth, my mother's German-Mennonite family raised her in places where you could ice skate, and now we all lived in Minneola.

As a child, I understood clearly that a person could be from more than one place at the same time, just like some of my classmates were "town kids" and some rode the bus to school: once in the classroom, we were all third-graders learning cursive handwriting. I crayon-colored buffalo, meadowlarks, and sunflowers, sang "Home on the Range" to celebrate Kansas Day each January, and relished the feeling of hot wind on my face as I pumped my legs to swing skyward on the playground. I felt tornado emergency practices were superior to and far more exciting than fire drills, and although I was a "town kid," I shared a vicarious thrill when I saw long lines of wheat trucks stretched out across the road to the grain elevator at harvesttime.

Kansas was known, our teachers told us, as "the breadbasket of the world." Our farmers grew more wheat than any other state or nation, which meant Kansas was taking care of everyone. It was a place to proudly claim as home.

I adored the fact that Kansas was the real-life site of Laura Ingall Wilder's "little house on the prairie" *and* the home of Dorothy Gale (intrepid visitor to the Land of Oz) *and* the Great Plains tribes who hunted buffalo and crafted beautiful bead moccasins. I frequently contemplated the difference between being an Indian from India, and Indian from the American tribes who'd been erased from the land now occupied by the asphalt-paved playground at my elementary school. We knew about *those* Indians from the Thanksgiving story and book illustrations that displayed the regalia of Comanche, Kiowa, and Cherokee kinship bands. They were wonderful with their teepees and war paint and honor—but there were different kinds of wonderful, and I felt lucky to be the most faraway kind of Indian. As much as I liked the idea of beaded moccasins, the allure of the East, with its sequined surfaces and kohl-painted eyes, appealed to the fashion lover in me. Besides, all the American Indians had been killed, according to the history books.

By fifth grade, that certainty had begun to fray, perhaps in part because I felt an undercurrent of Otherness, a term I wouldn't hear for another ten years. Tanning was a much-pursued summertime activity—high-SPF sunscreen was another thing still to be conceived—and I prided myself on growing ever darker with never a sunburn. In class photos, my black hair and brown skin stood out amid rows filled with blonde-headed, brown-haired, blue-eyed, light-complected classmates. I never heard a spoken slur; never heard affirmation for my heritage, either. Yet we were all inching toward that age when attractiveness carries currency and anxiety can easily trump achievements.

Asking my father was no help, partly because I was too shy to pose the burning questions in my mind: Did people think Indian girls were pretty? Did I look Indian? *Was* I Indian? Instead, I mused aloud about the possibility of getting a pixie cut like my mother's effortlessly chic style. Dad said he thought I could do that, then showed no sympathy when I cried over the disastrous results. It was a lonesome way to progress toward junior high. In retrospect, I find it funny and a little sad that I always assumed my hazel-eyed, white-skinned brother's popularity resulted from an innate likability that I simply did not possess. Perhaps that is true, but it's also possible I recognized a sense of reserve that is common in small-town America, where populations cohere around sameness.

It's no wonder my father was ill-equipped to shore up my sense of identity. India, for Dad, was a boyhood haven filled with train trips to the seashore or The Hills—an absurd Anglo-Indian slang term for the Himalayas—and boarding school exploits at Sherwood College, where he and his twin brother lived in Friar Tuck House and sang treble parts in Latin in the boys' choir. India meant ease and pleasure reserved for those who landed on a certain rung on the social ladder. The United States meant new adventures and opportunities, especially for immigrants who were Commonwealth members and wishfully British, if dark-complected. Assimilation was the way to success.

My mother, who had always viewed me with the slightly dazzled, loving eyes of a first-time parent, may not have recognized my growing sense of uncertainty. Strong emotions were to be expected in a pre-teen. Like all rough patches in life, challenges could be overcome through prayer, positive thinking, and the passage of time, especially for her bright, beautiful daughter. Mom had come to love this part of the world, "her" country. Driving back to Minneola from a mother-daughter shopping trip one late afternoon, she pointed out the golden bands of sunlight that fell across waves of feathery grass. It had taken years for her to appreciate the beauty of the landscape, and now "I love it," she said. My restless ears took note, even as I silently questioned whether it was my country, too.

Minneola was not a hotbed of newsworthy activity, so the arrival of a young couple who had purchased the modest motel just south of the highway intersection set the town abuzz. They were foreigners, is probably how folks phrased it at the post office. Anyone brown would be seen as such. It was a reality my father encountered in the early years that he walked to pick up the daily mail and was met with silence at the post office: people weren't inclined to return the greeting of a "foreign stranger" in town. After seven years, he evidently passed muster, and now everyone called him "Pastor Bob." By the time the Tucker Motel opened with new ownership, Dad had become one of the regular coffee-drinkers at the local café with church members and farmers waiting for the rain to stop, or spring to arrive. He attended the Ground Hog Suppers each year, eating "calf fries" and rattlesnake meat. He even drove a John Deere harvester one summer, focused on strengthening bonds with his church members. He only had to hear the name of these newcomers to know: the Patels must surely be from India.

When Mike and Daksha opened their front door to greet our family, the scent of their home would have lured me in, "foreign" or not. There was the pungent kick of incense, a hint of hot tea like my father drank every afternoon, and something more. A mosaic of fragrances danced in the air: cardamom, coriander, mustard, chili pepper, cloves, cumin, garlic, and ginger, all ingredients I did not know by name. Still, they entranced me like the vibrant, sparkling tunic-like top and baggy pants Daksha wore (I soon learned those were called *shalwar kameez*). Daksha herself smelled of coconut and sandalwood, a red bindi on her forehead, an ornate gold stud in her nostril, and bangles jangling softly down her arms. I don't remember much about Mike; I was teetering between awkward girl and eager teen and smitten with the glamour and beauty that evidently accompanied being Indian.

My mother was more interested in getting past the formalities. A skilled listener, she knew how to meet people on their own terms. In no time at all, Daksha had invited her to the kitchen to demonstrate how to make chai with fresh-grated ginger and loose tea leaves boiled in milk. My brother and I tagged along with the men as Mike hosted a tour of the motel's front desk area and living quarters, including a cupboard papered with vividly colored, shiny postcards of elephants, monkeys, and blue-skinned beings.

Mike and Daksha were Hindu, Dad later explained, distinct from Hindi, which was a language and not a religion, and which meant they prayed to hundreds of gods instead of the one true God, aka Jesus. As devout Hindus, they made daily offerings of food and flowers in their home altar, or place of puja. I'm pretty sure Dad would rather not have guided us through this ad hoc intro to Hinduism, but we'd already seen the pictures. I found them thrilling and secretly wished to study them longer, but Dad hustled us past as quickly as was polite—just as his mother had covered his eyes with her hands when they passed by Hindu temples festooned with explicitly sexual carvings in India. It wouldn't do for mixed-race, Anglo-aspiring children to see such uncivilized images then, and my dad was determined to be a good parent now.

For the next few years, Daksha schooled my mother in Indian home cooking that quickly surpassed the possibilities contained in *The Art of Indian Cooking*, a battered paperback that had served as her compass until now. Mom learned to make samosas, the triangular, crisp pastry pockets stuffed with peas, potatoes, and carrots, beginning with how to mix and roll fresh chapatis, a whole-wheat flatbread nearly identical to tortillas. Since the Patels were vegetarian, Daksha did not offer guidance about how to prepare the never-ending supply of feedlot beef my mother had at her disposal, but she demonstrated the things Indian cooks know: how to fry spices to intensify the flavors, how to cut vegetables into identically sized pieces so that everything cooks evenly and looks beautiful, and how to taste as you went along, creating your own unique *ger-ber*, or cook's signature taste.

There's no doubt Daksha found comfort in having a kitchen-table friend. In later years, she confided to Mom that she had told far-off relatives in other motel-operating locations that "we found family here in Minneola."

Scarcely more than twenty years old, Daksha had little control over where her husband's family required someone to run the business, no matter how out-of-the-way it might feel for his wife. I'm sure my mother recognized the emotions of a newcomer in a small Kansas town: displacement, loneliness, loss—and the importance of putting on a brave face and making friends. "Bloom where you are planted," is the way you heard it in Sunday School.

Daksha's presence shifted my sense of cultural uneasiness to something like confidence. When our music teacher selected *The Jungle Book* as the spring musical production for junior high students, excitement bloomed beneath my fading tan. The story of Mowgli and his friends was no creation of Walt Disney, I told classmates, but a tale written by Indian author Rudyard Kipling, a man who knew perfectly well that Baloo is the Hindi word for "bear" and Bagheera the term for "panther." Shere Khan? That meant "tiger king."

Everything in the musical interlocked with my family's personal history, and I was the most qualified class member to serve as resident expert. Better yet, our household connection to Daksha and Mike meant we had access to actual Indian clothing. Inside Daksha's closet, stacks of storage boxes held saris of every conceivable color, just waiting for the pleats and tucks that would transform them into graceful garments of silk and cotton. Would she help us stage the best *Jungle Book* ever presented by southwest Kansas junior high vocal students and provide costumes and sari-folding know-how? She would.

After my debut as the "village girl" who beguiled a swimming-trunk-clad Mowgli, there was no going back. I embraced anything Indian I could claim, though anything Indian was scarce in Clark County, Kansas. Still, I did my best. I let my thick black hair grow long and straight after years of recovery from my ill-considered haircut and fruitless efforts with the curling iron. I scarfed down the spicy, crunchy snack mix called *chaerlo*, and selected samosas to fill the Little Playmate cooler I toted to track meets.

Every long-distance runner needed an energy boost to make it through a long day on the field awaiting the mile and half-mile contests. I was certain samosas gave me a competitive edge, blissfully unconcerned about the labor-intensive prep time. Mom had to mix and roll out the chapatis, chop, cook, and mix the filling, then assemble the packets and seal them with flour paste before she fried them in single layers in the hot oil. There's no doubt I felt my mother's love. It's likely the sense of identity and family support fueled my wins more than any biochemical boost provided by the pocket-sized delicacies.

Food shows up as a game-changer in folk tales and traditions worldwide. There's the ancient honor code of protecting anyone you've invited in for a meal, mentioned both in classic tales such as *The Iliad* and *The Odyssey*, and in the Old Testament, when God himself shows up at the tent of Abram and Sarah (or, more darkly, when Lot offers up his daughters to the lustful men of Sodom in lieu of the handsome angel he is hosting and thus cannot surrender). On the other hand, eating or refusing what strangers offer can have unforeseen consequences, as depicted in cautionary tales about avoiding fairies' food or the refusal of the Babylonian captives Daniel and his friends to eat delicacies offered first to idols. In the first instance, greedy consumers found themselves trapped forever in the magical realm; in the second, the faithful Hebrew prisoners risked death.

And food becomes part of the one who chews and swallows. Alice in Wonderland felt herself shrink and then enlarge after she sampled unknown substances labeled "Eat me" and "Drink me." And we can't forget the miracles of Jesus Christ: first, he changed water into wine; next, he fed five thousand picnickers with five loaves and two fishes multiplied into more. Finally, in a tradition now known as holy communion, he commanded his disciples to eat the bread that "was" his body and drink the wine that "was" his blood in order to remember him, yes, but also to be transformed into something more like God himself.

It was not the Indian food that changed me so much as the access to Indianness provided through my father's stories, my mother's cooking, and our family friendship with the other strangers in town. Dad's retrieved memories transformed my mother's cooking into a feat of time-traveling alchemy as she sought to replicate dishes that transcended borders and languages and politics and religion. Her chicken curry, carefully crafted with cookbook guidance and her newfound *ger-ber*, brought the disparate parts of Dad's life to the family dinner table. There, in the parsonage kitchen with its yellow gingham wallpaper and speckled linoleum tiles, my mother brought the treasure home and worked magic for us all.

And magic—even kitchen magic—has a way of breaking barriers. While its population has neither grown nor vanished, twenty-first-century Minneola is a more cosmopolitan place, thanks in part to our family's thirty-five-year sojourn. Mike and Daksha moved to Florida; my classmates grew up and took over family farms; others sought their fortunes elsewhere, including my hazel-eyed, brown-haired brother, who moved to India. New people who came to town were seen not so much as strangers but as welcome additions who kept the town from dwindling away.

Still, it was unexpected to receive an anxious phone call from the Minneola town librarian one winter afternoon. My parents, still posted at the community church, had traveled to India to visit my brother and his family. The trip coincided with the fifty-year-anniversary of Dad's immigration and was slated to last nearly a month. Now, network news had interrupted local programming to cover a natural disaster: a massive 7.8 earthquake in Gujarat that eventually left more than a million people injured and tens of thousands dead.

Had I heard from Pastor Bob and Ruth, the librarian asked, real worry in her voice. "We're here looking at the world atlas to see if the earthquake is close to them," she added. I could hear voices in the background—the coffee shop gathering had migrated to Main Street and pulled out maps.

I was sure my parents were safe, I said, though I had not yet received my daily email message from them via the brand-new dial-up service America Online. India is a huge country, and they were far from the state of Gujarat, at a Bible conference on the coast. The library patrons wanted location names. And a rough outline of their travel plans across the perilous subcontinent. "We're all so worried," the librarian said. When my parents eventually returned, they were met with a hero's welcome.

My own multiracial children, born and bred Kansans well versed in tornado survival and *Wizard of Oz* trivia, have grown up with food I cook because my mother taught me. The savory tang of *khicheri*, a lentil-and-rice combo baked to crispy goodness and served with caramelized onions, hard-cooked eggs, and any leftover meat you fancy, was a favorite of one daughter before she could talk in complete sentences. As teens, my curly-haired, African American offspring often found themselves defending their Indian credentials to friends who expressed doubt. "Black, not Indian" elicited a recital of their best-loved Bollywood movies and favorite foods; the mention of popadams and saag paneer usually ended all debate. Combine such culinary know-how with the simple statement that "I grew up in Kansas," and you've got an irresistible conversation starter anywhere in the world, whether waiting in line or stuck in slow traffic. Throw in the kicker that you make beef korma like a pro and you may find yourself seated at a table of strangers who are about to become friends. Breaking bread together, it turns out, is just as powerful as lore claims. It only makes sense, here in the Bread Basket of the World.

Girls on the Land
Raylene Hinz-Penner

In many ways, my sister and I were isolated and insulated from mainstream culture during our 1950s and 1960s southwest Kansas Mennonite girlhoods. The openness and flexibility we experienced in attitudes about gender roles and prescriptions surely were directly connected with the needs of our family living on the land. The rural lifestyle made specific demands on a farm family, no matter whether children were girls or boys. Our primary community was the Oklahoma Mennonite church family who prized rearing children who had developed a work ethic, no matter the gender of the child.

As a 1950s girl I had internalized certain mainstream cultural norms: for example, the belief that marriage was a girl's highest priority. I realized only after marrying at age twenty, before I had graduated from college, how unconscious this marriage priority was for me; I had never seriously thought about myself as a professional. Now I was married. Who else was I? I must have chosen to become a teacher because that profession appeared to work well for married women (and our parents guided both my sister and me into the field of education, which they so admired). My community, school, church, and peer groups all believed a girl's success began with a good marriage. I knew I would never come back to the farm after college.

Division of labor by gender was not firmly fixed on a Mennonite farm like ours. I did not have brothers to do farmwork; when work needed to be done, it was simply all hands on deck. Also, my mother and father ran the dairy together, modeling for us the division of responsibilities as needed. My father never went to the dairy barn without my mother.

My mother's parents' model running a farm must have been an important influence on her. Her father alone controlled the purse strings in their Depression-era farm household; my parents both reacted against that model. They openly lamented my grandmother's lack of financial independence. By contrast, Mama paid the bills and kept the books. I often heard Daddy ask her for the checkbook. They were generous givers to the church, especially after harvest or for special events, and I heard them discuss and decide together how much they could afford to give. I know my father was the one who asked the bank for major loans (official "head of household" required) and was also the primary decision-maker on big equipment purchases, but never without my mother's input, and, of course, he often needed her help as a driver if they went to get a new piece of equipment.

My mother may have gotten her start doing farmwork because of her place as the third of three girls born before the boys in their family. The first boy, born after my mother, was nearest her age, and the two of them did farmwork together while the two older girls worked in the house with their mother and helped to care for the younger children.

I cannot think of a girl—whether she had brothers or not—in our church who did not drive tractor for her father, haul grain, and do farm chores. We all saw our farms as family operations, and gender seemed irrelevant when work needed to be done, especially at harvest.

This was probably especially true on our marginally arable farm. Hired help was not an option. What we four could not do, we had to ask the help of extended family or neighbors to do. Because our operation was small, if we had two trucks hauling grain as my father drove the combine, Mama always drove our truck until we girls were old enough to drive into town to the elevator, delivering harvested grain; a neighbor or relative would haul the harvested grain with another truck to keep the combine going nonstop. Then Daddy would take his truck and return the borrowed services to the neighbor who had helped him.

Probably, learning to drive very young was one way we could prove ourselves worthy contributors on the farm, and we all wanted to be mature and responsible enough that our fathers and mothers valued our contributions.

We began driving as soon as we could see over the steering wheel of the small work tractor or the pickup. First, we sat on our father's lap while he drove around the yard, carefully observing how to start, shift, brake, and manage the switches and levers. He took the time to teach us, anticipating our help when we were old enough. Then we began to drive across the yard, at the age of six or eight, believing ourselves important and helpful if our father said, "Go get the pickup and bring it here. Can you do that?" Or, Daddy might inform us that he needed to build a fence around the Sudan patch and he needed someone to drive the pickup from fencepost to fencepost as he walked, dug holes, and strung wire. We carted his equipment and learned to drive the panel truck. With a standard shift, we might kill the engine repeatedly until we got the hang of it, but we lived for our father's praise: "Ah, that was a nice smooth takeoff."

We were humiliated when he had to come restart the engine we had killed through ineptitude or had to come get us out of the sand if we got stuck. One of my life lessons was when I was plowing a sandy field north of our house and somehow got the plow clogged and twisted in field debris. I stopped the tractor and tried to dig out with my hands! Soon I saw my father come walking across the field.

He assessed the damage. I think I may have even broken something on the plow. But before we set about fixing it, the lesson. Never panic and do something stupid, my father said, like try to dig this out with your hands. (I suddenly had the image of myself as a desperate varmint trying to dig that plow out with squirrel "hands." I felt immensely foolish and inadequate.) Always come get me, my father continued. You could tear up your hands digging in this field debris.

We were farm laborers, but not tomboys. Dress, makeup, and adornment were important parts of our lives. Our mother loved nice clothes, was an expert seamstress, and delighted in custom designing clothes for us for church and school. Mama loved shopping and buying good fabric and combining patterns, and she often stayed up late at night to finish new outfits we could wear to church or a special school function. Daddy too took time to admire our clothing, shoes, and hair before we left for church or school, complimenting us on our appearances (and later, begging us not to wear our skirts so short). As I look back, I think girls and women in our church took pride in working as hard as the men did during the week and looking like they had not done any farmwork on Sundays.

In fact, my mother worked longer hours than my father because she did her work as a dairy woman and in other ways assisting my father with farmwork, and after that, all the work necessary for good housekeeping. Though Mama did "men's work" on the farm, Daddy seldom did "women's work," which is not to say that he didn't work hard. I realize now that women like my mother on the farm in the 1950s were amazingly versatile, skilled, and integral to a successful operation. After I left the farm, I read the old adage, "Man's work may be from sun to sun, but woman's work is never done," and recognized my mother's life. Mama worked late nights sewing or doing food preparation or house maintenance in addition to raising children, helping to run the dairy, gardening, preserving food, or helping us with homework. Daddy, of course, helped to raise the children. It is much easier to send a child outside to be with her father if he is doing something on the farm than if he has a job away from the home.

One very clear role for women on our farm was doing the laundry and ironing. I remember helping my mother do the wash with the old Maytag on the south end of the screened porch and hanging the clothes on the line in the early years. But when the washer finally broke down, for several years we drove into Liberal to the laundromat on the east edge of town.

Mama, my sister, and I went in to do the wash. We loved this outing. Mama loved it because it was a time saver: she could take the laundry in during the afternoon and complete it in a couple of hours, stop for groceries, and easily be home for evening milking. She taught us to sort the clothing carefully and efficiently in the washers; we happily put quarters into each machine, and then we each got a bottle of pop and a magazine from the table and sat reading and commenting on the magazines the laundromat provided while the laundry was being washed. *Life* magazine was our favorite, and Mama loved to show us pictures of the British royalty, Grace Kelly, and Elizabeth Taylor. We felt somehow like sophisticated women out on the town. I greedily scavenged those magazines for news of the world until Mama called me to help fold the warm clothes tumbling out of the dryers.

We also loved going along with our daddy on errands into town. As I remember going to the Golden Gloves boxing ring with Daddy, to the male bastion of his cousin Sherman's Mobile station, or just hanging out in our tin shed as Daddy talked with his uncles when they stopped by, I realize that one of the greatest gifts our father gave us was never to insinuate that he wished either of us had been a boy to help him on the farm. On the contrary, Daddy loved girls. It always seemed to me that he wouldn't have known what to do with a boy.

My sister and I drove the tractor, milked cows, ran, and jumped the high jump Daddy helped us to build each spring. I was shocked to learn from other Mennonite girls that the boys in their homes got more respect than the girls. My father was very competitive and expected us to win out over every boy in our class, whether in a foot race or a history exam; his attitude instilled confidence in us. In fact, I always had the sense that my daddy, despite his dignified masculine bearing and military demeanor, was closer to his mother and sisters than to his brothers. He seemed proud, in awe of, and totally appreciative of the wide-ranging skills and competencies of his wife.

Years after I left the farm I heard a Colorado park ranger speak on women in the West; she described a Southern Cheyenne woman warrior who took up her butcher knife to avenge her rage after the Sand Creek Massacre. The butcher knife was what a woman had, and in this case she used it. In a moment of epiphany, I thought of the butcher knife as an ironic symbol—the farm woman's primary tool and weapon. Mama butchered chickens, used her butcher knife as protection—maybe even thought of it as a weapon of self-defense.

I have a very early image of my mother's strong hands on her butcher knife, as I sat on the kitchen floor watching her sharpen the knife on the stone edge of the bean pot she had received as a wedding present, a squat gray crockery pot with a pink rose on its front. The pot sat high atop the refrigerator (where it still sits in her home today). Mama reached to remove the lid carefully, so as not to chip it, and with the knife in her right hand set about to create a ringing twang akin to the noise created by "playing" a woodcutter's handsaw as she smoothed the edge of her butcher knife, alternating one side and then the other, back and forth, sharpening the knife blade against the crockery edge, long ago gone gray with metallic rubbings.

My mother hated butchering chickens, and so did I, but she insisted that I help her. After she had retrieved the largest fryer from the chicken house, she grabbed the chicken by its scaly yellow legs and marched herself grimly to the old elm tree near the barn, where she hung the fryer from the hanging tree by its legs with the piece of wire that always dangled conveniently from a lower branch.

Upside down and helplessly flopping from its wired feet, the chicken dangled as my mother grabbed its neck to stretch it taut, then quickly hacked off its head before she retreated a few steps, allowing the chicken to flop to its death, spurting blood and reddening its flapping wings. Mama threw the head to the dog, though she noted that in the hard times of her youth, they had cooked the head and legs of the chicken.

Next, Mama dunked the bloody fryer into a bucket of boiling water and called me to the scene to help pluck feathers, a smelly job I never got used to. Nor to the smell of chicken guts on newspaper, the naked bird degutted on the drain board in the kitchen while Mama disposed of its innards. I fled this ghastly sight until the chicken was clean for frying—or maybe to help in the fine cleaning of an occasional missed pinfeather after Mama had singed the naked bird. What I remember most is my mother's adept hands wielding the butcher knife.

Other prairie women used the butcher knife in more dramatic, even legendary ways. My great aunt, who had come to the Oklahoma Panhandle long before my parents arrived in 1950, lived on a desolate farm in an unpainted house that looked as haunted as the stories that were told of her—the way her husband awoke to find her standing over him with a butcher knife when she was on one of her jags, for example. Today, I know that she must have suffered bipolar disorder or some other untreated mental illness of the kind that plagued lonely women whose lives got chronicled under the heading of "women and madness." I never met my great aunt, a total recluse, though she didn't live far away.

The story I heard most often was of the time the "cops" came to her house to collect on speeding tickets my great uncle or one of his sons had been issued. One glance at the lonely, unpainted farmhouse should have told those cops not to go to the door. My great uncle himself had alternative sleeping quarters in the round-top tin shed. Supposedly, the two uniformed policemen knocked on my great aunt's door.

She opened it, brandishing a large butcher knife. Pointing her knife at the combines on her yard, she reportedly said to the officers, "There are two dead men in those combine bins, and there might be two more if you don't get off this place right now." As it was told to us, they didn't check the bins in their haste to get to their car. I thought about that story repeatedly as I grew up, making a mental note that if I needed a weapon in self-defense, the butcher knife at least could serve as a threat.

Our little four-room house had a lock on the south door, which faced the road. However, our back door, which faced east and was entered through the screened porch, had no lock. I watched every night as my mother, the last one to bed, took an old twelve-inch, tough-bladed butcher knife and stuck it snugly sideways, handle in front of the door, blade inserted into the door frame so that pushing the door from the outside would thwart an intruder. I always wondered if it would hold. So far as I know, it was never tested.

Girls in our community were the inheritors of a long tradition of women's lives on the land. The women who were our models were tough but not hard, competitive problem solvers who had known hard times long before my 1950s girlhood.

Long after I left the farm I learned the story of my favorite Sunday school teacher, a tiny wiry woman who probably did not weigh a hundred pounds. Leona lived to be 107 when she died in 2021. A woman of humor, intelligence, and grace, she was a profound influence on me. As the oldest child in her family, she had helped to save them during the Dust Bowl. Fresh out of high school with a provisional certificate to teach in the Oklahoma Panhandle during the Dirty Thirties, she brought her earnings home to help the family survive while her father took the horses to help build a bridge on Highway 83, working off the farm trying to save it for his family. Feeding themselves and their animals was their all-consuming task. They could not consider leaving the area despite one child's illness with dust pneumonia because they simply did not have the money to go. "We could not have afforded the gasoline," she told me.

Tiny Leona wore her overalls to school, hauling a five-gallon can of water for the children to drink from and wash in. She changed to her professional clothes in the outdoor toilet before the children arrived. She cleaned acres of dust out of the school and built the coal fires in winter. School was called off for a week once when the wind blew hard for seven consecutive days. Leona's family survived on bread, butter, eggs, and Leona's salary while many of their neighbors left the area. Leona never got her college degree. She later married a college-educated teacher and farmer, and though she had always hoped to finish her degree, she was needed on the farm, and after marriage she had children. She poured her heart into teaching us in Sunday school and Bible school. Women like Leona taught us to believe that farm girls had grit, were both tough and intelligent.

(Not) There

Rachel C. Jackson

For S. H., all who struggle in addiction, and all those who love them.

I only know Kansas through coming and going and the drive back and forth between here and there. As a child, I loved the ride from our home in Oklahoma because Bangy lived in Lawrence. Bangy, so named by my middle brother while he was still the youngest child in the years before I was born, lived in an enchanted two-story house with an attic and a basement and a clawfoot bathtub the size of a swimming pool. As a little girl, the details of the hundred-year-old historic house, so different from our own 1960s model in suburban Oklahoma City, sent me into untold imaginary realms of my own making.

My launchpad, the carpeted landing of the staircase between the two floors, radiated in the morning sun through a tall eastern window. I propelled myself down the wooden banister through a field of rainbows cast by the beveled glass window. I was six, seven, or eight, shooting through Rachelspace on a cosmic Candyland slide, and when I touched down the immediate task was to twist the inside clapper on the Victorian doorbell to announce my arrival on the pretend planet of the day. In the afternoons, the staircase landing became a make-believe classroom or kitchen or apartment or library or toy store, wherein I constructed stories so entertaining they kept me occupied by myself for hours.

It was because of my grandparents that I spent so much time as a teenager transfixed on the infinitude of the southern plains through a car window, but it was because of my mother's Cherokee family that I knew all of it was Indian Country. Her family had a whole different set of stories than my dad's, one I identified more with my whole life. I am the brownest of my parents' children, and as the only daughter I am an image of my mother, slightly lighter. Now that she is gone, I think it spooks my brothers.

My parents grew up in Shidler, Oklahoma, in the northern portion of Osage County, fifteen miles south of the Kansas state line. Momma was born in Webb City at a Phillips Oil camp. Her parents regularly attended the local pow-wows in the summertime. The first time I danced a Round Dance was at a Kaw Nation pow-wow outside of Kaw City, Oklahoma, in 1980. Grandma Vann, my mom's mom, had a close friend who was Kaw and who made my first shawl for me, but my mother wore it mostly until I was grown. I laid it across her casket when we buried her.

My family spent summer vacations on Kaw Lake, and when we were not swimming or fishing, we were picking wild blackberries with Grandpa Vann or chasing rabbits in the back pasture or collecting aluminum cans along the Shidler streets with cousins. From there, we would often leave for Kansas. I never saw the state border between Kansas and Oklahoma despite (or perhaps because of) the many times I crossed it. I understood the two states as one landscape; the sheer expanse of prairie made it obvious. It made innate sense to me that Kansas be named for the Kaw people, the Kanza, the people of the wind, because I was always told it was theirs.

I learned how to drive on dirt roads cut through those prairies, first the ones linking pump jacks around the old Carter 9 Magnolia Oil camp between Shidler, Grainola, and Fairfax, Oklahoma, the oil fields where both my grandfathers once worked. Dad also worked in the oil fields when he was a teenager, doing dirty, dangerous work the older men either would not or could not do. I suspect the oil field was where he learned to tell a good story—what he liked to call a "big windy." Once I progressed to paved roads, we would take Oklahoma Highway 18 to the state line, just so we could tell everyone I drove to Kansas and back.

Bangy was born Agnes Drexie Jones, and both she and my grandpa, Lawrence Lee Jackson, were born in West Virginia. The men in both families got work in the Oklahoma oil fields sometime in the late 19-teens. Grandpa was a roustabout, and Bangy ran a kitchen in the Magnolia Oil camp in Quay. It was a rough place for a young woman, I imagine, but soon enough she took the skills she learned there into town. She worked in food service her whole life and even owned a restaurant by the time Dad was a boy in school.

Recollecting Kansas, I remember Bangy's illuminated staircase landing as a transitional place, lifting, transporting, and transforming me even now somehow. I attribute these same characteristics to Kansas, not as much to the political state proper but to the landscape and light itself, qualities of space and place and, of course, time—and also my storied imagination. Kansas marks my earliest years, when my grandparents were still alive. Kansas was a place in my life, and then it was not. Losing Kansas brought its own peculiar grief when Bangy passed.

The long light and golden line of the Kansas horizon fold time for me still. Waking up alone in a tent in Wilson State Park after the first night of a long road trip west approximates passing out of life and transcending into heaven. The unbroken prairie wind and open breadth of the Kansas plains reconfigures the linearity of life, somehow dislodging me from a stable sense of clear trajectories. The land becomes a living map, and state borders do not matter much in memory. The places of our lives become one place in our hearts. The past lives on in the present, and Kansas, as Oklahoman as I am, lives on in me.

Rolling through the Flint Hills in the back of an '80s model Ford Crown Victoria or Buick LeSabre at any given time of year all throughout my childhood was a lesson in the spaciousness of patience. An eternity arose during these roughly five-hour commutes, it seemed, both in space and time. The drive was endless because the land was endless. The two were one. I remember long stretches where the car stood still and the road rolled by underneath us.

As a child it was easy to enjoy it, particularly in anticipation of seeing my grandparents, Bangy and her husband, my step-grandfather, whom I got to name PapPap. As we drove, our parents entertained us with stories and sing-alongs, and we stopped often. I could set record time at bathroom pit stops along the way. Dad liked to take different routes—up the turnpike past Wichita to Topeka, or on back roads through towns like Coffeyville, Independence, Chanute, Yates Center, Emporia, Ottawa. He knew every route and every Dairy Dream. For as many ways as he drove us from Oklahoma into Kansas, it came to seem there was no line between the states at all. It was more of an overlay of grasslands with cornfields.

At fourteen, fifteen, and sixteen years old, I felt increasingly captive to my grandparents' imminent deaths, dragged away mercilessly from my teenage social life in Oklahoma City almost every other weekend to attend to their increasing needs. Getting to drive at least offered some sense of power. This was in the late 1980s and early '90s, well before cell phones, and leaving for two nights meant disappearing completely from any number of ongoing sagas among my circle of friends, for which my presence was clearly crucial. It was hard not to be resentful, selfish as it was, but I soothed myself knowing that my grandparents had cable, and thus MTV, which we never had.

Yet Lawrence felt like home in ways Oklahoma City did not. It was a college town. Everyone was well-read and radical. The culture and coolness available to me there far exceeded the limited opportunities of the milquetoast suburb of OKC where we lived. Walking down Massachusetts Street,

I felt myself in ways I didn't at home. In the dark midst of my grandparents' decline and eventual deaths, Lawrence gave me space to explore future possibilities.

Being from Oklahoma puts Kansas in perspective. Certainly Thomas Frank's observations, questions, and complaints in *What's the Matter with Kansas?* coincided with my own early inquiries into Oklahoma's political history, marked in many ways with the same trajectories as Kansas. From robust labor organizations and American socialism to industrial capitalism and right-wing Christian conservatism, the two states comprise their part of a complex region of political, racial, and economic histories. When during the Civil War the United States failed to support the Native American nations after removing them to Indian Territory in the 1830s, the Confederate States of America took full advantage of the subsequent military vacuum. This mattered to Kansas.

Long-standing tensions between factions and families in tribal governments translated into militant divisions between those that supported the North, abolition, and emancipation and those that supported the South and slavery. Without Northern reinforcement, many tribal and tribally enslaved peoples aligned together with white missionary abolitionists against the South. Members of my mother's Cherokee family participated in the mass exodus of those who fled north to Kansas, where the men joined the United States Indian Home Guard and Colored Voluntary Infantry Regiments. Under the direction of Colonel William A. Phillips of Kansas, it was these fully integrated Northern regiments—Native Americans, Blacks, and whites fighting together for the first time in the war—that stripped the Confederacy of its colors on the Honey Springs battlefield in July 1863, right here in Indian Country. These alliances changed lives and history.

Of course, I knew none of these facts or intricacies as a kid. Few people know them now. My dad—by no verifiable means the least bit Native American—was a seasoned, skillful storyteller, which was one of the reasons my mother liked him from the beginning. As I drove north toward Kansas, the backseat became a stage for him to hold forth at length on any number of topics, usually while chomping mercilessly on a stick of Big Red.

Many times he told the story of the terrible attack of Quantrill's proslavery Raiders on the abolitionist Jayhawkers' headquarters in Lawrence, which was only a month after the Battle of Honey Springs. While Cherokee Confederates had trained William Quantrill in guerrilla tactics a few years earlier in Texas, even the Confederacy withdrew its support from Quantrill as a result of the Lawrence massacre. Same for my father—although he was always one for outlaws, when it came to Quantrill and the reckless, ruthless, racially motivated violence of the bushwhacker guerrillas from Missouri, he saw the difference. By now my own political orientations departed far enough from my father that our discussions were often fraught. Had we lived in Kansas at the time, he would have been a Dole Republican.

As I advanced in school, I found the Jayhawk mascot much preferrable to an Oklahoma Sooner. Both groups were outlaws at points in history, but one was right and the other wrong, in that order. In my mind, this righteous, radical Jayhawk spirit rested over the town of Lawrence. A strident ferocity for freedom found a deep-rooted repose and remained somehow in place. During my teenager visits, it called me from Bangy and PapPap's porch. I walked down to Mass Street and wandered around anonymously as though I belonged there, envisioning what it would be to live there as a college student, pretending to be the me I hoped to become.

The Casbah on Mass Street—a hollowed out, open-concept, three-story building transformed into a Moroccan-inspired market with a loft and a basement—provided a parallel paradise to me. Somewhere between a fair-trade boutique and Shakedown Street, it offered a primordial, maternal, feminist space, like an ancient predecessor to World Market much closer to the source of life. Teeming with trade beads and imported jewelry, vibrant textiles and handmade housewares, broom skirts and tie dyes, incense and oils, and art and instruments from all over the world, it also included a marvelous natural foods café in the lowest level.

I ordered China Colas and ate vegetarian chili or curry and yearned to become as counterculture and conscious as the older bohemian goddesses who worked there. I sat for hours in the basement and wrote poetry both sad and bad. I listened to conversations around me about art and literature and music, boyfriends and parties, babies and breastfeeding. I imagined a future where I would know as much as they knew, where I would walk in my body as they did, where I would live in a space of freedom so vast I could get my nose pierced, a time when I would belong to me.

You realize after your parents pass how much lies buried with them. I know now this must be what my father felt as we buried his mother at Oak Hill Cemetery in Lawrence. Our visits there, once the house on Maine Street was cleared out, stopped. Most of the furniture stayed in PapPap's family or was sold. Bangy's organ and piano were donated to their church. I got the lava lamp that sat on the top of their cabinet TV, billowing and bubbling in soft blue light while I watched MTV. I also got their 1976 Chevrolet Caprice Classic as my first car. There was no smoother ride. I named it Rosemary after a Lenny Kravitz song on his first album. I didn't know then what it was like to lose your parents, and the thought of it terrified me. Dad cried in front of me for the first in a handful of times in my life at Bangy's funeral. She passed in December 1990, and I felt the depth of his sorrow inside me, too, down at the root.

I've lost my father now, and I understand how generational experience regenerates across time. The stories of our grandparents and parents encode our bodies genetically, biologically, psychologically. We carry their stories with us as we go on without them. Just as Dad's stories live in me, so Bangy's stories lived in him. We may lay our loved ones in the earth, we may try to bury history, but stories live on in and around us, sometimes beyond our knowing. Even with stories we may not wish to tell, knowing them at least brings us closer to healing from them. This is how families change. This is how the world changes.

After graduating Shidler High School as valedictorian, my mom attended Oklahoma College for Women in Chickasha on a Phillips Petroleum scholarship. My dad went to Germany to help the Army Corps of Engineers with the postwar reconstruction of roads and bridges. They timed it so that when he returned in three years they could marry. Mom graduated a year early with a bachelor's degree in elementary education to make their nuptials possible ten days after Dad landed back in the States.

They married at the Shidler Methodist Church on September 1, 1956, and drove Highway 18 straight through Grainola, Oklahoma, to Arkansas City, Kansas, and on to Topeka. It was two years after the *Brown v. Board of Education of Topeka* decision, and Mom had been recruited to teach kindergarten at an early integrated Head Start program. Dad took a grueling job at a rubber plant, which nearly broke his back. After that, he attended barber school and worked his way through college at Washburn University. It took him ten years. By the time he graduated, my parents had two sons—my much older brothers.

I look at pictures of this time in my family's earlier life with perpetual puzzlement, perhaps because I am not there. My parents look like people I never knew, yet who feel hauntingly familiar. Or rather, they look like people I have always wanted to know while also thinking I did. I suspect this is in part because my parents are young in these pictures, even mid-century stylish. I was born in 1974, eighteen years after they were married. I never knew them as young, and certainly not as stylish. One brother was nine and the other fourteen when I arrived, I imagine, quite unexpectedly. No one planned to have a baby at age forty in the mid-1970s, and no doubt my parents, who always claimed to be pleased, thought they were long done.

Kansas always sounds and feels idyllic in pre-me stories passed between my parents and my brothers: a faraway dream, a kind of perfect past prior to the move back south. My family moved to Oklahoma City about six years before I was born, and Oklahoma has been the only state where I have lived. Kansas will always be the storied mystery, historically before me and geographically above me, an experiential standard I cannot attain but somehow remember from tales handed down. It is a familial fantasy space, free from the burdens of the present, but present still.

My oldest brother, Lee, born in Topeka in 1960, recalls Bangy as magical. She ran the Pawnee Café in Oklahoma for several years with Shorty, a Tonkawa man who brokered pawn deals on behalf of other Natives. Lee remembers jewelry and beadwork, drums and hides, paintings and pottery for sale in their living room.

When her marriage to Shorty went bust sometime around 1964, Granny, not quite yet Bangy, took off for southern California, where she worked in the kitchen at the Lawrence Welk Ranch. She had always been a hard-working woman with an interminable taste for nice things. She had a glamour that my mother's mom did not. She was also, according to my brother, far more fun. Her hair, red, wavy, and perfectly piled on her head with barely any backcombing, crowns her head during this time in the memories I do not technically have of her. To me, she resembles Endora, Samantha's mother on *Bewitched.* Magical, yes, and feisty. Her upward horn-rimmed glasses, punctuated with tiny pearls and crystals, complement the downward angle of the sharp white collar on her wild taffeta dress, and a wide satin belt bright with color accentuates her tiny waist. She gracefully balances on kitten heels. Her laugh, always loud and full, resonates in mine. I want her to be happy.

I always knew her as happy. That is, until I was nineteen and expressly unhappy myself. As my teenage years wore on and my grandparents kept dying and my parents were preoccupied with estates, and grief, and other trappings of death, I found myself increasingly alone and unable to cope. The pressures of public high school in the early 1990s converged with rave culture and grunge culture, all of which proffered a preponderance of diversionary substances. I never quite fit in this scene, but I tried. After graduation, friends left for college elsewhere or otherwise took off for bold adventures and better places. I stayed in Oklahoma.

During my sophomore year at the regional public college, while imagining myself free and taking great risks, I got ahold of some bad acid and found myself trapped in a terrifying trip-induced neurosis that took months to wear away. When it lifted, I was left dangerously depressed. My world was changed. I was changed. It would never be the same. Everyone was gone. I dropped out of college for a semester and worked in a natural foods café.

In 1965 my brother Vann, who would soon revise Granny to Bangy, was born in Wichita. During this time my father determined, after finally securing his own bachelor's degree in education, that two teachers' salaries would not suffice to raise two boys. My family moved back to Topeka, where Dad took an entry-level sales job with Dewey Portland Cement. Just as they were getting resettled, a call came from Southern California, the first contact from Bangy in months.

My grandmother, bereft and senseless on the other end of the phone, needed a way out of San Diego. She was desperate to get away from trouble. A morphine addiction that began when Dad was in junior high had returned, and ever-flowing alcohol in California added to her struggle. The Lawrence Welk Ranch, despite all the bubbles, was a bust. With two young boys at home, my mom couldn't teach, work, and take care of both alone, so my father took Vann west with him to Escondido. He drove Bangy home to Topeka, where she went through weeks of harrowing withdrawal in my parents' bedroom.

Dad waited until the lowest point in my young life to tell me this story about Bangy, who by now had been gone four years. In the moment, it seemed like thoughtless timing. Hearing it did not make me feel better. I think now, though I look nothing like her, he recognized his mother in me. I was a holograph, a portal, to a Bangy whom until that moment I never knew. The details of the story, like the details of her house on Maine Street in Lawrence, stay with me today, alive and intimate.

To hear my dad tell it—and he was the only one I ever heard tell it, and then only once or twice—the depression that set in once the physical withdrawals ended hung heavy around Bangy and the family once he got her back to Topeka. Her bright, blue-eyed spark, the one I would know later as a child, was gone for a long while. Dad took Bangy to the Menninger Clinic, the once-famous psychiatric hospital just outside of town. Mental health resources, particularly for addiction recovery, were hard to find. In Topeka, however, of all the places in the country, sat a world-renowned, innovative practice and school. It was worth a shot.

Dad tended toward skepticism, but he grew desperate enough to believe that the Menninger Clinic could help. He brought Bangy to the clinic and waited outside in the car during her intake appointment. He never knew what the clinician said to her, but after forty-five minutes Bangy came blasting out of the inner offices hot as hell, angry to her core, and absolutely unwilling to return. She never told him what happened or what was said, and it did not matter. I will likely spend my life imagining. They drove home in combustible silence. Within the week she had a job at the lunch counter at Arlen's Department store. Lee says she brought home caramel popcorn every night.

Home in Kansas, Bangy slowly regained sobriety, then stability, then her indomitable independence. After a few years, she took a better job running a dormitory cafeteria at the University of Kansas and moved to Lawrence, just as my parents moved to Oklahoma City. She met PapPap through his sister Lena, who lived behind him across the alley on Missouri Street. PapPap was a meat salesman soon to retire and, thankfully, a longtime member of Alcoholics Anonymous. Bangy and Ed, not quite PapPap, became friends fishing in the early mornings at Clinton Lake for several years before marrying a few months before I was born. They were both in their early sixties, a testament to love at last.

Bangy and PapPap grew backyard sunflowers and cockscombs as high as the garage roofline, and they always had a jar for fireflies waiting on their porch for our late-night summer arrivals. Bangy made famous meringue divinity trees at Christmas, homemade chicken cordon bleu any time of the year, and played dominoes to best any man in the family. She was whole and healthy, huge-hearted and happy, changed and free. Because of her, so now can I be. When she healed, my whole family took a new road.

With Bangy, my mom, and the next-door neighbor taking turns playing duets on the piano and organ in the front room, the voices of family, friends, and neighbors fill the front room of 715 Maine Street in the Kansas of my heart. They laugh and sing and lean into each other. Their joy stays in the walls and in my bones, and the coming and going continues. I am down from the landing where I have been waiting while listening, now twirling and dancing among them. My dad swings me around, winding me up to sing solo for the grand finale from his shoulders, "This Little Light of Mine." Death is as the prairie where no division remains within or between us. Stories lay the road home in all directions.

Nothing Better to Do

Matt Perrier

As a teenager, we all said it at some point, "Why not? *There's nothing better to do.*" Ranch kids knew better than to say it very loudly, as the nearest adult would quickly offer a task, lesson, or workout to fill the void.

As Kansans, we know the scenario: no mountains, no beaches, and fewer of life's "finer things" than some of our more urbane neighbors. For *rural* Kansas kids, the nearest movie theater might be thirty minutes away. The mall? Try an hour or two.

If they could talk, the vast pastures and prairies of Kansas that are home to our state's most valuable agricultural product, 6.15 million beef cattle on ranches and feedyards, might utter the same thing. You see, most of the land where we raise cattle was not deemed fit for farming and other food production. It was too rocky, steep (yes, even in Kansas), dry, or of poor soil type to be plowed for crop ground. So following settlement from the Homestead Act, the ranchers took what was left. After some of the land was plowed and then found to be of poor farming quality, grass was replanted, and the rancher got that castaway as well.

There was nothing better for it to do.

The men and women who populate Kansas ranches are usually a conspicuous bunch. Every few decades, our fit and fashion are adopted by popular culture but rarely changed by us: a wide-brimmed hat, long sleeves, denim jeans, and leather boots, all to protect us from the daily elements. Our job description is straightforward, as well: care for the cattle, so they'll feed and clothe us and our hungry world. Abstractions such as hobbies, vacations, 401(k)s, and even our retirement age are less clear-cut, or nonexistent. Our investment strategy: save enough for a down payment on that adjoining piece of land that might come up for sale once in a lifetime (if our neighbors pass on and don't have kids who want to return to their family business).

If the ranching community had a mission statement, I believe it would be something like this: We care for God's land, so it will care for His cattle and we can care for His people.

While cattle care seems to suck up most of our time and energy, it's likely the faith and family components of that statement that keep us going. We may not always be in the pew each Sunday, but most of us agree that without our partnership with the Good Lord above, we are lost in this expanse of grass. And as any ranching spouse or children can attest, family time may be short in quantity, but we try to balance this with quality time.

Quite often, the isolation of the prairie may be exactly where ranchers feel closest to our Creator. It is certainly where He demonstrates His works most vividly. Regardless of where I travel, I believe that Kansas is blessed with some of the most beautiful sunrises and sunsets in the world. The rolling Flint Hills in the springtime, the magical colors of the grass as fall paints its hues. . . . Ranchers get to see many blessings of nature.

But, at times His works seem anything but picturesque. Though ranchers fret about weather, wildfires, and other woes, I believe that God uses these instances to strengthen our resolve, humility, and faith in Him. And although we don't always hear His voice amid these "lessons," I know He is there to help guide us through each of them according to His plan and His timing.

There's nothing better for us to do.

According to the US Department of Agriculture, 95 percent of American farms and ranches are owned and operated by families. As anyone involved in a family-owned business can attest, this can be a blessing and a curse. There are few better feelings than seeing our young sons and daughters work together to complete a ranch task on their own. Conversely, there are few things more challenging than having a disagreement with a family member on the ranch on a Saturday afternoon, knowing that you will certainly sit across from them at dinner later that evening.

Some folks determine ways to carefully walk these blurry business and personal lines. Others, unfortunately, do not. Interpersonal communication is not usually a rancher's strongest trait, and therapy is not part of our vernacular. So one critical member of the ranch team, the rancher's spouse, has another line added to their already lengthy—and certainly unwritten—job description. I use this term intentionally, and not as some politically correct signal of virtue. While the vast majority of ranchers have historically been male, it has never been solely so, especially today.

In fact, my family's ranch was carried into its second and third generations by the respective daughters and sons-in-law. And while these male spouses did their share of the daily ranch duties, the wives had plenty to do with both ownership and management, especially during times of war.

Today, there are plenty of ranches owned and/or operated by women. Some may share responsibilities with their father or husband. Other times, they're on their own to capably do the tasks required. Regardless of which spouse puts in the bulk of day-to-day work on the ground, their "plus one" is much more than simply their "better half." To properly list the roles and responsibilities may require a second essay.

No two ranchers are the same, nor are their spouses. If they don't work full-time on the ranch, the spouse will quite often hold a job in town. This job serves multiple purposes, the first of which is largely financial. You see, most ranchers receive the bulk of their income once a year, when they sell their calves or yearling cattle. A spouse's monthly paycheck can provide some much-needed cash flow during the lean months. In addition, a spouse's health insurance or retirement package can be a valuable benefit for ranching families. Plus, social interaction, personal growth, and a sense of accomplishment are often critical for spouses who are otherwise surrounded by a few thousand acres of grass, a few hundred head of cows, and a tired, often grouchy, rancher.

Whether the spouse works five- or fifty-hour weeks at their "side hustle," their days likely start and end on the ranch's timeclock. They may make breakfast, get kids on the school bus, enter bills in the ranch's accounting program, update the family calendar, and order vaccines for next week's cattle work. And since they are going to be in town already, they pick up a few bags of feed and extra groceries for the meals they're bound to prepare for extra cowboys and family who may stop by. After cleaning up dinner, the real work commences: piles of filthy laundry, homework with kids, and often a high school ballgame (which can involve a three- to four-hour round trip in rural Kansas).

While this list is already lengthy, I haven't touched on this partner's most important job: *spouse.* Although the remoteness of ranch country appears peaceful to the casual observer, it can be an endless source of stress for the rancher. Most of us rarely, if ever, "leave the office." We work on the ranch. We live on the ranch. We occasionally play on the ranch. So, while it seems we are out here "away from it all," we are rarely away from anything. The endless challenges of financial risk, animal health concerns, government regulation, and weather extremes are seen and felt with each glance out the window or step off the porch, and they can often overcome us.

Right or wrong, ranchers are not usually the sort to seek professional help. According to the Centers for Disease Control, US farmers and ranchers have a suicide rate 3.5 times the general population. Often embarrassed by our feelings, we are not usually comfortable sharing the thoughts and concerns that often should be expressed. Our spouse is one of the few folks who knows what is on our mind. And often, it takes months or years for them to finally get it out of us.

So after they have worked in town or beside us on the ranch all day and kept our house in order (both literally and figuratively), they then get to hang their mental health shingle out pro bono. Ranchers rarely express appreciation for the myriad "little things" that our spouses do, but when caught at a weak moment, we'll admit that we couldn't do this without them.

There's nothing better to do.

Ranchers have always been a proud bunch. Whether it's the horse we trained, the bull we bought, or the steak we produced, we strive for quality—especially when hard work is associated with it. There are few things that make ranchers stand taller than when their calves "top the market," fetching the highest price when sold into the beef supply chain.

But note, I said "few things." The one exception: that rancher's family.

Ask any rancher what he or she produces, they might say something like cattle, hay, crops, or beef. And yes, this is what we monetize. It is what (hopefully) pays the bills, feeds us, and allows us to keep our generational businesses afloat. But if we're honest, our most valuable asset is never sold. It has immeasurable value. Its time to market is roughly eighteen years, and every May, most of it is exported from the rural ranchlands onto the global market.

It's our kids.

We're pretty good at raising food, fiber, and fuel in rural Kansas. But in my opinion, we are even better at raising families. Honestly, I'm not sure we can take much of the credit. The same forces that we often view in a negative light—long hours, loss of life, exposure to the harsh misfortunes of weather and markets, and even the daily risks that ranchers take when they walk out the door each morning—build character for all those involved. I once heard someone say, "Parents can raise good kids on concrete . . . it's just harder to do it well."

Ranch kids accidentally pick up a valuable education outside of the school day. Though they generally graduate with a class of fewer than forty students, they're exposed to many hard lessons to build what are ironically termed "soft skills" today.

Employers have recognized that the lessons taught by Mom, Dad, 4-H, FFA (formerly Future Farmers of America), the three sports they played, and all the clubs that they led have prepared them to excel in the workplace. When a rural high school with a few dozen kids wants to field multiple sports teams, a band, choir, and put on a school play, students don't get to specialize in one area. As a result, our kids learn early on the mantra, "If it is to be, it is up to me." Consequently, employers hire them in droves, and these kids fuel the creativity, drive, and growth of our nation, both within and outside of agriculture.

While "upstanding citizen development" can't be quantified anywhere in my financial statements, it has significant value. Frankly, it's the main reason that my wife, Amy, and I decided to return to my family's ranch and replant our roots more than twenty years ago. We both had very successful careers, owned a split-level home, commuted thirty miles to work each morning, had two weeks' annual vacation, health insurance, and a 401(k). For a decade or so, we were normal.

Then our first child, Ava, was born. Up until then, any magnetism to the rural lifestyle was more than offset by our steady paychecks, plentiful coffee shops, and all the luxuries that a two-income household could attain.

But as we did the benefit analysis of our situation, prayed, and tried to imagine our future, we decided that we had an opportunity that could not be passed. So we left our comfortable positions in the city to, as a friend of ours terms it, "raise kids, cows, and grass."

There was nothing better to do.

Amy and I now have five children ranging in age from five to twenty-one. By historical standards, they have seen fairly lucrative times in agriculture during their childhoods. Granted, "fairly lucrative" is a relative term, since most ranchers could work fewer hours and still make higher wages doing any number of town jobs. Regardless, I watched my parents and their counterparts struggle through the farm crisis of the 1980s. My father recalls the drought of the 1950s. His father exuded the typical resourcefulness of children who survived the Great Depression. Because of these constant reminders of the many challenges of production agriculture, I had little interest in returning to our family's ranch after my schooling.

My kids, on the other hand, *all* expressed interest in a possible return to our ranch, Dalebanks Angus, in Greenwood County. This place was started by my ancestors in 1867. I'm the fifth generation of this family to own and manage it. Like nearly every other rancher I know, the decisions that I make today are governed by the overarching question, "How will this affect my kids' ability to operate this business decades from now?" That test rarely allows black-and-white answers, only vast shades of gray. In the constant battle between short-term profit and long-term sustainability, it pushes me to choose the latter.

And while there are always plenty of complaints about the endless monotony of ranch chores, the twelve miles of bad road to and from town, and the countless challenges that surround ranch life, our kids still claim that we made the correct choice.

There was nothing better to do.

While a rancher's short-term focus may be consumed with cattle, land, weather, and bank notes, these are all means to a longer-term end: their next generation of family. While annual financial analyses and budgets are critical to success in business, they are often not the focus of the rancher. This could be viewed as a poor business model, but there may be good reason for this inattention to the short-term bottom line: their priority simply lies further into the horizon.

The biological makeup of the cow forces a rancher to be an eternal optimist. When I turn a bull with my cowherd, it will be at least 283 days before any of those cows deliver a calf. That calf will be roughly 210 days old before it is weaned from its mother. That calf will usually spend ninety more days on some sort of forage before leaving pastureland and entering a feedyard, where it will receive a nutrient-dense ration for roughly 175 days until harvest. That's around a two-year time span before monetization—and our investments in equipment, land, and most other lines on our balance sheet require decades before they are amortized.

So why do we continue this business model? I guess you could say it's our vocation. I've heard a rancher alter the phrase, "I didn't choose the ranch life, the ranch life chose me."

There's nothing better to do.

As a ranch kid, it was easy to look to the bright lights of town and see how much "easier" my friends had it. They could ride their bikes a few blocks to a friend's house, and then go a few more blocks to the video game arcade or swimming pool. After school or sports practice, they could be home on the couch before the country bus had made its first of many stops along a twenty-five-mile loop through the boondocks.

As a parent, I also have concerns about my kids growing up in rural

America. Their schools cannot offer the level of coursework, arts, or activities of their suburban counterparts. With a class size of fewer than forty kids here in our consolidated district (some schools have significantly fewer than that), rural Kansas kids don't have the opportunity to experience much of the culture and opportunities of their urban and suburban peers. However, the practical lessons of science, economics, and community give these ranch kids a keen understanding of the realities of life and our connection to nature. And I believe that this basic sense of place is one of the most important lessons they can learn in their formative years.

As mentioned earlier, the multifaceted nature of ranch kids' childhood makes them highly marketable to companies looking for new employees. While we are pleased when our "best and brightest" become the next crop of doctors, engineers, or business executives, it can also lead to a drain of intellectual capacity from rural Kansas. Rural development councils, concerned citizens, and groups like the Kansas Sampler Foundation continue to put immense effort into finding ways to reinvigorate rural Kansas.

For our part, ranchers continue to make sure rural Kansas is an option for youth who want to live and work here. By caring for the natural resources, while finding ways to make each acre as productive as possible, we strive to improve both the environmental and economic sustainability of these ranchlands for our future generations.

There's nothing better to do.

Sustainability has become a buzzword synonymous with environmental stewardship. In my opinion, it has been misinterpreted—maybe even hijacked—in recent decades. Kansas ranchers have defined it for years: care for the resources around you (land, water, air, and people) and operate a business that is viable for the next generation to steward. And while this certainly has an environmental component (if the land is abused, it won't sustain its productivity for long), it also has financial and social components.

We depend on this grass for our livelihood. The cattle under our care are ruminants, meaning they have a four-compartment stomach. This stomach, and the rumen microflora within, enable cattle to graze forage, allow the microbial "bugs" to convert this roughage into useful nutrients for the bovine, and enable it to convert otherwise low-quality grass into high-quality protein.

What's more, this properly managed grassland can simultaneously accomplish a multitude of tasks along the way. It is a carbon sink, sequestering

CO2 from the atmosphere and returning it to the soil through photosynthesis. It provides cover for countless birds, wildlife species, and microflora beneath the soil. What's more, its vast landscape and remote vistas provide inspiration for artists, tourists, and even the occasional rancher who takes a few minutes to remember why we love this place.

There's nothing better to do.

While the hardscrabble image of the weather-beaten cowboy with a stiff gait and even stiffer scowl pervades our culture, ranchers are a bit of a walking paradox. Beneath all the denim and leather is a worried human being. For some reason, we worry most about things mostly out of our control: the weather and the market prices paid for our cattle or charged for our feed and other inputs. Will we get enough rain to grow grass and have water in our ponds and streams for cattle to drink? Or will rain come too quickly, washing away our fences and flooding our hayfields and bottom ground?

After a multiyear drought like we recently experienced in Kansas, we are a bit more tolerant of mud and thunderstorms. Otherwise, we subscribe to the Goldilocks theory: not too much, not too little. We want it just right.

We're an independent bunch—fiercely so, at times. We spend the bulk of our time alone. We feed cattle in the winter, mend fence in the spring, check cattle in pastures during the summer, and drive a tractor when necessary to raise feed. When we need extra help for a job, we often "neighbor" (as this essay may indicate, ranchers are nothing if not free with our noun-verb conversion and other grammar blasphemy) with others to do big jobs like prescribed pasture burning, vaccination of calves, weaning, and fence construction.

This neighborly nature pervades the ranching culture. While many of us prefer the solace of the saddle, we recognize that we're a single member in a seemingly endless list of partnerships. A few are likely obvious: our spouse, our business partner, our corporate board (these first few are usually the same individual, which makes marital communication a bit challenging at times). Other partnerships are a bit more ambiguous, but significant: those with the land, the Lord, our lender, even a good horse or dog.

Since we're accustomed to pitching in when needed, we're usually willing partners on everything from the volunteer fire department to the county cattlemen's association to the local school board. Our hobbies are limited, but usually include what most would call "service hours" today. In rural Kansas, nearly every community development council, hospital board, civic group, or church organization will have a rancher or rancher's spouse on it.

There's nothing better to do.

For decades I have tried to determine if ranching is a business or a lifestyle. Honestly, it's a mix of both. And this is the first of many ironies that have pervaded ranch life since the American West was settled more than 150 years ago.

Ranching is a constant balancing act of paradoxes: tradition vs. progress, chemistry vs. biology, technology vs. labor, risk vs. reward, short-term risk for long-term reward, just to name a few. Long ago, most of us traded in our *Old Farmer's Almanac* for a smart phone. Today, my screen time rivals that of my teenage children, but my leading apps are the Weather Channel, Google Earth, Angus Mobile, and CattleFax instead of TikTok, Snapchat, and Instagram.

Since the 1930s, US agriculture has greatly increased its production efficiency. Today's ranchers produce more beef with fewer cows, and we do it with significantly less manpower. While this seems like a desirable business trend, these improvements in labor efficiency mean fewer ranchers and farmers living and working the land. Fewer ranchers mean smaller schools, more vacancies on Main Street, lower tax bases, and often a bleak economic picture in much of rural Kansas.

And while remote work continues to enable more folks to maintain well-compensated careers while living away from the office, the lack of broadband Internet and other communications issues still makes telecommuting from rural Kansas a challenge for the next generation of Kansans who would like to support and live in their rural communities. But ranchers are a resilient bunch, and we will continue to find solutions.

Right or wrong, we generally put lifestyle before livelihood and people before profit. We work extremely long hours to complete the tasks put before us, but our strength comes from our faith and our family. Without them, we often lose direction, drive, and determination to withstand the challenges from a far more fickle group of "extended family": Mother Nature, Father Time, and Uncle Sam.

While rural Kansas provides bountiful blessings, it also delivers its share of hardships. But it's these struggles that build our character, our resolve, and our faith in those around—and above—us. Often attributed to Willa Cather, it has been said that "anybody can love the mountains, but it takes a soul to love the prairie." The same could be said about ranching. For all the violence, vulgarities, and vitriol that Hollywood has brought to our profession through the decades, reality shows something quite different.

A Kansas rancher may be one of the more misunderstood folks around. Risky and rambunctious, yet careful and caring when needed. We're proud of our past, yet focused on our future. Our long-term investments are in land and livestock, but our true legacy is our family. Our business visions may not be stated, but most would parallel the mission statement listed above: Trust God to provide. Care for land, livestock, and family. And leave *all* of these in an even better state than when we found them.

There's nothing better to do.

The Day the Great Plains Burned

Ian Frazier

Slapout, Oklahoma, at the intersection of a county road and a much used east-west state highway, has a population of five. The town's name used to be Nye, but in the 1950s its residents, who were then more numerous, changed it. Locals explain that there was a store in Nye where, if you asked the owner for a particular item, he often went to look for it and came back and said, "We're slap out of it!" How this inspired a name change, no one knows. Now the store is gone, and the town consists of a single building that's a combination gas station, truck stop, convenience mart, café, and improvised community center. In the dark of early morning, it's jumping with truckers, oil-field workers, guys who drive the county road graders, and farmers who have been baling hay all night. A hand-lettered sign on the door reads: "Please hang on to the door." This is so the howling prairie wind won't keep yanking it open and undoing the feeling of comfort inside.

Just to the south on the county road stands the Slapout firehouse, a metal building with three bay doors and six enormous fire trucks behind them. These vehicles, acquired from the military and the forest service, have been modified for prairie firefighting by the firemen themselves, all of whom are volunteers. Charlie Starbuck is the fire chief. He objects to being called Charles; it's Charlie on his birth certificate. Starbuck has a drooping, Emiliano Zapata mustache and green eyes, and he wears overalls, end-of-the-nose spectacles, and a rumpled army-fatigue hat. His father was a fire chief before him. On his muscled forearms are multiple reddish burns made by sparks from welding, a regular occupation at his ranch, not far from town, as well as at the firehouse.

On the morning of March 6, 2017, Starbuck's pager went off at 10:53 and informed him that a grass fire was burning in the Mocane oil field, by County Road 141 in Beaver County, north of Slapout. Its cause was a downed power line. With three trucks and eight of his crew, he drove to the fire and saw that it had already blown up to a size where, given the conditions, he was going to need help. He called neighboring fire departments. Texas County, just to the west, sent trucks—"I will praise Texas County till the day I die," Starbuck says. He also called Mark Goeller, the director of Oklahoma Forestry Services, who, needing a name for the fire, used Starbuck's. Sometime afterward, Starbuck's sister in Virginia called him to ask about the Starbuck Fire she had heard mentioned on the news. That was the first he learned of his fame.

For weeks, the National Weather Service out of Norman, Oklahoma, Amarillo, Texas, and Dodge City, Kansas, had been sending alerts. The conditions were perfect for wildfires. There had been almost no precipitation for six months; before that, however, a lot of rain had fallen, and now the plentiful prairie grasses stood up tall and tinder-dry. On some days, like this one, the winds blew at fifty-plus miles an hour, while the humidity dipped down into the single digits. An ice storm in January had damaged scores of power lines, making them more vulnerable. Often, the Weather Service alerts are mainly precautionary. But on this day the south-central Great Plains did indeed catch fire. Huge wildfires spread over the Texas and Oklahoma panhandles and in western Kansas, with a smaller burn in Colorado.

This is a part of the world where extreme weather hangs out. Meteorologists refer to the prevailing late-winter "dry line," a phenomenon found almost nowhere else, which in this case is produced by hot, dry air from the Mexican plateau colliding with moist air moving up from the Gulf of Mexico. In March and April, if there's an incoming storm system as a trigger, the combination of wet and dry explodes above the plains. High winds generated by the dry line contributed to some of the dust storms of the 1930s. Plowed ground on the plains blew away during those years; later, the government encouraged agriculture that returned the land to grass.

The big dust storms haven't reappeared since, but now when the winds come, the grass holding the soil in place is sometimes thoroughly ready to burn.

A megafire is considered to be one that burns more than 100,000 acres. In Oklahoma, the total burned in the March 6 fires was 781,000 acres. Moving northeast with the wind, the Starbuck Fire soon crossed into Kansas. Eventually, the Starbuck and other nearby fires would be given an official, bureaucratic handle, the Northwest Complex Fire, but to the people most affected, the fires that burned 608,000 Kansas acres are still called by the name of a fire chief in Oklahoma. In the Texas Panhandle, fires burned 482,000 acres. Seven people are thought to have died in the March 6 fires. The expanse of burned land on the south-central Great Plains amounted to almost two million acres—roughly three thousand square miles. Rhode Island, that useful state for comparing geographic measure, covers about one thousand square miles of land. The March 6 fires burned an area about the size of three Rhode Islands.

Ashland, Kansas, is almost fifty miles from Slapout, if you follow a straight line across the prairie. As the county seat of Clark County, Ashland grew along the gentle valley of a creek, with ambitious streets as wide as big-city avenues. After going through a familiar Great Plains cycle of boom and not quite bust, the town today has a population of about 850. Two water towers rise at either end of town; swallows swoop and dive around the tall, white grain elevators at Ashland Feed & Seed, by the train tracks at the end of Main Street. A twenty-foot-high bas-relief map on the front of the courthouse shows the county's historic sites, including the place where one of Coronado's men lost a bridle bit when they were looking for the rumored Cities of Gold in the vicinity in 1541. The intricate, rusted, ancient object is on display in a glass case next to the district court clerk's office.

Millie Fudge, Clark County's head of emergency-management operations, is in her late sixties. Mildred Barnes was her name growing up; she has lived her entire life in the western part of the state. Dark-eyed, with short, light-brown hair and black-rimmed glasses, she walks leaning forward a bit, as if successfully towing a great weight. Her twanging, slightly gravelly voice projects calm, and her silences have formidable presence. Everyday attire for her includes a dark-blue T-shirt, blue jeans, running shoes, and a camouflage holster on her belt containing a radio. From time to time the radio squawks, and she answers it. She works with the volunteer fire departments and the police, not only in Ashland but also in the county's two other towns, both of which are smaller. Her office is in the ambulance building, because she is also the emergency medical services (EMS) director for the county.

Millie's husband, Gary Fudge, is a retired truck driver. The couple married in 1970 and moved to Ashland in 1979. They had three boys and a girl. Their third son, Brannon, born in 1981, suffered from a brain disease called Rasmussen's encephalitis, which caused him to have as many as three hundred seizures a day. When Brannon was seven, his parents took him to the Johns Hopkins Hospital, in Baltimore, where Dr. Ben Carson (later the secretary of the US Department of Housing and Urban Development) performed a brain operation called a hemispherectomy, which cured the seizures and allowed the boy to function. Brannon learned how to talk and take care of himself, and did well until his late teens, when another operation was necessary. He graduated from high school in 2000, but because he required monitoring he stayed in Ashland and opened an ice cream shop called Fudge Man's. "He and I ran it together," Millie says. "He loved people, and they loved him. In fact, he enjoyed visiting with customers so much that he sometimes ignored business and I'd have to remind him about it."

In 2002, because of complications resulting from a hairline fracture in his skull, Brannon went to a hospital in Wichita, and while recovering from surgery he lapsed into a coma. After thirty-three days, his family made the decision to take him off life support. The experience led his mother into despair. She got through this period only by the grace of God, she says. Her family's ordeal left her with love for her Ashland neighbors for patronizing Brannon's shop and supporting her family and being with them as they grieved. In a way, Brannon was why she got into public service in the first place. She had signed up for her first EMS course back in 1983, partly so she would be able to take care of him and her other children.

On the morning of the fires, Millie was checking the Weather Service updates. At about 11:30, she got a notification about the Starbuck Fire and a request for Clark County to send whoever was available to Oklahoma as reinforcements. With her daughter, Brandy Fleming, who is the assistant emergency manager, she set out in the department's pickup, but before they'd gone twenty-five miles it became obvious that they would have their own problems closer to home.

They stopped near Englewood, two miles from the state line, the county's southern border. By that time, the fire was approaching a ranch owned by a man named Frosty Ediger, who has raised cattle and wheat there for fifty years. The Englewood volunteer firemen had already given up trying to stop the ranks of flames rolling across the prairie and were focused on saving people and structures. An Englewood fireman saw Frosty Ediger on his tractor trying to plow a firebreak around his house. The fireman looked at the oncoming inferno and thought, *That old man is going to die.*

In conversation, people out here bring up God a lot, but that could be because a self-evident mighty power—the sky above—demands attention almost every day. At any minute, this humongous sky might smash you with hail or whirl you away in a tornado or bless you with rainbows and cloud-piercing sunbeams evocative of celestial choirs and the angels ascending and descending. Now, to the southwest, the gray-and-black smoke was boiling up toward altitudes where airplanes are tiny white X shapes with pipe-cleaner contrails. The smoke mounted in gray cumulus-like eruptions or redacted everything above the horizon line to black, while the underside of the billows glowed orange from the flames. Embers flew through the air, and the fierce heat added its own force to the wind, which blew with such a noise that people standing four feet apart had to shout to talk.

On a quirk of the wind, the fire jumped over Frosty Ediger and his house and outbuildings. In Englewood, directly in its path, some trees already blazed. The Englewood firemen retreated to defend the town. Millie saw the arm of flames sweeping north and realized that she and her team would have to manage the disaster from Ashland. They drove back on Highway 283, along which the telephone poles were soon burning. The Englewood firemen had advised her to go, but as they watched the flashing lights recede they felt completely alone.

Millie Fudge did, too. She had called the sheriff's office in Ashland and asked them to call Mutual Aid, an organization of neighboring counties that help one another in emergencies. But fires caused by sparking or downed power lines had broken out all over. When the sheriff's office called her back, they said that all trucks had gone to other fires and none were available. Millie then asked them to call counties farther out, but the same answer came back. Eleven separate fires burned in Kansas that day, though none the size of what was approaching Ashland. It hit her that Clark County's three volunteer fire departments (in Englewood, Ashland, and Minneola) would be defending their towns and county entirely on their own. For Millie, this was the most frightening moment.

Garth Gardiner, a rancher who raises cattle and quarter horses west of Ashland, watched through the window of his ranch's office as the smoke plumed skyward and figured the fire would miss him. He got in his pickup and drove west on a dirt road for a better look, then pulled over and gauged the smoke's distance—still pretty far off, he thought. Suddenly, a wall of flames came leaping over a ridge about three hundred yards away. "I saw it and hauled butt out of there," he said. Speeding back toward his house, he saw the smoke engulf his family's cattle operation, to the southwest, causing the photo-sensor floodlights above the corrals to turn on. Soon, only those lights, tiny pinpoints, were visible. Within the smoke's blackness, Garth's brothers, Mark and Greg, and Mark's wife, Eva, each escaped without knowing if the others had made it. Mark drove out on a lane so dark with smoke that he had to hold the truck door open so that he could follow the gravel road edge below him.

On folding tables in Ashland's ambulance garage, Millie Fudge set up the Emergency Operations Center for Clark County. She gave her daughter and two volunteer assistants the job of listening to all the police and fire dispatch calls and writing them down. Computer records would do for later; now, in the rush of events, she trusted paper. Other volunteers recorded the comings and goings of first responders on T-cards, which they inserted in a multi-pocket organizer that hung on the wall so the cards were visible at a glance. At 3:11 in the afternoon, Millie ordered the evacuation of the nursing home and the Ashland Health Center. She also ordered the evacuation of the entire town of Englewood and, about twenty minutes later, the evacuation of Ashland itself. Residents grabbed what they could and drove southeast, to Buffalo, Oklahoma, or east, to Protection, Kansas. (The town's name comes from its Republican founders, who espoused protective tariffs; it was later among the first towns in the United States to be inoculated with the Salk polio vaccine.)

Still the fire came on. Burning tumbleweeds flew forty feet above the ground, and the red cedars in the hollows roared as their resinous boughs ignited like kerosene. The wind swept up the dry grass until the air itself was on fire. Ashland's firefighters had never seen a blaze that could not be outflanked and subdued. "But what could you do against this monster?" Millie asked. Like the Englewood firemen, Ashland's tried to save structures and people. In outlying areas, they hosed houses with a flame-retardant foam. Some houses could not be saved. Here on the prairie, fires are fought from trucks, not on foot. Bumping over rough ground, the trucks threw the firemen around, banging them up and bruising them as burning sparks went down their necks. Several times, the fire's front line jumped over the trucks, and the firemen kept from burning by spraying a mist around themselves.

Cattle, for no known reason, sometimes ran into the flames. A man and his eleven-year-old son became separated while trying to move their cows to safety. The father, bouncing on an all-terrain vehicle, lost his cell phone; the son, driving a pickup, couldn't reach him and thought he had died. The son almost went back into the flames to try to save him; in another vehicle, his mother, who still had her phone and kept her head, insisted that the boy not do that. Horrible minutes passed before both father and son made it out of the smoke OK.

Several ranchers set out to plow firebreaks, as Frosty Ediger had done. Mike Harden, a farmer and rancher, got his tractor and heavy-duty disk plow and began to plow all around Ashland. He disked along the state and county roads on both shoulders, and along fences, and all around the health center, on the town's west side, and around the southwest side of the high school, and around the house of his former math teacher, and around piles of hay bales. When a transmission hose on his tractor broke, he started blading dirt and making firebreaks with a road grader. Once, Harden graded so close to the flames that the dirt he threw put them out. He also bladed a firebreak around his tractor and his disk plow so they wouldn't burn. He drove the grader to his house, quickly ate a supper his wife had fixed for him, and went out again.

At about 4:00 in the afternoon, the wind shifted from out of the west or southwest to out of the north. David Redger, the Ashland fire chief, conferred with Millie, decided that Ashland was most vulnerable from the northwest, and sent trucks there. At Garth Gardiner's, the firemen told Gardiner they would try to save his house, and they did. It touched him to know that some of these men, neighbors of his, helped him when at the same moment they were losing property of their own. The fire department now had more reports of houses on fire than it had trucks. Nothing was burning yet in town. The last evacuees made it out on roads with fire so close on either side that it blistered the paint on their cars. By 6:48 p.m., fire surrounded Ashland on all sides, and it was impossible to enter or leave the town. Those evacuated to Buffalo and Protection had to be evacuated farther, to the towns of Woodward, Oklahoma, and Coldwater, Kansas. As the flames closed in, Millie considered moving the Emergency Operations Center to a field of new wheat on the town's north side, just past the golf course. Too green to burn, the field could provide a refuge.

In Englewood, Bernnie Smith, the fire chief, was looking for water. A fire truck had run over a hydrant, draining the town's water tower, and he couldn't pump from wells, because the electricity had gone out. Meanwhile, his daughter was trying to bring his wife, who suffers from severe asthma, out of the smoke and to a hospital. Without treatment, she could die. Smith told his daughter to drive her south, to Woodward; half an hour later, his daughter called back to report that fire was blocking the roads in that direction. He told her to try the town of Beaver, Oklahoma, northwest of there, but when she got to the clinic it didn't have the necessary medications. She turned south, toward Perryton, Texas, but another fire, later called the Perryton Fire—also caused by power-line sparks—ruled that out. Then he told her to go north again, to the town of Liberal, Kansas, even if she had to drive through fire to get there. She finally reached the Liberal hospital, and her mother received treatment.

On the front line in Oklahoma, Charlie Starbuck and his crew fought on. When the wind changed to out of the north, flames suddenly surrounded them on three sides. Starbuck always drives with both windows of the truck cab open so he will feel the same heat as those riding on the back. Now the encroaching flames leaped through the cab, in one window and out the other. Starbuck ducked. By misting around themselves and blasting the fire with their hoses, they reached safer ground upwind. "We almost got overrun," he told me later. "To this day, I'm amazed that we didn't end up going to a lot of firefighters' funerals."

In Texas, the wind shift led to three of the state's deaths. A rancher, a cowboy who worked for him, and the cowboy's girlfriend were trying to rescue cattle when flames from an unexpected direction suddenly caught up with them and brought down their horse and four-wheeler. The three burned to death as they tried to escape on foot.

As night fell in Ashland, the few people remaining in town looked out at flames in every direction. Not all were sure they would ever see their families again.

People give different explanations for what saved the town. Some point to the firebreaks that Mike Harden disked and graded. In places, you could see where the fire had come up to one of those and stopped. The wheat field where Millie had thought of moving the Emergency Operations Center seemed to have been crucial. An aerial photograph from a day or two later shows the soot black of the incinerated prairie meeting the spring green of the four-hundred-acre field in a straight, uncompromised line. The fire kept threatening the town into the next day, and Ashland's firefighters stayed on the job without sleeping, some of them for thirty or forty hours. Millie remained at her command post, getting only a few hours' rest during the same period. On nature's part, the humidity increased, and the wind died down at night.

The only fire fatality in the county (or the state) on March 6 occurred when a truck driver on Highway 34 tried to turn around, jackknifed his truck, got out of the cab, and died of smoke inhalation. His name was Corey P. Holt, and he came from Oklahoma City. In the low visibility, two cars then crashed into the truck; the cars' occupants were injured, but no one died. Englewood lost about a dozen houses, nine in the town itself, and an Englewood man whose house burned down died of a heart attack two weeks later.

Losing buildings and fences and vehicles and stored-up hay was bad, but the suffering of the cattle grieved the ranchers' souls. Thousands of cattle died in the fire, but thousands wretchedly survived—blinded, their ears gone, ear tags melted, udders burned off. Many had little hair left, and their feet were burned so badly that they walked out of their hooves. Herds stood swaying slightly, moaning or mute in agony. Shooting cattle occupied the ashy days afterward. Ranchers whose guns and ammunition had burned up had to borrow them or ask neighbors to do the killing. Bulldozers and backhoes dug pits for mass burials.

Ashlanders said God had spared the town and its residents. Miraculous escapes were attributed to God's plan. Even the few older citizens who had been around for the Dust Bowl storms declared they'd never seen anything as awe-inspiring as this. Everybody said they hoped never to experience anything like it again.

But, in a sense, they soon did. Immediately after the fire—even as it still burned—unsolicited and generous aid started arriving from around the country. The outpouring amazed them even more than the fire had. News outlets did not cover the prairie fires extensively, the way they do California fires. But rural America found out about the March 6 fires on social media and followed their progress in real time. That day was a Monday. By Wednesday, hay to feed the cattle now without pastures started to arrive. For weeks afterward, convoys of flatbeds loaded with large cylindrical hay bales, up to $5,000 worth of hay per truck, all decked out with American flags and hand-lettered messages of support, rolled in, night and day. In Englewood, the fire department couldn't unload all the trucks at late hours and left a skid-loader and a sign by the firehouse asking the truckers to please unload their bales themselves. In the mornings, new piles of bales had appeared.

Replacing a mile of fence costs $10,000. The Gardiner ranch, for example, lost more than 270 miles of fence. Trucks from Iowa and Michigan arrived with donated fenceposts, corner posts, and wire. Volunteer crews slept in the Ashland High School gymnasium and worked ten-hour days on fence lines. Kids from a college in Oregon spent their spring break pitching in. Cajun chefs from Louisiana arrived with food and mobile kitchens and served free meals. Another cook brought his own chuck wagon. Local residents' old friends, retired folks with extra time, came in motor homes and lived in them while helping to rebuild. Donors sent so much bottled water it would have been enough to put out the fire all by itself, people said. A young man from Ohio raised $4,000 in cash and drove out and gave it to the Ashland Volunteer Fire Department, according to the *Clark County Gazette*. The young man said that God had told him to; the fireman who accepted the donation said that $4,000 was exactly what it was going to cost to repair the transmission of a truck that had failed in the fire, and both he and the young man cried.

Farm and ranch organizations and an association of rodeo cowboys gave tens of thousands of dollars to fire sufferers. Residents of Ashland, who had farsightedly established their own 501(c)3 foundation several years earlier, could accept the donations and distribute them without having to route them through another nonprofit, such as the Red Cross. The president of the Stockgrowers State Bank, Kendal Kay, who is also the town's mayor, offered low-interest loans so ranchers could restart their operations. But, as one rancher noted, all those who rebuilt acquired extra zeros on their debt line.

Even more contributions arrived: newborn-calf formula, veterinary medications, protein cake for cattle, winter clothes, frozen casseroles with scriptural messages taped to them, a shipment of cheese curds from Wisconsin, and more hay, of all kinds, in bales whose quantities had never been seen in the region before. After the 24/7 task of managing the hundreds of fire trucks and crews that showed up in the days after the fires, Millie Fudge turned to making note of all the donations, so that people could be acknowledged and thanked. Kansas's governor, Sam Brownback, made a visit; nobody chided him for the state's recent to-the-bone budget cuts. The fire had moved so fast that no agency outside Clark County could have done much anyway, Millie believed. In fact, the state's Incident Management Team had showed up on March 7 and provided excellent practical assistance, she pointed out (although the county had been careful to retain local control).

A young woman whose family's ranch houses had burned told a livestock-association meeting in Wichita, "The government didn't help us, but America did." From the point of view of Clark County as a whole, the government did play a part: the National Weather Service sent warnings about the wind shift; the states of Colorado, Nebraska, and South Dakota dispatched firefighting teams and aircraft to help squelch what was left of the fire; Ashland used a FEMA grant to buy two of its fire trucks; and the Department of Agriculture later provided ranchers with payments of up to $125,000 for livestock losses and up to $200,000 for fencing. And, of course, Millie and her team, as county officials, were part of "the government" themselves. None of that, however, was to the point, which was the unexpected nongovernmental love that the fire sufferers felt coming at them from around the country, as if out of nowhere.

A gun-store owner in Oklahoma who raffled off a 9 mm. pistol, an antelope hunt, and a custom rifle explained, "They're all my people." A stranger sent a cash donation and a handwritten note directly to Garth Gardiner after reading about him in the news. She said she wanted to do this for him even though he was a rancher and she was a vegetarian. "Our country's in a pretty turbulent political situation nowadays, but people are still good," Gardiner told me.

One afternoon last summer, I talked with Bernnie Smith in the shade behind the Englewood firehouse. He rolled some office chairs out the back door for us, because the metal building was stifling. Smith is a compact, green-eyed man with a level gaze and a quiet demeanor, and he wore a Western shirt with mother-of-pearl buttons, blue jeans, square-toed cowboy boots, and spurs. My call had interrupted his workday; he'd been moving cattle on his ranch. His horse stood in a stock trailer nearby, behind his club-cab pickup. Smith said that dealing with the emotions that the firefighters went through after the fire had been kind of a PTSD experience, because, honestly, they thought the fire had kicked their ass. They held meetings after it and talked about it and sometimes cried, and invited post-stress counselors a time or two. The guys on his crew range in age from nineteen to over seventy, and they stayed on the fire for, in some cases, two days straight. He worried about one young guy because Smith thought his eyes had been burned, but he turned out to be OK. The generosity of people in the aftermath had meant an enormous amount. "That hay movement after the fire is the greatest thing that's happened in America in my lifetime," he said. He still loves to look at a pasture full of good grass, but he remarked, "It's pretty until it burns," adding, "That grass is your livelihood and a hazard at the same time." He and I talked for hours, until his horse was whinnying with impatience and kicking the slats of the trailer. Smith never mentioned that while he fought to save lives and houses in Englewood the fire had burned up a third of his cattle herd.

I learned that fact later, from Cara Vanderree, the librarian in Ashland. She is originally from Comanche County, next door, and her family has been in the state for generations. The Ashland Library is the best small library in Kansas, in the judgment of the Kansas Library Association, which recently gave it an award. Vanderree speaks in a sweet, soft voice. A lot of her job, especially in summer, consists of superintending kids who want to use the library's computers. With sweetness and patience, she requires that if a child wants to play on the computer for half an hour the child must read a book for half an hour, and she watches to make sure the child actually reads. Sometimes she decides a difficult child must go, and she says, "Darlin', I can feel your home callin' you."

Before the fire, Vanderree did some archival work for the Kansas Humanities Council (now Humanities Kansas), transcribing recorded recollections.

After the fire, when everyone was going through a period of talking about it, trying to come to terms with it—a period that has not yet ended—Vanderree got the idea of recording as many survivors of the fire as wanted to participate. Then she would put the recordings on the library's website, and make the transcriptions into a book. The Kansas Humanities Council liked the idea and gave her a grant, as did the Kansas Health Foundation. With the assistance of Diana Redger, who has a master's in history and is also the Ashland fire chief's sister, the library has interviewed sixty-nine people.

Vanderree had thought she could ease the chore of transcribing by downloading an app she bought online. She soon discovered that the app couldn't understand a Kansas-Oklahoma accent. When a speaker said the word "town," what the computer somehow heard was "Tehran." The repeated appearance of the Iranian capital in the first-person accounts of a Kansas wildfire gave the project a certain international flavor, but these and many other mistakes became a pain to deal with. She and two assistants went back to doing the transcriptions themselves.

Redger conducted most of the interviews, and at the end of each one she asked the interviewees if anything good had come from the fire. They replied that it made them know their neighbors better, it drew people closer together, and it strengthened the town. I know all these answers are true. If you drive on the plains a lot, you see towns in decline: store windows boarded up on Main Street, houses becoming run-down, local schools closed. Our rural places are emptying out. The frame of a sign with no sign in it could be an emblem for much of small-town America, not only on the plains. Sometimes a town will even lament its fate publicly: "Pray for Fowler," read a sign I drove past in Fowler, Kansas.

Ashland used to have dozens of businesses, a passenger-railroad station on the Santa Fe line, and a movie theater that showed films every day. All are now gone; but the town nonetheless continues, with the courthouse, an office of the US Department of Agriculture, a public swimming pool, a lumberyard, a good restaurant, the grain elevators, a motel, two bed-and-breakfasts, a public school for K-12, four churches, two banks, the health center, a veterinary clinic, and the library. The March 6 fires affected other towns, but I know of none that did a local-history project about the experience. Ashland's collection of fire stories is like the town's immune system kicking in.

The prairie greened up quickly after the fires, and in some places the grass came back better than before. Then, on March 5, 2018—almost exactly a year after the fires—a wind-driven fire broke out just north of Ashland.

Incredulous, the fire department pounced on the blaze, put it out, and watched indignantly lest it make another peep, which it did not. No major fires had threatened Ashland in 2018. In April, however, big fires burned again in Oklahoma. One that officials called the Rhea Fire started near the town of Seiling and consumed about 300,000 acres, with two deaths. I drove through the area just afterward. Wind turbines in great and stately numbers populate the prairie there—Oklahoma gets more than a quarter of its electricity from wind-generated power. The blades were turning slowly overhead as ashes drifted in the air and made the whole landscape look smudged and blurry. Black skeletons of scrubby trees stretched to the horizon south of Seiling; in other places, the flames had turned open prairie into Sahara-like dunes dotted with spiky black sagebrush stumps.

Since 2005, the prairie states have seen a lot of fires. Several that burned in 2016 now look like preludes to the giants of 2017; other record-setting fires had preceded them. The biggest prairie fire in Texas history burned about a million acres on the Panhandle in 2006. Deke Arndt, a meteorologist and a climate scientist for the National Oceanic and Atmospheric Administration, has written on NOAA's website about prairie fires. I called him and asked if he saw the fires as part of a pattern related to climate change.

Arndt grew up in Oklahoma, and his mother still lives there, so he understands the immediacy of weather in people's lives on the plains. He thinks that may be why Oklahoma produces so many weather scientists. Arndt explained about the dry line and said that it has been creating wild weather in the region since before humans lived there. But the weather and the climate are two different things, he added (as meteorologists often do). Extreme weather has always occurred on the plains. What is new, and derives from climate change, is that the atmosphere has become hotter and wetter, bringing more rain, causing wetter years (2016, for example), which produce more fuel in the form of grass. As the atmosphere warms, it is also thirstier, so that when dry periods come the air sucks more moisture from the soil and the plants and makes the land more susceptible to fire. We may be witnessing a slow process of desertification in drier parts of the region, but nearly half the people in Arndt's native state doubt that climate change is real.

No one I talked to in Kansas told me that he believed in climate change. Prevailing opinion holds that nothing about the recent extreme weather here is much different from what's always been. People say that Native Americans sometimes used prairie fires as an environmental tool. Some claim that government policy is partly to blame for the recent fires, and often single out the CRP—the Conservation Reserve Program, a federal initiative that since the 1980s has paid farmers to replant and maintain grass cover on their land. The argument resembles the one applied to the long-standing policy of fire suppression in forests: that is, fire suppression and the CRP both create dangerous buildups of fuel.

As Adam Elliott, who administers the program in Clark County from the US Department of Agriculture (USDA) office in Ashland, told me, the CRP was intended to be a continuation of government efforts to put marginal land back into grass so that it wouldn't blow. A subsequent increase in deer and game-bird populations has become another justification for it. (That increase is evident on summer mornings, even in the middle of Ashland, when you awake to the dulcet "bobwhite" call of the quail.) People say that the fires resulted from a unique combination of a rainy period followed by a drought, with the land made more flammable by the CRP. Evidently the government agreed with this analysis, because soon after the 2017 fires the USDA expanded the time frame for grazing on otherwise closed CRP land.

When I asked Millie Fudge her opinion about climate change and the fires, she deliberated so long before answering that I thought I'd offended her. Then she said, "I'm not knowledgeable about that. Climate change, if it exists, might have something to do with the fires. But, whether it does or not, I know God is in control. He allows or causes the increase in fires to happen for a reason."

Again she fell silent. "What is the reason?" I asked.

More silence. Then: "The fires are a wake-up call. They will get worse. We humans think we are in charge. We think we are indispensable to God, but he is showing us that he is in control. He is telling us that we need to find God."

When I talked to Mike Harden, the man who plowed and bladed the firebreaks, he also said he did not know if climate change existed. "But I'll tell you, it's never boring trying to raise cattle or crops out here," he went on. "My great-grandparents came out and homesteaded in the 1890s, and we've seen everything. Floods. Hailstorms. Grasshoppers. Ice storms. Tornadoes. Dust and more dust. And now these fires. Living here takes it out of you, but every year is a little bit different. Whatever the weather is going to do in the future, that's not up to me. All I know is that the Bible says man will eat his bread in the sweat of his face, and that's certainly true if you ranch or farm in western Kansas."

I drove hundreds of miles trying to make geographic sense of the fires. After going back and forth between Oklahoma and Kansas several times, I noticed the name of the river I crossed in Oklahoma near the border: the Cimarron. How could it have taken so long for me to notice the Cimarron River? On the whole Great Plains—in all the West, for my money—no other river name coincides with Western myth so closely or so lyrically. Almost ninety years ago, Edna Ferber wrote a novel, *Cimarron*, about the opening of the Oklahoma Territory. The book was made into a movie, starring Richard Dix, which won the Academy Award for Best Picture in 1931. That movie, in turn, was remade into another *Cimarron*, which starred Glenn Ford, in 1960. There've been any number of other movies, TV shows, songs, and albums with "Cimarron" in their titles. It comes from a Spanish word that means, in this context, a runaway horse that lives in wild places.

For years, the Oklahoma Panhandle was No Man's Land, a refuge for outlaws. For complicated reasons, no state had jurisdiction there. A branch of the Chisholm Trail, which the cattle herds followed northward from Texas after the Civil War, crossed the Cimarron River not far from present-day Highway 283. Englewood, just north of the river in Kansas, where law existed, offered entertainment and hotels and a railroad connection for cowboys riding the trail. Outlaws used to commit crimes in Kansas and then escape back across the Cimarron to relative safety. Western-style shoot-outs, where the bad guy drew on the lawman and the lawman shot the bad guy, occurred on the dusty streets of Englewood. From the even more civilized town of Ashland, marshals set out across the Cimarron to catch and bring back wanted men for trial.

In wet periods, the Cimarron runs at about the volume of a respectable creek back East. I stopped and watched its clear, buckskin-colored water flowing through the willows and the red cedars. A few cottonwoods held up their blackened branches, but otherwise you'd never know that fire had recently raced along this valley. If I were younger, I would have swooned farther back into lonesome-cowboy fantasies, into all the *Cimarrons* of my childhood. But that Wild West past happened to other people. We are of a different time and place—on our own, like the Ashland and Englewood firefighters in the firestorm. As I looked at the Cimarron River, my thoughts were of the present and the soon to come.

Amazon Army

Megan Kaminski

December 1921

A solitary voice reverberates
when joined with 6,000 others,
demanding a horizon better than
the status-quo forecast. In Franklin, Kansas,
a 500-women meeting blossoms into a mine-to-mine
protest for the right to strike—the right
to safe working conditions, to feed families,
to make a living from one's own hands.
Met by fire hoses and mine guards firing,
their feet marched on, carrying children
and flags for three days to sixty-three mines.
Unflinching women united to refine the future.

And Governor Allen responded, like those
who fear justice continue to, by discharging
the National Guard on his own people, on
women and children asking for a better life,
asking the lives of those they love be
valued in the calculus of corporate profits.
Their actions in the coal fields of Southeast Kansas
extracted labor reforms and changed minds.

It's still dangerous to strike in Kansas; the average
American CEO now makes 320 times that
of the average worker. But there are more
of us than them.

They'd like us to forget
the power we hold together: when we

listen to each other's stories, when we
share resources in mutual aid, when
we know both that our neighbors' backs
ache as violently as ours and also that
pain doesn't have to spread this way.

When a gathering of women became an
army, when word of their bravery spread
across the country, when that story
still burrows into our own hearts the power
of we speaking truth. When we value
lives over profit, when we are many and we
care fiercely, when your children and your
children's children matter as much as my own.

How I Fell in Love with Kansas—and Spent the Next Five Years Trying to Change It

Davis Hammet

It's 2013, and I'm a twenty-two-year-old queer who's moving to Kansas to paint a house rainbow colors directly across from the notorious Westboro Baptist Church hate group. I don't know much about Kansas except that it's in the middle of America and famous bigots live there. It doesn't matter, though, because I won't be there long.

I never left. Over the next five years, I learned that the politicians are more dangerous than the hate groups, and that the people of Kansas are nothing like the politics that dominate.

I arrived to a state in crisis and ordinary people doing whatever they could to try to fix it: a mom walked more than sixty miles hoping someone would pay attention to schools, a student chased legislators through the statehouse trying to keep guns off college campuses, a rabbi was arrested holding a sit-in against voter suppression. I fell in love not with a physical place but with a community that was starting to shape the future. A community I could be a part of.

After arriving in Kansas, I didn't find the inhospitable attitudes I expected. Neighbors brought us food they'd grown, and strangers invited us to spend holidays with them. I couldn't find much of anyone who agreed with what was going on in the state: a radical economic experiment had cut income taxes dramatically and eliminated taxes on hundreds of thousands of businesses. Rather than boost the economy, this devastated it. From the gas station clerk to folks chattering in restaurants, everyone was concerned about where Kansas was headed.

Not to say that everyone was pleasant, but this wasn't the backward place I anticipated. Kansas quickly grew on me. Wanting to meet more activists, I went to a protest at the statehouse; only a half-dozen people were there. I started to realize that many of the organizers who did the work in the past had burned out or fled the state after the 2010 election.

I didn't know where to start, so I began connecting with any and all individuals and organizations I could. I showed up to their events, advocated for their causes, and held candles at their vigils. My own purpose in Kansas grew as I developed friendships with those affected by various state policies. Their causes became my causes.

In 2014 the most one-sided government in Kansas history was elected. Coincidentally, this was the first election under a "voter fraud prevention" law Secretary of State Kris Kobach pushed through, which required Kansans to provide official copies of their birth certificates to county clerks in order to vote. The law only applied to new, mostly young, registrants. Kansas dropped into the bottom five states nationally for youth turnout, with 14 percent of eighteen- to twenty-four-year-olds casting ballots.

In 2015 Governor Sam Brownback rescinded LGBTQ protections by executive order, making it legal to fire and harass LGBTQ state workers. Gay state workers messaged me about how they were scared for their safety and future. In response, we organized. Two years prior, I had protested alongside fewer than six people. This time, six hundred showed up. Most weren't LGBTQ; they were people affected in different ways who stood together as moral witnesses, declaring that this decision was wrong.

The Kansas government increasingly used prejudice and scapegoats to distract from the headlines of its failing economic experiment, of struggling schools, of critical services being cut. As the state struggled to pay its bills, legislators made claims that welfare recipients were going on luxury cruises, that undocumented immigrants should be shot like swine. They even tried to strip a Black representative of her elected status because she said a racist bill was racist. All of this nonsense was distracting from the reality that the far right, which branded itself as conservative, was driving the state into debt, roads were crumbling, and job growth was declining. Kansas was a very dark place in that moment. After one rally, a state senator walked by me and softly mentioned how wrong the attacks on the LGBTQ community were, how wrong all of this was. I wouldn't forget this moment because I so badly needed to be reminded that what was happening wasn't okay.

I decided to leave LGBTQ activism to create a nonprofit, Loud Light, and devote myself to voter registration and turnout. Convinced that if more young Kansans voted, things would be different. I ran around college campuses trying to register students, but it was difficult given the burdens of Kobach's laws. Then a judge issued a preliminary injunction against Kansas, saying the state couldn't require birth certificates for those who registered using the federal registration form. I began registering hundreds of students with it.

In 2016, as the nation was taking a plunge to the right, Kansas was going the opposite direction: a third of the Kansas legislature was newly elected, mostly Democrats and centrist Republicans. We knew politicians were reactive, so we gave them something to react to. We traveled the state gathering input from hundreds of folks to create a platform of sorts called the Kansas People's Agenda. The first week of the session, legislators arrived to a statehouse filled with Kansans screaming, "Whose House? Our House." Hundreds of people individually delivered the agenda to their own legislators. The new legislature began turning things around. Finally, the economic experiment was repealed.

I met all kinds of people who wanted things to change. One was Brian "BAM" McClendon, who created what became Google Earth. We talked about voter registration obstacles. Immediately, he created ksvotes.org, a digital federal form that bypasses the obstacles and makes registration easy. Another was a woman who messaged me to talk about the state's future; a coffee meetup turned into an hours-long discussion about human dignity.

Tens of thousands of Kansans were re-added to the voter rolls as a federal judge ruled that Kobach's law violated the US Constitution. Kansas could no longer require birth certificates to vote. Loud Light registered thousands of young Kansans to vote, and more young Kansans voted early than had voted in the entire previous midterm.

In November 2018 the woman I had met for coffee, Sharice Davids, was elected the first LGBTQ congressperson from Kansas and one of the first Native American women elected to Congress. She gave a victory speech surrounded by LGBTQ youths. I was there, overwhelmed, thinking how most of my life I thought accepting my sexuality meant forfeiting my future. The same night, Brandon Woodard and Susan Ruiz were elected the first LGBTQ Kansas state representatives. They went to work in a chamber that has spent close to a decade blaming people like them for every ailment under the sun. Kobach lost his bid for governor. The state senator who whispered words of solidarity to me back in 2015, Laura Kelly, beat him. She promised a new tone in Kansas and declared her first executive order would be restoring LGBTQ protections to state workers.

In Kansas I learned that nothing happens by accident. Every drop of decency is fought for. We pushed a boulder slightly up the hill, yet the moment we stop pushing, we will again be flattened. In fact, the Kansas legislature is worse now—Republicans retain supermajorities in both chambers, and more moderate Republicans were ousted by those adhering to the far right. The challenges can seem insurmountable, but there are hundreds of individuals doing whatever they can, devoting their energy and talents to make change, and becoming a community as they show up for each other. Now I know the power of that.

Unraveling the Myths of the Chicano Movement in Kansas

Valerie M. Mendoza

No one associates the Chicano Movement with Kansas, yet activism reverberated throughout the state during the 1970s, '80s, and into the '90s—what I call the Long Chicano Movement—when Topeka, Kansas City, Wichita, and other municipalities experienced a surge in advocacy on behalf of the Latinx community. This advocacy ranged from politics and voting to education and economic opportunities. Notably, too, Chicanos in Kansas stood at the forefront of organizing services for Spanish-speaking elders. These stories have yet to be told. Too many myths about the Chicano Movement need to be dispelled. The creation of Topeka's League of United Latin American Citizens (LULAC) Council 11071 and the LULAC Multipurpose Senior Center are a small story in that larger framework.

In recognition of the fiftieth anniversary of many organizations and events related to the Chicano Movement in Kansas, I interviewed individuals involved in organizations throughout northeast Kansas. As I did, I gradually remembered people, places, and events from my own childhood in Topeka. I connected the dots between memories of the past and my actions today. Interviewing these folks felt like time traveling.

I became a historian and teller of stories because of my grandmother Hazel Gomez. She was a child of the Depression and saved everything. I remember as a child being with her as she pulled out her ivory-colored silk wedding dress. It had a princess neckline and long, sheer sleeves. She wore it in 1944 at the height of World War II when she married my grandfather Robert Gomez just before he shipped out with the Navy. He wore his Navy dress uniform. Her dress told a love story of the past, and I was captivated.

I also remember years later when she was clearing out her attic and came upon a huge pile of vintage postcards from the 1940s. They were gorgeous pieces of artwork in and of themselves, but in those days I was interested in the stamps. Written on the back of the postcards were literal stories of the war, but she told me not to read them, so I didn't.

Fast-forward to my grad school days in history at UC Berkeley—I needed a topic for my PhD thesis and longed to tell my family's immigration story from Mexico to Kansas. But I was reluctant to reveal something so personal for fear of seeming biased. Instead, I decided to tell the immigration story of Kansas City's Mexican community. It was close enough to be similar, but not my own personal community. I wrote about how men and women experienced migration differently. Men came to Kansas City first, looking for jobs and leaving women behind. Because Kansas City was away from the border and did not have an established Mexican community, this caused a role reversal: men cooked and cleaned for themselves in Kansas City, and women served as heads of households in Mexico.

Fast-forward again and I'm a public historian, writing and researching for the education of the general public rather than academia. StoryCorps came to Topeka. I knew that my dad—the son of immigrants, who went to college and eventually earned his master's degree—had a unique story that needed to be told. I convinced him to let me interview him about his days in the Chicano Movement. I was eager to ask him how one person could accomplish so much. I learned about how his community came to rely on him to fix or change things, so much so that he had to step back so others could learn for themselves.

I also knew that a centerpiece of my dad's activism was LULAC, the League of United Latin American Citizens. Fifty years later, the anniversary of the LULAC Multipurpose Senior Center in Topeka offered me a chance to continue my research when Kathy Votaw, executive director of the senior center, asked me to speak about the center's history. That's when it hit me that not only does the story of the senior center need to be told, but the story of Topeka's LULAC Council and all of their works should also be shared. I applied for and received a Sunflower 70s grant from Humanities Kansas, then got to work interviewing the remaining founding members of the council. I also went through my grandmother's papers, which I had donated years before to the Kansas Historical Society.

Part of my research revealed myths about LULAC and the Chicano Movement that need to be addressed.

Myth 1: LULAC Was a Conservative Organization

The League of United Latin American Citizens was established in 1929 in Corpus Christi, Texas. Its name was purposeful because it included the word *citizens*. Mexican Americans in Texas, as elsewhere, were discriminated against due to their dark skin, last names, accents, and more. The organization formed to combat discrimination, which the founding members felt was unjust because they were United States citizens. Early advocacy centered on desegregating schools, voting rights, officially classifying Mexicans as white in the census, and desegregating public spaces. The organization and its membership were considered assimilationist from the start because of these focus areas. Despite the negative impression some harbored, LULAC gained traction throughout the country for its work helping Mexican Americans. Soon after its founding, chapters spread throughout Texas and into other states.

Because of LULAC's emphasis on equal rights for citizens of Mexican origin and its use of the courts to gain those rights, most people during the era of the Chicano Movement considered LULAC to be an establishment organization filled with middle-aged conservative folks. For the most part, councils and their members were not protesting in the streets, participating in walkouts, or organizing boycotts. However, over the years the organization as a whole accomplished a lot, particularly in Texas and California. In fact, I later learned that two of the founding members of Topeka's council, Ascension and Rosemary Hernandez, learned of LULAC while they were living in California during the late 1960s.

When the Hernandezes moved back to Kansas in the early 1970s, Ascension suggested starting a LULAC council in Topeka. Arguments for this idea were plentiful. My mom, Virginia Mendoza, recalled that one of the reasons she supported forming a council was because of the clout they would have with the backing of a national organization.

My dad, John Mendoza, remembered, "The Chicano Movement galvanized everybody. It served as a catalyst for everyone who wanted to change things—inequality, education, and in jobs." The need for change was ripe in Kansas and Topeka, and LULAC and its members led the charge, creating a wave of organizations that had a profound impact at the time, and many of which are still in existence today.

Myth 2: The Chicano Movement Only Happened in the Southwest
Kansans knew what was going on in the national Chicano Movement. Articles about Cesar Chavez and the United Farm Workers began appearing in local newspapers as early as April 1966, with news about the grape boycott and the United Farm Workers march from Delano to Sacramento. Indeed, Chavez himself visited Kansas City in November 1969. Local newspapers also reported about Reies Lopez Tijerina and his raid on the courthouse in Rio Arriba County, New Mexico, in 1967. The raid was meant to publicize

the cause of returning land back to New Mexicans that dated all the way to Spanish exploration and settlement in the sixteenth century.

In addition, in 1970 Chicanos in Kansas and Missouri learned of Corky Gonzalez and his Crusade for Justice when one of the leaders of that organization spoke at a student Raza Unida Conference at the University of Missouri in Columbia. That same year, *Los Angeles Times* reporter Ruben Salazar was murdered during the Chicano Moratorium, a protest march against the war in Vietnam and the disproportionate representation and deaths of Chicano soldiers serving in the military. Headlines such as "Probe into Riot" and "Riot Toll Up to 2" dominated the newspapers.

Therefore, Mexican Americans in Topeka knew of the Chicano Movement and events happening on a national scale. This knowledge influenced how these activists viewed their community and the changes that they wanted to see. Through local mainstream newspapers and regional and national Chicano newsletters, Kansans knew that Chicanos throughout the country demanded changes, and they knew that they needed to participate.

Myth 3: Only Youths Were Active in the Chicano Movement

In Topeka, active members of LULAC were in their late twenties and thirties, married with young children. My parents, John and Virginia Mendoza, were both in their late twenties when the Topeka council received its charter; they had two children under five years of age. Other charter members were solidly middle aged, such as my grandparents Robert and Hazel Gomez. Robert was a World War II veteran and Hazel a professional volunteer all of her life. They were in their late forties during the early 1970s. They weren't the only ones, either. John and Leocadia Navarro, two additional founding members, were also in their forties.

The early council was formed based on the cultural capital of the founding members. Most were related. For example, Hazel recruited her nephew and his wife at the time, Jim and Pat Gomez, who had three young children. Council members also invited childhood friends and neighbors. My father and Ediberto Gonzalez attended school together.

Women participated in equal numbers to men, with many couples joining together. Women served in leadership roles and organized many of the fundraising events, such as food sales and rummage sales. My mom, Virginia, came up with the idea of the Sweethearts Dance to raise funds for the senior center and scholarships. The dance continues to this day, having raised hundreds of thousands of dollars over the past fifty years.

The council thrived due to the connections, dedication, fundraising acumen, and sheer charisma of Hazel Gomez. She mobilized the "comadre network" (woman's network) to recruit volunteers, LULAC members, and senior center participants. A running joke in her family was that her phone was always busy and she could never be reached because she was constantly organizing one thing or another. Indeed, her son Bill recalled, "I joined [LULAC] because she told me to."

Myth 4: The Chicano Movement Is a Thing of the Past

Most people, myself included before this project, think that the Chicano Movement is something that happened "back in the day," with no relevance to today. However, many of the accomplishments from that era still reverberate. Activists achieved many important goals in a short amount of time, most of which happened against long odds. The list of accomplishments for Topeka's LULAC Council is impressive and falls broadly under the following categories: education, advocacy, and community engagement. However, all of these categories are interrelated. Getting people into college so that they can get good jobs, for example, will in turn develop strong communities and lead to civic engagement.

The first issue the Topeka council tackled was servicing the elders of their community. According to my father, John, "There was a senior group at Our Lady of Guadalupe church established by Mr. Lopez, but they had limited resources." At the time Spanish-speaking elderly faced many barriers due to language difficulties and lack of translators. This caused them to be isolated. The LULAC Council decided that establishing a senior center for this group would be their top priority.

In March 1973 LULAC filed articles of incorporation with the state of Kansas, and by May its members hosted the first state conference on aging along with Justicia, an advocacy nonprofit founded by LULAC member Ediberto Gonzalez.

Ascension Hernandez learned about the Older Americans Act, which supported the founding of the senior center. John Mendoza said, "I didn't understand the funding, bureaucracy of it all, but he somehow understood. We stood first in line to grab some funding and became successful."

I am astounded by the profound matter-of-factness of his statement, which belies their perseverance, as if what they did was easy.

Virginia Mendoza, my mother, said, "Ascension found the grant to expand the senior center and purchase the building, and we got it." Ascension and Rosemary Hernandez recalled, simply: "John wrote the grant and we got it." They each credited the other, and neither mentioned the hard work and hours of research and writing that went into it.

This put the LULAC Council on the ground floor of funding from the Older Americans Act, which in 1973 authorized grants to local community agencies for multipurpose senior centers. Indeed, the LULAC Multipurpose Senior Center predates the Kansas Department of Aging, which was not established until 1977, and the Kansas Area Association on Aging, which began in 1974.

LULAC Council member Patricia Gomez was hired in December 1973 and became the senior center's first long-term director. The center provided noon meals, transportation, and recreation activities; nearly all participants were retired Santa Fe Railroad employees or their spouses. A year later in December 1974 the center had seventy regular participants, and their space was suddenly too small. This prompted Ascension Hernandez, then the LULAC state director, to contact the superintendent of the Santa Fe Railroad to request a donation for the center.

While it is unclear whether he received the donation, what was clear was that the center needed a new space. The council worked with the Oakland Neighborhood Improvement Association (NIA) to purchase a former church building at 1205 Seward Avenue for $25,000. Both the council and the Oakland NIA approved the funds in January 1978. Council members worked tirelessly to refurbish it from a church into a senior center by pooling skills such as carpentry and soliciting donations such as office equipment. The council members and the community answered the call. The center uses that building to this day.

The senior center spawned two state conferences and a national conference on aging. The LULAC Council also applied for funds from the then Department of Housing and Urban Development and opened a housing complex for the elderly in the Oakland neighborhood in the early 1980s.

Although the center experienced ups and downs over the years in terms of funding, it has become a neighborhood mainstay. Today it provides medical transportation, meals, and recreational activities like karaoke, art lessons, cooking classes, and parties. A recent Cinco de Mayo celebration featured a piñata shaped as a taco.

Like our parents, today my brother J. R. and I continue their work. I recently joined Topeka's LULAC Council, and he presides over Council 4871 in Dallas. His work garnered him LULAC District III Man of the Year in

2024. Much remains to be done, and we are fortunate to build from the solid foundation of the Kansas Chicano Movement begun more than fifty years ago. *Si se puede!*

Parsons Brings the Pride Flag Home

C. J. Janovy

The iced tea was flowing, and the women of Parsons High School's class of 1969 were on a roll.

A handful of them were circled up at a table in the fellowship hall of St. John's Episcopal Church, where yearbooks from fifty years ago were spread out on display at the front of the room. Laughter from old stories grew louder. One of the women at the table had purple hair—not the subtle tint of elderly ladies' salon rinses but the declarative violet in vogue among queer kids.

All of these women had clear recollections of a classmate who got the hell out of Kansas as soon as he could and went on to change the world.

Gilbert Baker, born in Chanute, Kansas, on June 2, 1951, designed the rainbow flag, now flown all over the world to signify support for LGBTQ equality and pride.

"He always was into the arts," one of Baker's classmates remembered.

"He was a personality unto himself," another said.

"He was always at our lunch table. He really did feel comfortable with us, and we felt comfortable with him."

"He loved to act, and help us do the plays."

They remembered a dark-haired boy with thick Buddy Holly glasses. "You know, he would be the kind to wear a scarf or shawl, whatever you'd call it."

"A snappy dresser."

"This may not be etiquette, but in '69, we didn't know what gay was. So Gilbert was just different," said Debbie Sailsbury Burke. "People would make fun of him because he was different, but he set the stage way before it was ever a norm."

One time, he asked Patty Eakins Edgington on a date. "I'd evidently broken up with a boyfriend. I don't know what I'd done, I was sixteen or

seventeen, who knows. And I don't know why he said—that's just Gilbert—
he said, 'Let's go to the drive-in.' So we went to the drive-in movie and it was
a quote, *date*, but I kind of knew it wasn't really a date."

Everyone agreed: "Just a friend—just a friend."

"The next day," Edgington continued, "I got yellow roses delivered to my
house: 'Thank you for a great time.' He was just a nice guy."

In the decades since they graduated, people began to realize what Baker
had done after leaving Kansas. Eventually Facebook came along.

"I shot a request to him, and he accepted," Edgington said. "I posted some
stuff over the years because I fiddled around in art, and he'd comment."

At some point there was talk of inviting Baker back for one of the re-
unions, but that brought up other memories.

"At our lunch table, the guys, the jocks, would come by with their trays,
and they would slap him in the back of the head," Burke said. "I mean, some
of them were cruel to him. I always felt sorry for him."

They pointed across the room to Sandy Salyer, who remembered Baker
doing cartwheels. Salyer said she read an interview where Baker talked
about being bullied as a kid.

"When I heard that, it broke my heart," she said. "We were just innocent
and didn't understand what a gay person was. He was a free spirit, loving
life."

A lot of people didn't know where Baker went after high school, but he
seemed destined for greatness.

"I'm just so proud of what he did and the movement he was part of,"
Salyer said. And she began to tear up. "I'm really sorry people treated him
that way."

"Take Me Away!"
Kansas has a rough time staking a claim to Gilbert Baker. By the time of his
death, at age sixty-five on March 31, 2017, his legacy belonged to the world.
"The rainbow flag has become a universal symbol for inclusion, peace, and
love," the *New York Times* noted in his obituary.

In his autobiography *Rainbow Warrior: My Life in Color*, published post-
humously in 2019, Baker devoted a grand total of eight pages to his Kansas
upbringing. He titled that chapter "Dreaming of a Life Over the Rainbow."

"I was born gay and I always knew it," Baker wrote, before detailing the
pain of that knowledge in 1950s Kansas.

As a child in his bedroom, Baker pulled sheets off his bed to fashion outfits for a kindergartner's imaginary drag routine, dancing to songs on the radio until he heard someone coming, and scrambling to put the sheets back on the bed. Later, when his parents discovered him twirling in his aunt's old prom dress, his father spanked him. On Sundays at the Methodist church, his soul burned with questions. "Did God make me gay and love me, or was I going to hell for a sin?" He considered killing himself.

Still, his work was inspired by a quintessentially Kansas phenomenon: when President Dwight D. Eisenhower ran for reelection, Baker's mother let him watch the convention on TV. "I was mesmerized by the hoopla of bunting and balloons and thrilled by the pageantry," he wrote. "I especially loved the parade of state delegates, each group carrying signs and banners created in crepe paper. There were crazy hats and pretty girls in washes of stars and stripes, the national anthem and the Pledge of Allegiance. I was especially moved by the sight of the American flag."

Armed with crayons, young Baker became obsessed with drawing what he'd seen. But "it was not considered normal to imagine greatness and beauty," he wrote. "Being an artist was bad in the same way that homosexuality was bad."

Baker's family moved to Wichita for his father's law practice. By the time he was nine, he was in such distress that he went to the library to try to figure out what was wrong with him; in a book about Sigmund Freud and abnormal psychology, a description of "delusions of grandeur" seemed to explain his feelings. Fearing his parents would send him to a mental institution, Baker, like so many other Midwestern kids of his time, tortured himself with efforts to be something he was not. He grew obsessed with death. "Only one thing seemed certain about my life in Kansas: I would either be blown up by a nuclear bomb or die from boredom."

Peak mid-twentieth-century TV provided a bit of salvation: Phyllis Diller on *The Tonight Show*; the political, passionate, and kooky Barbra Streisand; the long-haired Beatles and the Rolling Stones. "Old people said they looked like girls, so they were definitely pushing a button on the taboo of homosexuality," he wrote.

Baker took up the trumpet, and music became his teenage means of survival—"the way I could compensate socially for being so effeminate and being known as the class queer." Nobody wanted to play Sousa marches, so Baker pressured music teachers to include arrangements of Herb Alpert & the Tijuana Brass and Blood, Sweat & Tears.

"My efforts succeeded," he wrote, "and I even became popular with my classmates because of it."

But fights with his parents intensified, and he grew riveted to news from the 1968 Democratic National Convention. The streets of Chicago were exploding, "but the only thing taking over the streets in Kansas was tumbleweed."

He left when he was nineteen. "Unlike Dorothy, when the tornado came I ran right for it, saying, 'Take me away!'"

"We Just Act Like It's Normal"

Parsons is about thirty-five miles south of Baker's birthplace in Chanute, in the far southeast corner of the state. Home to around ten thousand people, it can feel like a city to kids from nearby towns of just a few hundred.

It's the kind of place where people remember ZaSu Pitts, an actress who started out in silent films and worked through *It's a Mad, Mad, Mad, Mad World* (1963). Pitts has a star on the Hollywood Walk of Fame and a bronze star in front of the Parsons movie theater. It's also the birthplace of jazz trumpeter Buck Clayton, who played with Count Basie, Benny Goodman, and Billie Holiday and has been honored with a local jazz festival. Cherryvale, twenty-some miles away, has bragging rights to two people: Vivian Vance from *I Love Lucy*, and Frank E. Bellamy, a high school student who claimed to have written the Pledge of Allegiance.

"We jump on every little tiny thing we can to get people to our towns," said Scotty Zollars, the library director at Labette Community College. "But why has there never been any mention of Gilbert, who had much wider representation than that?"

One answer might seem obvious: that a conservative small town in Kansas wants no part of international gay culture. But reality has more nuance.

Zollars, a gay man in his early sixties, has lived around Parsons almost his entire life. "I don't hide it. Everybody at work knows; my boss knows," Zollars said. He goes to college events with his partner. "We just act like it's normal. And there's other couples in town who are the same way." People in southeast Kansas, Zollars said, "really don't care as long as you don't shove it in their face." Gay people in small towns throughout Kansas say the same thing. Flying rainbow flags does, of course, put something in people's faces.

But by leaving Kansas so early and so thoroughly, it's as if Baker helped erase his own legacy in the state.

Zollars had never heard of Gilbert Baker until 2017, when Aaron Casserly Stewart was elected to the Parsons city commission. Stewart was an anomaly in Parsons for two reasons.

"As a gay Black man, to be honest, I didn't think I was going to be elected,"

Stewart said. He had newly returned to town for family reasons and ran for office to honor his father. "He was the city building inspector, so anything that was built in the town he had to sign off on it. A lot of people knew him."

During Stewart's own high school years, a couple of generations after Baker's, Stewart had been the president of the student council, and popular enough to be president of all the southeast Kansas student councils. But some kids found his diary, in which Stewart had been trying to deal with his sexuality. They took it to a party and read it out loud.

"Being outed at seventeen in rural Kansas in 1983 was more than I could deal with, so I left," he said. Stewart finished his senior year in Lawrence and, like Baker, joined the military. He ended up in Minneapolis, where, possessed of a soulful baritone, he found a gig singing with the Sounds of Blackness, a three-time-Grammy-winning group whose members ran in the same circles as Janet Jackson and the esteemed producers Jimmy Jam and Terry Lewis. From there he moved to Los Angeles, where he worked as an assistant for the keyboardist Morris Hayes, who'd been in Prince's New Power Generation.

By the time he came back to Parsons, Stewart had been gone for twenty-two years and didn't need anyone's validation. Dealing with people's conservative views was hard, but Stewart was also surprised to find a lot of support. "Because my husband is British, and we're an interracial, intergenerational couple," he said, "there was a bit of, how do I say, just, *interest* in that because we were kind of a novelty."

Recognizing an opportunity, Stewart got in touch with Gilbert Baker and extended an invitation. He and Baker's old classmates would give him a key to the city, and the college would host a Gilbert Baker Film Festival. Baker was reluctant because of his experiences growing up there, Stewart said, but both men seemed struck by the fact that no one had ever asked Baker to come back. Finally, he agreed.

A month before his celebrated return, Baker died.

The film festival went on as planned. Zollars screened the hits *Milk* and *Pride*, as well as *Out Here in Kansas*, a short documentary about a gay football star from Andover named Burt Humburg, and he gave an award to one of the student submissions. Few people attended. "It was not a good showing," Zollars said, "but we did it."

In the year that followed, Stewart immigrated to England, where he and his husband were married. But he stayed in touch with a few people, and in 2019 he asked one of the city commissioners if they'd fly a rainbow flag at City Hall during June. He got no response.

By then another gay couple had moved to town. A doctor named Shawn Zimbrunes had taken a job at the hospital, bringing his husband, David Matthew, from Washington, DC. When he learned it was Baker's hometown, Matthew told a reporter for the *Parsons Sun*, he was surprised. "I wondered, where is the memorial? Where is the honor of his legacy? Where are the pride flags?"

Matthew couldn't let Pride Month pass without honoring Baker. He bought three dozen rainbow flags and put the first one up in his yard, an act that felt so momentous it brought him to tears. He also approached businesses along Main Street, and Dave Pawlus, the owner of the popular Kitchen Pass restaurant, offered to fly two flags out front and one inside in support of LGBTQ friends and employees. There were some questions about affixing flag-holders to city light poles, and in general all of this was a lot of drama for Parsons. Pawlus was a little worried at first. "I'm not sure why," Pawlus said. "I've never really been political or an activist type of person." A lot of people were grateful. "A good friend called and said, 'Thank you, I don't know if you know, but my son is gay.' That kind of hit me, made me realize that was the right thing to do."

Two flags outside the Kitchen Pass were stolen, then returned. Other than that, Matthew wrote in a statement to the *Parsons Sun*, the response was overwhelmingly positive. One city commissioner agreed that the town should consider a way to honor Baker.

Fifty Years Later

As Les Hammett put it, "It's not often that you rub shoulders with a person who changes the world."

Hammett, who spent his career in Parsons as a State Farm insurance agent, figured it was twenty or so years ago that he learned his classmate had designed the rainbow flag. His own memories of high school suggest a nearly universal truth: that teenagers don't have any clue how others perceive themselves or each other, which is especially sad in Baker's case.

"He talked about being picked on in high school," Hammett said. "I'll be honest with you—I just never saw that. I thought Gilbert was well liked. He was in theater and that kind of thing, he was a fun person. I think everybody liked Gil."

But Hammett was preoccupied. "My mom died right before I started high school, and I lived with my grandparents. I was just trying to survive. I didn't go to dances and that kind of thing. My social skills and my social life in high school was not like a lot of folks."

Maybe everyone feels like an outsider in high school, one way or another. Certainly it's easier for queer kids today, even in a town like Parsons. Over reunion weekend, one rainbow flag hung along Main Street. It was a mile west of downtown, where the thoroughfare is lined mostly with houses, attached to a white bungalow with potted plants on the front porch.

"We have it up all year," said Alyson Delich, who had lived in the rental house for a couple of years with her girlfriend, Bailey Collins. Once or twice she'd been outside and someone in a passing car yelled an obscenity, she said. But in June, she said, "like five people drove by and hung out their windows and yelled 'Happy Pride!'" That was really cool, she said, "because there aren't a lot of flags."

Delich described her landlord as "an older man, really nice, sweet, soft-spoken." When they first put up the flag, she said, "We heard some older people were making comments to him and he was like, 'They're nice girls.'"

Now in her twenties, Delich has lived in Parsons since she was a kid; she and Collins got together in high school. "When I was a senior there was probably seven people who were out," she said. "I felt like that was quite a few people for a small high school."

"The younger generations are out and living their lives," said Scotty Zollars. Before Gilbert Baker died, the conversations about his return inspired Zollars to start a Gay Straight Alliance (now called the Gender Sexuality Alliance) at Labette Community College. Sixteen people were on its roster in the fall of 2019, though as with any club only a few were active. "We have a trans man, gender queer, nonbinary—a whole bunch of them who have come out since the GSA started," Zollars said.

But for some of those young people, Parsons still felt like it did for Gilbert Baker. "I think the L, G, B part of the spectrum is becoming old hat, in a way," Zollars said. But that's not the case for his trans, nonbinary, and queer students. "Their abuse is so massive right now."

Since 2015, when the US Supreme Court legalized same-sex marriage, the backlash to LGBTQ progress intensified across the nation amid escalating culture wars. Lawmakers in dozens of states worked to pass hundreds of increasingly virulent laws, many of them specifically targeting transgender people. Kansas was one of those states.

Covered in Rainbows

In the years after the 2019 class reunion, Les Hammett approached city officials about creating a Gilbert Baker memorial and flying a rainbow flag somewhere on city property. The Parsons High School Class of 1969 liked the idea of installing it at the old Carnegie Library, now the Carnegie Arts Center. At first, city commissioners seemed in favor. That didn't last.

"People came out of the woodwork to oppose it," said Sherri Spare, a retired elementary school teacher. Spare was a few years younger than Baker's high school classmates, but she'd had a lot of conversations with Les Hammett after her father died, because Hammett was the family's insurance agent. Her parents had been civil rights activists. They'd met Martin Luther King Jr., and had taken Spare to Vietnam War protests as a child. She'd had gay friends in high school who couldn't be themselves.

"It was like the door got slammed in our face," she said of the city commission's reversal. But they started thinking about other ways to honor Baker and came up with the idea of a scholarship in his name at the high school. Unlike a plaque, Spare said, "You can't vandalize a scholarship."

Joining them on what they eventually called the Gilbert Baker Committee was Lauren Shepard, then in her late twenties. She'd left home and come out as a lesbian in Kansas City, but moved back to Parsons to attend college thirty-five miles away at Pittsburg State University.

"I heard the lovely townspeople who came out to speak against it, and that lit a bit of a fire in me," Shepard said. "Even though this is not where I want to live forever and I couldn't get out of here fast enough when I was younger and it was hard moving back, I wasn't going to sit and wait until I could move some place more accepting. I was going to stay here and make this place more accepting."

Shepard wrote letters to the editor and organized people to ask more downtown businesses to fly rainbow flags that June. A couple of business owners refused, but this time there were more flags than just at the Kitchen Pass. "That was fun," she said. "Every time you drove through that little strip it was covered in rainbows."

By 2022 Shepard was working as an academic adviser at Labette Community College, where she'd graduated more than a decade earlier and had known Scotty Zollars. She signed on with Zollars as a cosponsor of the Gender Sexuality Alliance, which had essentially gone dormant in the pandemic years. Soon there was once again a small handful of students who got together once a month for educational and social activities. "Just fun stuff to hang out and have a sense of community and feel connected," Shepard said.

At the high school, meanwhile, something profound had been happening since Tracey Elliott hung a rainbow flag outside her classroom. New to town after her then husband got a job in Parsons, Elliott at first taught a half day at the high school and a half day at the middle school. She hung flags at both.

"I knew we had students who needed to know that somebody in the school supported them just for being who they are," Elliott said. Statistics suggested that would be the case, but it was also obvious to her "on day one at the high school." She knew how some students felt. "I've been bi since I was in my twenties," Elliott said. "Having gone through the experience of feeling completely alone in my gayness, I couldn't stand the thought that students would feel that way."

Administrators at both schools were overwhelmingly supportive, she said. The only negative response came within the first few weeks at the high school, when someone yanked down the flag and tore it up. But that was one kid out of four hundred who were enrolled. Elliott hung another flag, this time with a zip-tie, and nobody tore it down.

Although Tracey Elliott had never lived in Kansas until she moved there in 2018, she had family in the area. Her mother was from Edna, twenty-five miles away, and her father was from Caney, fifty-five miles away; they'd met at Pittsburg State in the 1960s. She had aunts and uncles in Parsons and other relatives in Chetopa and Oswego.

Still, when she hung that rainbow flag, she had no idea of its connection to the place where she now taught. "All of this isn't new to me," she said. "I've gone to huge gay pride parades in Dallas, Austin, been all over the world almost with my own rainbow flag." When she learned about Gilbert Baker and Parsons, she said, "I was completely blown away."

By the end of the year, a group of students asked if Elliott would sponsor a club for LGBTQ folks and their supporters. She immediately said yes and got to work helping them start OQA (Out, Questioning, Allies).

"There was a lot of homophobia going around my school. It was bad to be someone like me and my friends," said Adian Marshall, the president of OQA. "We just wanted to create a good, safe space for people like me to get to know each other."

Marshall had known since sixth grade that he liked boys. Walking down the hall at school, he'd hear kids calling him names. He absorbed religious messages that he was going to hell. He was terrified when he finally came out to his mother, but she supported him. By high school, he decided he would force people to accept him, and he set about finding like-minded peers. He was a sophomore when he and Olivia Martinez, a junior, started OQA in 2022.

So many people signed up that they had the first meeting in the school auditorium. By Marshall's senior year, OQA was one of the biggest clubs at Parsons High School, with forty or fifty students.

"I felt like I was finally doing something helpful," said Marshall, who is also on Student Council and a couple of other clubs. "It was so empowering for me to have all these people joining—even though most of them are not queer and they're there to be allies and friends—to be so loving and open."

At club meetings, Marshall educates students about LGBTQ culture and history. One time, Les Hammett and Sherri Spare came to talk about Gilbert Baker.

"I was baffled that someone so famous is barely spoken of in their hometown," Marshall said. "I couldn't wrap my head around why." Still, he said, learning about Baker was empowering for club members. "A lot of them feel like they're stuck here in a town that doesn't want them," he said, so it helped to know there was someone who felt the same way and went on to change the world like Baker did.

By 2023 the Gilbert Baker Committee had something more than stories to empower students: it had raised enough money to award the first Gilbert Baker Scholarship, $500, to a senior graduating from Parsons High School. For now, each annual scholarship will go to one qualifying student in OQA. But someday, committee members hope every graduating senior who qualifies will receive a scholarship in Baker's name. "The whole idea is for this to be his legacy here," Shepard said, "and we don't want it to be exclusionary."

It's an extraordinary thing to dream about: a scholarship for everyone who graduates from Gilbert Baker's high school, regardless of whether they're a member of the LGBTQ community, regardless of their religious, social, or political views. In any case, it'll be a while—and a lot of work—before they can raise enough money to make that happen.

But Marshall, who graduated in 2024, could already see a difference since starting OQA: more pride flags at school, same-sex couples walking hand-in-hand in the hallways. More than one pair of same-sex couples going to prom. "I still encounter discrimination at times, but not as much as it used to be," he said. "I don't think it's enough until I'm considered normal, just as if I was holding hands with a girl. I shouldn't have had to start a club to feel safe and welcome."

Change can be maddeningly slow, especially for young people. But these days, the pride flag has new colors: pink and white to represent trans people, brown and black for people of color. And considering the difference between Marshall's high school experience and Gilbert Baker's, progress is undeniable. Marshall started a club and felt love in return. Baker left and created an international symbol of love, even if he never got to feel the love of his hometown—which still hasn't fully embraced him.

"There's no sign on the edge of town that says 'Home of Gilbert Baker,'" said Lauren Shepard.

But maybe someday, after more Kansans understand their native son's extraordinary contribution to the world, that sign will be at entrances to the state.

Section IV:
Astra: Imagining Traditions

> Idealism must always prevail on the frontier, for the frontier, whether geographical or intellectual, offers little hope to those who see things as they are.
>
> —Carl Becker, "Kansas," *Essays in American History Dedicated to Frederick Jackson Turner*, 1910

The Kansas past is populated by idealists and creators of traditions. But even more important is how we manifest those traditions: continuing, re-creating, and even imagining new ones. Over a hundred years ago, William Allen White, a true Kansas idealist, wrote: "When anything is going to happen in this country, it happens first in Kansas. Abolition, Prohibition, Populism, the Bull Moose, the exit of the roller towel," and his list continues. People scratch their heads over the roller towel, but that is a tribute to another Kansas idealist, Dr. Samuel J. Crumbine, who rid Kansas of the shared towel, and also the common drinking cup, polluted water, and a tolerance for flies. In fact, during Crumbine's "Swat the Fly" campaign, a Weir City Boy Scout troop, in their fight against the pests, nailed a square of screen to a yardstick and invented what they called the "Fly Bat." Their troop leader, Frank Rose, brought it to Topeka, and Crumbine changed the name to "Flyswatter" to match his campaign slogan. So Kansas contributed another gift to the world.

Another head-scratching first that White might have included: the piggy bank. In 1913, when ten-year-old Wilbur Chapman, from White Cloud, was inspired to raise money to fight leprosy, he tried to raise $250 to give to visiting William Danner, first secretary of the American Leprosy Missions. He failed, but Danner gave Chapman $3, which he used to buy a pig. He fattened it, sold it for $25, and sent the money to Danner. Impressed, the American Leprosy Mission made cast-iron pigs, with slots in their backs, to encourage people to save for the cause. E. B. White, in *Charlotte's Web*, was inspired by the story, and named his pig Wilbur.

Though flyswatters and piggy banks are perhaps small gifts, they illustrate White's notion of Kansas firsts, and in *Astra: Imagining Traditions,* we move toward some of the substantial Kansas contributions born in a place of innovation, experimentation, and idealism, and carried forward by tradition bearers, whether through teaching, performing and writing, or Kansas institutions.

Kelly Erby teaches and writes about the persistence of John Brown in terms of Free State Kansas and our nation's quest for racial equality. Libby Schmanke puts Kansans at the forefront of innovative art therapy. J. T. Knoll remembers a grandfather of a mining past through the lens of one tool, the shovel. Wes Jackson tells the story of imagining a school, the Land Institute, then sustainable agriculture, and perennial grains. Robert Rebein helps us experience two eras of Dodge City: the Wild West of cowboys and the parking lot of today's Boot Hill, where teenagers meet to drag Wyatt Earp Boulevard, putting off thinking about a future of "getting out of Dodge." Andrew Milward writes about James Naismith, the inventor of basketball, and Phog Allen, the originator of basketball coaching, and the long association of basketball with the University of Kansas. "SpiritDancer" Dennis Rogers witnesses his journey on the path of his spiritual tradition, Native dancing: through "knowledge, research, study, practice, and presentation," he has become what he calls "An edu-cultural specialist of dance." Jim Hoy gives Texas a boot, claiming for Kansas the best boots for working cowboys, country singers, and celebrity actors. Rolf Potts advocates a new practice, encouraging people like himself to move from "digital nomadism" to "digital homesteading," from being nostalgic for Kansas roots to putting down roots in Kansas again. The last essay in this book, then, moves us from one version of "O give me a home" to another, from where "never is heard a discouraging word" to a place where all of us, near or far, can make our words heard.

The list of Kansas firsts, of Kansas traditions and the expression of them, has the power to inspire us "to the stars," defining for us what historian Carl Becker realized was more than a "geographical expression." Kansas, he wrote, is a "state of mind."

—Thomas Fox Averill

Why I Like to Drink at a Bar Named after John Brown, and Other Musings on Why John Brown Is Everywhere

Kelly Erby

A bar in Lawrence, Kansas, where I live, is called John Brown's Underground, or JBUG as some affectionately refer to it. It has a speakeasy vibe in a basement on Seventh Street, down one flight of stairs from the sidewalk. The heavy wooden door features a small window at eye level covered by an iron grill, as in Prohibition times, when visitors would be allowed inside only once they were vetted.

JBUG is quite popular and always tops the yearly roundups of best bars in the city and region, and it was named a semifinalist in the "Outstanding Bar" category of the 2025 James Beard Awards Restaurant and Chef Semifinalists. This popularity undoubtedly stems from its topnotch, creative craft cocktails. (I personally recommend the "Free Lawrence.") But I believe the ways in which JBUG references and celebrates the radical abolitionist John Brown as a local folk hero and freedom fighter also have something to do with it.

JBUG evokes Brown through its eponymous name, obviously—John Brown's Underground. But why "Underground"? Well, the bar *is* physically located underground. And there's the allusion, again, to JBUG as a hidden speakeasy evading the law of Prohibition. But the name also conjures Brown's involvement with the Underground Railroad, a secret network of safehouses that similarly evaded the law by providing shelter and assistance to runaway enslaved people before the Civil War. The bar's logo, a chair, more directly references Brown's specific involvement with the Underground Railroad in Kansas: he dozed in such a chair one night in December 1858 in a safehouse along the Lane Trail in Kansas Territory while accompanying eleven enslaved people who were escaping to freedom. The actual chair in which Brown slept is now in the collections of the Kansas State Historical Society.

In addition to the bar's name and logo, the dominant feature inside JBUG is a colorful mural portraying Brown as a 1920s cocktail lounge singer. This mural is a clear riff on John Steuart Curry's *Tragic Prelude* that stretches across several walls in the Kansas State Capitol, only in the JBUG version Brown's outstretched hands hold a gleaming gold saxophone instead of a Bible and a Shure 55S microphone (like the kind Elvis used) in place of the "Beecher Bible" rifle he holds in *Tragic Prelude*. While Curry's mural is set amid an ominous Kansas prairie, tornado blowing through on one side and grass fire raging on the other, in JBUG Brown towers over throngs of stylishly dressed revelers carousing on Massachusetts Street in Lawrence. Where dead Civil War soldiers lie in Curry's painting, a beautiful flapper (that speakeasy reference again) perches on a whiskey barrel and caresses Brown's bearded face.

I am a historian of the nineteenth-century United States. At Washburn University where I teach, I have developed an upper-level history course called "John Brown" that examines Brown's abolitionism and seeks to understand Brown as a man of his times. The course concludes with a unit about Brown's place in American historical memory and popular culture and the many ways his story has been appropriated, both during his own lifetime and in the years since his execution. For me, JBUG is a perfect example of how ubiquitous and compelling Brown remains even now, more than a century and a half after his death. In that time, he has been the topic of countless historical studies, novels, poems, works of art, plays, music—there's even a full-length opera simply called *John Brown*—films and television shows, museum exhibitions, and other cultural works. I routinely see Brown's bearded face (though he was unbearded for most of his life) on T-shirts, vinyl laptop stickers, and novelty license plates. My own college class, which draws curious students from many different majors and interests, serves as another example of Brown's relevance in America today.

As JBUG suggests, Brown has become something of a pop icon, a symbol of resistance who transcends time. But not everyone views the abolitionist so favorably; to the contrary, Brown is as deeply controversial now as he was in his own lifetime. Americans continue to dispute Brown's memory and whether he was fundamentally "good" or "evil." Was he a martyr who gave his life to end slavery, or a radical fanatic and terrorist who caused a war that killed millions?

That Brown is both so compelling and so controversial is not a coincidence. He remains as relevant today as he does because he left a complex legacy with beliefs and actions that remain open to interpretation and debate. He forces us to grapple with questions as significant in the twenty-first century United States as in the final years of his life. What is the purpose of this republic? What does freedom mean? When is violence justified? What difference can one person make? Are interracial coalitions effective in achieving racial progress? The fact that Americans remain as divided about whether Brown was on the right or wrong side of history suggests how far we are from settling these questions.

Brown's Road to Infamy

Brown's celebrity in twenty-first century America is surprising given his utter obscurity for all but the final few years of his life. Until then, he was known only to his own large family and immediate circles of business clients and community members. He was born in 1800 and grew up in an America that became increasingly divided over the issue of slavery. After the murder of abolitionist editor Elijah Lovejoy in 1837, Brown, who had been raised to consider slavery a sin, took an oath promising to dedicate his life to eradicating the "peculiar institution." But his efforts did not become noteworthy until he was an old man (by nineteenth-century standards anyway), when his exploits in Kansas Territory during the contentious early territorial period known as Bleeding Kansas catapulted him to the sudden political and cultural relevancy he continues to have today.

In May 1854, when Brown was fifty-four years old, the federal government opened Kansas Territory for white settlement and left the question of whether the practice of slavery would be permitted there to the white male settlers of the territory to decide. Brown was living with his family in North Elba and assisting formerly enslaved African Americans in farming the generally inhospitable land of upstate New York. Initially he had no intention of uprooting himself to go to Kansas Territory; he hoped to live the rest of his life in North Elba. His older sons, however, saw Kansas as a land of economic and political opportunity so long as it was kept free from slavery. Brown's unmarried sons Owen, Frederick, and Salmon arrived in Kansas that October. John Jr., Jason, and their families followed in the early spring. Brown's sons wrote to him from Kansas Territory to share the grave conditions they and other antislavery settlers faced there. These hardships, according to his sons, included open violence and intimidation from proslavery settlers. His sons asked Brown to come and help them secure Kansas as a free state.

Brown accepted his sons' call to join them in Kansas, leaving his wife, Mary, to tend to their younger children and farm in North Elba. He arrived in Kansas Territory in November 1855. En route, Brown stopped at an abolitionist convention in Syracuse, New York, where he shared letters he had received from his sons and successfully raised a small amount of money and the promise of guns to help support and defend his fellow free-state emigrants.

Once in Kansas, Brown quickly began to attract attention through his radical abolitionist beliefs. In contrast to most of the antislavery settlers there, Brown was an *immediatist*, meaning he called for an immediate and not a gradual end to slavery. While gradualists thought that simply preventing the practice of slavery from spreading west to Kansas Territory would eventually strangle the institution itself, Brown's abolitionist principles called him to do more than vote for free-state territorial legislators who would uphold a free-state constitution. Brown demanded that slavery end *now*. But even that would not be enough to satisfy Brown's abolitionism, rooted as it was in a combination of Calvinism and the influence of Black militant intellectuals such as Reverend Henry Highland Garnet and Frederick Douglass, both of whom Brown knew personally. Brown's abolitionism called him to also assist Black Americans in becoming equal to white people in the United States, just as they were already equal in the eyes of his God. This meant that African Americans could not wait for slavery to end peacefully, or through the political maneuverings of white Americans as other antislavery Americans hoped it would, but must instead take bold and decisive action to throw off the chains of their enslavement. They must demonstrate their unfitness for slavery by every means possible, including violent insurrection. They must seize freedom as white patriots had seized it in the American Revolution. In Kansas Territory, Brown hoped to show that the process through which slavery would finally end would be—must be—violent. And Brown, for one, was ready for the fight.

These attitudes contributed to Brown's decision in May 1856 to order the deaths of five proslavery settlers in what has become known as the Pottawatomie Massacre. Up to this point, five free-state settlers had been killed in Kansas. Brown and the posse he convened to carry out these deaths evened the score in a single evening. Brown's resolve to employ violence in combating an institution he recognized as inherently violent and evil unleashed the simmering hostility between anti- and proslavery settlers; the territory immediately became engulfed in a full-out civil war. Brown was wanted throughout the territory for his crimes at Pottawatomie. Still, the abolitionist lingered in Kansas that summer, evading those who pursued him and adding to his notoriety at the Battle of Black Jack in June. Then in August, Brown and his men were forced to retreat at the Battle of Osawatomie as proslavery men set fire to the town. Brown's son Frederick was among those killed.

Brown may have remained infamous only in Kansas had he not turned up in Boston in early 1857 at the offices of the Massachusetts Kansas Committee, where he met the committee's young secretary, Franklin Sanborn. Sanborn shared Brown's immediatist abolitionist beliefs. He had briefly visited Kansas himself in 1856 but quickly returned home to Boston, deciding he could better serve the free-state cause with his administrative and organizational skills. Sanborn introduced Brown to prominent Boston abolitionist families who extended speaking invitations to Brown and agreed to contribute to his stated cause: to raise money, rifles, and ammunition to assist the free-state settlers of Kansas Territory in securing Kansas as a free state.

Brown was able to thoroughly capture the attentions and imaginations of Sanborn and other Boston abolitionists by sharing his stories as a guerrilla warrior fighting the slave power in Kansas Territory. He did not disclose his grisly deeds along the Pottawatomie Creek that night in May (and word of these acts had not spread beyond the territory), but he made it clear he had done and would continue to do whatever was needed to stop slavery from expanding into Kansas. Northern abolitionists at this point had written and talked in support of their antislavery views. Some had given money to the cause of antislavery or voted for antislavery political candidates. A few had even boycotted products created through the institution of slavery, like sugar and cloth made from cotton. But Brown had put his life and the lives of his sons on the line. Indeed, he had lost a son in Kansas. He had left his family and farm to live out his principles. In the wake of the *Dred Scott* decision in March 1857 in which the Supreme Court declared Congress had no authority to ban slavery from federal territories and that African Americans nowhere in the country had rights that white men were bound to respect, some of the more radical abolitionists clearly felt that the traditional tactics of combatting slavery were not working. Brown represented a refreshing and compelling change of course in the fight to eradicate an institution they considered sinful and contrary to the founding principles of their country.

Brown stockpiled what he could raise from his Northeastern benefactors not for Kansas—where the free-state settlers had mostly won the upper hand anyway—but for a raid on the federal arsenal at Harpers Ferry,

Virginia, that he was secretly planning. And it was this final exploit against slavery that proved pivotal in Brown's life and legacy. After seizing the arsenal, his plan called for him and his band of twenty-one men to hide out in the Allegheny Mountains and lead periodic raids onto plantations. They would distribute weapons, including guns and ammunition taken at Harper's Ferry and iron pikes Brown had commissioned for just this purpose, to enslaved people so these men and women could claim their freedom. Brown's plan failed, however, when ten of his men were killed, including two of his sons, and Brown himself was captured. He was quickly put on trial by the state of Virginia and convicted of treason. Brown received the sentence of death by hanging.

In the six weeks between his arrest and execution, Brown saw to it that he became more politically and culturally relevant than ever. From his jail cell, he scribbled letter after letter justifying his cause and his actions. While his many detractors throughout both the North and South painted him as bloodthirsty and insane, Brown's letters and his stoic conduct throughout his trial and as he was led to the gallows suggested he was instead a selfless martyr dedicated to a cause much greater than his own life.

This idea of Brown as a martyr for the abolition of slavery became a source of inspiration for some white Northern literary luminaries like Ralph Waldo Emerson, Henry David Thoreau, Herman Melville, Walt Whitman, John Greenleaf Whittier, Henry Longfellow, Lydia Marie Child, and others. Painter Louis Liscom Ransom was moved by an apocryphal story that appeared in the *New York Tribune* of Brown's final moments to paint the abolitionist kindly greeting an enslaved mother and kissing her child as he was being led to the scaffold. In this and other works depicting Brown as a martyr, the abolitionist was stripped of any trace of his revolutionary violence. He became, instead, a grandfatherly figure, dignified in his absolute dedication to antislavery work.

That even a limited number of Northerners admired or approved of Brown's actions at Harpers Ferry helped convince the South that the region must prepare to defend slavery and the Southern way of life at all costs. It is paradoxical that Brown and his ideas about securing racial equality became most significant in the wake of his failed insurrection, one that certain Northern abolitionists sanitized of its violence; it is further paradoxical that admiration of this more pacific Brown ultimately helped to bring about the bloody Civil War. In the end, of course, the war that Brown had both predicted and foreshadowed proved his ideas about the necessity of violence in ending slavery to be correct. The war legitimized the shedding of blood in the pursuit and achievement of this end. After four long years, slavery was finally dead.

On Brown, Violence, and Interracial Coalition

In the many historical and cultural appraisals of Brown since his death, he has often been used to mediate reflections about the role of violence and racial progress. His beliefs and actions have been frequently manipulated. White Americans have tended to either ignore Brown's violence while praising him for his willingness to die for his principles *or* condemn him as a violent lunatic with no regard for law and order. In the 1940 film *Santa Fe Trail*, for example, Brown is portrayed as a dangerous radical relentless in his personal agenda to bring on war. He cares nothing about his country or even his own family. The film also ignores the brutality of slavery and relies instead on racist tropes suggesting that slavery provided care and security to Black Americans, who were lazy and intellectually inferior to white Americans. These tropes were still very prevalent in the 1940s, as was the myth of the "Lost Cause." The film reinforces Lost Cause mythology by acknowledging that slavery was wrong and should end but that, if given appropriate time, Southerners would settle the problem of slavery in their own way and without a costly war. The film rejects the idea that Brown acted for a moral purpose and suggests he was instead an egomaniac intent on bringing about a war for reasons that were deranged and entirely self-serving.

Black Americans, however, have long celebrated Brown precisely *because* he was willing to be violent in his efforts to bring an immediate end to slavery. In the 1861 account *Voice from Harper's Ferry*, Osborn Anderson, one of Brown's Black followers and the only surviving African American member of the Harper's Ferry raid, admiringly compared Brown to enslaved rebels Gabriel Prosser and Nat Turner and called for a war to fulfill his mission to "dissolve the union between Freedom and slavery." Frederick Douglass also repeatedly praised Brown's willingness to fight and die to free the enslaved. He insisted on reminding people throughout the later years of his life, when the Lost Cause was becoming the dominant narrative of the Civil War, that Brown had begun the "war that ended slavery." Later generations of Black writers, artists, and intellectuals have similarly celebrated Brown's urgency in pursuing not only Black freedom but also equality. Langston Hughes, for example, who was born in Kansas and had family ties to one of Brown's Black raiders, called for Americans to remember John Brown "Who took his gun, / Took twenty-one companions, / White and black, / Went to shoot your way to freedom."

Black writers and artists have also commemorated the interracial coalition Brown assembled to combat slavery and his willingness to work *with* Black people in addition to working on their behalf. In some of Jacob Lawrence's many paintings of Brown from the 1930s and 1940s, for example, Lawrence depicts Brown praying alongside Frederick Douglass and Harriet Tubman. In other paintings, Lawrence shows Black men arming themselves to fight for racial justice while Brown distributes guns or conducts training drills. This was as radical a message in the 1940s when Lawrence was painting Brown as it was in the 1850s when Brown was alive.

But not all Black Americans are entirely celebratory of Brown. In Showtime's adaptation of James McBride's novel *The Good Lord Bird*, which chronicles the final years of Brown's life in Kansas Territory and then plotting the raid at Harpers Ferry, the fictional protagonist Henry Shackleford, known to Brown as "Little Onion," acknowledges that African Americans are also divided about Brown's legacy. Onion explains: "Some Black folks love him because they think trouble needed to be started. Some Black folks hate him, thinking he was some kind of bullshit white savior." This same tension shows up in Lawrence's work. As historian R. Gilpin Blakeslee has written, in Lawrence's paintings depicting Brown praying with Douglass and Tubman, the artist poses but does not resolve the question of whether he was the answer to Black Americans' prayers for freedom, or a result of years of Black struggle and resistance. Lawrence's 1941 series of paintings *The Life of John Brown* begins and ends with crucifixion scenes, clear references to Brown again as a martyr. Yet Lawrence does not shy away from highlighting Brown's violence and representing the struggle and sacrifice of Black men who fought and died for their own freedom.

Artist Kara Walker has further explored the limits or, as Onion put it, "bullshit" of Brown as white savior. In one provocative untitled drawing of Brown done in the 1990s, Walker portrays him dressed in S&M apparel performing fellatio to a Black baby whose mother watches while a little white girl runs out from beneath the mother's skirt. The drawing is clearly a contortion of the Whittier poem that describes Brown kissing a Black baby on his way to the gallows and of the paintings by Ransom and, later, Thomas Hovenden showing the same scene. In another of Walker's drawings, a Black baby suckles at Brown's breast but procures no nourishment or satisfaction from him. In this work, Brown dispassionately turns his head from the baby as if to say he has nothing to offer him. According to Walker, Brown is not a martyr, nor is he an ally or interracial conspirator; he is a deviant who misused Black Americans for his own gratification.

McBride also grapples with the idea of Brown as white savior throughout his 2013 novel *The Good Lord Bird*; the author portrays Brown as a violent, Bible-thumping religious fanatic. But McBride also describes Brown with great humor and warmth. There is no question in *The Good Lord Bird* that Brown was on the right side of history. In late 2020 when Showtime released the miniseries adaptation, the country was coping with national and international protest following the murder of George Floyd by Minneapolis police, systemic racial inequalities laid bare by the COVID-19 pandemic, and deep political polarization around the role of slavery in US history and in history education. Given these contemporary realities that made Brown's story more relevant than ever, it is significant that the miniseries promoted a view of the abolitionist not as a savior to Black people but to white Americans in need of redemption for their own legacies of racial oppression, brutality, and violence. As Onion explains in the miniseries to a white person regarding Brown: "He ain't trying to save us; he's trying to save you."

Brown's Legacy in and to Kansas

For Kansans, the many complexities of Brown's legacy are coupled with, and further complicated by, the meaning and significance of their own state's origins. Did the abolitionist come to Kansas as a visionary of a more egalitarian and just American republic, or as a radical fanatic intent on social upheaval? Was Bleeding Kansas a harbinger in the struggle to eradicate slavery, or a lawless land that presaged a terrible and tragic war that killed millions? What is the state's own history and legacy regarding radical social movements and violence?

Curry's *Tragic Prelude* answers these questions by emphasizing the deadly costs of moral righteousness and fanaticism. Curry, an isolationist who wanted the United States to stay out of looming conflict in Europe when he began the mural in 1937, selected Brown as its focal point to warn of fanatical, radical men and the futility of war. Curry's Brown is an angry messiah and extremist. In the artist's telling, Brown did not accomplish much in the name of racial equality or justice, either; Black women and children cower behind him as war rages and kills.

In contrast to Curry's conservative take on Brown, a marker erected in 1969 by the US Department of the Interior, the National Park Service, the state of Kansas, and the City of Osawatomie to commemorate Brown and the 1856 Battle of Osawatomie reads: "The blood that flowed in Kansas before and during the Civil War nourished the twin trees of liberty and union." This simple sentence acknowledges Kansas as integral to the cause of the war and honors the bloodshed that secured both freedom and the country itself.

And then there are the numerous tongue-in-cheek tributes to Brown throughout the state—the T-shirts, coffee mugs, and JBUG. Another good one is located at a coffee shop across from Washburn University's campus in Topeka. A mural in the entryway depicts Brown as a barista holding a portafilter in one outstretched hand and a Chemex in the other; it has remained in spite of ownership changes over the years. This version of Brown celebrates the abolitionist as a timeless local folk hero, someone who put Kansas on the map. The exact reasons for his (in)fame are not important. Perhaps he serves to congratulate the coffee drinkers for choosing a unique and locally owned café and not a chain they could find in any city, any state. Or maybe this Brown, who looks quite virile with his towering stature and flowing beard, suggests what is possible with good coffee. A rising orange sun shooting out rays of rainbows suggests a bright day is ahead.

Historian Drew Gilpin Faust wrote recently in *The Atlantic*, "As a nation, we are unable to get over John Brown." Americans continue to struggle to settle the questions and tensions to which the abolitionist simultaneously responded, reflected, and provoked in his final years. We are unable to "get over" John Brown as a country because we have not yet reached resolution on these questions. Brown continues to serve as both a warning and an inspiration. His memory helps to mediate our most sincere hopes, and our greatest disappointments and fears, for this American republic.

Strong Roots: Kansas and the Evolution of Art Therapy

Libby Schmanke

Art—from prehistoric cave drawings to Indigenous sand paintings, from masks worn by tribal shamans to religious icons—has played essential roles in rituals and healing practices from the dawn of time. By contrast, the modern profession of art therapy—with its own graduate-level academic degrees, independent accreditation procedures, extensive body of professional literature, national board for ethical standards and practitioner credentialing, and national and state membership organizations—is relatively young.

Around the turn of the twentieth century, a few European psychiatrists and art historians took interest in mental asylum residents who were using whatever materials they could find to make drawings. The process of artmaking seemed to have a healing effect on the maker, and the doctors viewed the art products as potential tools for diagnosis or psychoanalysis.

During the same era, Sigmund Freud and other pioneers of psychotherapy were interested in symbolism and dream interpretation. Artmaking came to be seen as a similar process to dreaming, in that it also could reveal the unconscious.

The psychoanalytic term *projection*, applied to artmaking, referred to the tendency of the unconscious to reveal itself in what and how the patient chose to draw. Specific tasks such as "draw a man" or "make pictures of a house, a tree, and a person" were developed by psychologists in the 1940s to provide assessment information. For example, a house drawing that featured a smoking chimney indicated contention in the patient's family relationships; a drawing of a person with full lips signaled hedonistic tendencies. The publication of several highly regarded (at the time) manuals on projective assessment for use by psychiatrists and psychologists led to the height of this approach in the 1950s.

Ultimately, the assumptions made in those interpretive manuals did not stand up to scientific research. Art is a language, but it is too nuanced and idiosyncratic to be confined to a symbol dictionary or applied generically to individuals.

Taking a different approach, pioneers in the emergent field of art therapy helped each patient explore their own personal use of symbol or metaphor. They also considered universal meanings and other variables of artmaking such as the formal elements of an artwork or use of media. The artmaking process itself, enhanced by verbal processing with the therapist, led to insight and healing.

The typical mental asylums of the early twentieth century provided an occasional session with a psychiatrist, but little else to treat residents or occupy their time. The innate value of activity, including artmaking, was recognized early on by the Menninger family of psychiatrists, who in the 1920s established a psychiatric teaching institute, clinic, and sanitarium in Topeka, Kansas. The Menninger Clinic rose to worldwide prominence by the mid-twentieth century, having been a pioneer of the milieu therapy model, wherein a range of activities and therapies were provided in addition to psychoanalysis. Still, even at Menninger, artmaking was destined for decades to remain the province of the painting teachers and activity therapists who hardly ranked in the established hierarchy of psychiatrists, psychologists, and social workers.

So it was that the contemporary discipline of art therapy was born not from the MDs and PhDs, but from the artists in their employ. And it was a handful of Kansans with ties to Menninger—Mary Huntoon, Don Jones, and Robert Ault—who played a key role in the development of the new profession during its formative years.

Mary Huntoon was a descendant of the Huntoon pioneer family in Kansas. She graduated from Topeka High School in 1914 and then studied art a few blocks away at Washburn University. With her husband, she moved to New York City and spent several years in the 1920s studying at the esteemed Art Students League. One of her teachers, Kimon Nicolaides, may have been the first to publish (in 1941) about the concept of blind contour drawing, a technique that would become seminal in the lives of Elizabeth Layton and Robert Ault. Another of her teachers, Robert Henri, encouraged students to paint subjects from their feelings and intuition, rather than according to naturalistic appearances.

In 1926 Huntoon was commissioned to travel to Paris for five weeks to create etchings of Parisian street scenes for a newspaper syndicate. She and her husband followed their own drummer, for her stay in Paris did not end until her return to Topeka as a widow in 1930. In the intervening period, she had mastered a rare etching technique, taught art classes, and solidified her identity as an artist through solo exhibitions in Parisian galleries.

Back in Topeka, Huntoon pursued her own art, primarily drawing and printmaking, and contributed to the growth of the arts in the community and its institutions. She was named the Kansas state director of the Depression-era Federal Arts Project, and under her management three hundred works of local artists were distributed for display in the Topeka public schools. She founded the Topeka Arts Center (now the Topeka Arts Guild and Gallery), which provided gallery space for local artists and art instruction.

Meanwhile, as the Menninger bailiwick continued to expand, Dr. Karl Menninger had become the manager of Topeka's Winter Veterans Administration (VA) Hospital in 1946. By way of their previous careers and experiences, both Huntoon and Menninger were convinced of the value of immersion in artmaking as a powerful form of therapy. Menninger appointed Huntoon director of fine and manual arts at the VA and gave her the freedom to develop the program from the ground up. She later wrote that she meant to stay only a year, for she longed to get back to her own artmaking, but it took her two years to get the program where she wanted it. At that point, a New York gallery rep told her she was too old (at fifty-one) to resume her art career, and she made the decision to remain at the VA.

Huntoon later wrote of her surprise to find that a high percentage of her patients possessed talent, but the hospitalized veterans probably would not have revealed as much "talent" in another setting. Mary Huntoon was a pioneer in conceptualizing a studio art therapy space as a *container*, or therapeutic holding environment, which provided psychic safety for patients' exploration and self-expression. She was insistent that patients be honored for their own way of using art materials or depicting reality, and that sessions were not to be interrupted by other staff or needs of the hospital routine. She would not use the term *patients* for those using her studio (although technically they were), but referred to them as students. These principles of caring and respect for the participants in a studio art therapy approach remain central in the subsequent literature and practice of the profession.

In monographs written during the 1940s, Huntoon described her approach as a unique form of therapy, to be distinguished from the art educational approach of occupational or recreational therapists. Nor was a patient's diagnosis of primary concern to her. She never employed a directive approach, as is now sometimes used to match certain art tasks to specific diagnoses or symptoms. She referred to what she did as "dynamically oriented art therapy," referring to the complex dynamics of the psyche. Huntoon was well-informed in psychodynamic theory, and she believed that when her students worked intuitively and without external prompting, they naturally projected unconscious needs or wishes into their art products. She observed this process as inherently healing; she saw herself not as a teacher or a psychotherapist, or not only as those, but as a catalyst who perceived and enabled the patient's own process.

As Linney Wix relates in a biographical article of Huntoon in *Art Therapy*, Margaret Naumburg, an East Coast artist and psychotherapist, upon whom history has bestowed the title "the mother of art therapy," once visited Huntoon in Kansas to learn of her work for Menninger. Shortly after returning to Philadelphia, Naumburg published a book, *Dynamically Oriented Art Therapy*, using terms and approaches Huntoon had described. On another occasion, she asked Huntoon to ship some of her VA patients' art for an exhibition back East, but after she had done so, informed her that there was "not room" for the work after all. Wix insinuates that Naumburg was achieving glory on the East Coast and had no desire to share the spotlight with an unknown Kansan.

Contemporary art therapists recognize in another of Huntoon's adverse experiences the dilemma of performing art therapy research for the purpose of gaining professional legitimacy. In 1947 Huntoon received research funding to use her VA studio as an *in vivo* laboratory. Eventually, she abandoned the project due to pressure to identify how the art worked for different diagnoses. She refused to misstate her impressions to satisfy the research objective. Her dedication to the uniquely artist-driven "art as therapy" approach was rock solid, being both personally and professionally informed. Although Bob Ault met Huntoon but once, he was of the same mind, and would later affirm her approach in his own work at the twenty-first-century iteration of the Creative Arts Clinic of the Topeka VA Medical Center.

Other pioneering elements of Huntoon's studio approach are now in common use. She provided space to display participants' work in the studio, and a museum project, which distributed artworks throughout the hospital in hallways, day rooms, and offices. She cited benefits to the artists themselves of experiencing pride in their work, as well as the edification of staff and the aesthetic enhancement of the surroundings for viewers. Additionally, she noted the sense of belonging experienced by non-artist hospital patients upon viewing the work in their otherwise sterile or fearsome environment. By 1959 the museum project had grown to include 3,900 works made available via an interhospital loan system. The emergence of multidisciplinary Arts in Health programs in the latter half of the twentieth century acknowledges Huntoon's pioneering philosophy and programming.

Any Topekan knows the name Huntoon, if only from a primary street by the same name. Joel Huntoon, of unclear relation to Mary, was an engineer and pioneer who arrived in the fledgling city of Topeka in 1856. He was responsible for the plotting of Huntoon Street on a true east-west latitude, to which all later streets ran parallel. Archival letter-writing stationery with a header for the Studio of Mary Huntoon lists its address near the convergence of Huntoon and Twelfth Streets, just off Huntoon Park. This appears to be where Mary Huntoon lived and worked after her retirement from the VA in 1958. There is no longer a building at that street number, and Wix has noted that Huntoon's home and studio were destroyed in the Topeka tornado of 1966. Huntoon died a few years later; some say, living in poverty. Sadly, then, as had nearly happened with the rest of her life and work, the premises where she finally had personal space in retirement for the pursuit of her own art was soon irretrievably lost.

Early pioneers of art therapy on the East Coast during the same era as Huntoon became better-known to history due to their published work or personal affiliation with prominent psychiatrists. The field of art therapy was not unified in any significant manner, nor were annual conferences held, which would document the sharing of ideas, until 1969, when the American Art Therapy Association was founded, one year prior to Huntoon's death. However, many of Huntoon's concepts about her studio model have made their way into our current definitions of "art as therapy." Kansas art therapy pioneers stayed close to these roots, maintaining their identity as artists, paired with a love of helping others by using a process they personally knew to be rich and meaningful.

As American engagement in World War II became inevitable, a young Pennsylvanian named Don Jones dropped out of college to volunteer for the Civilian Public Service as a conscientious objector. His college programs in both pre-med and pre-theology would have sufficed to keep him out of the draft, but as he later told the story, he felt called to serve, and his placement as a volunteer in the Marlboro State Mental Hospital in New Jersey became his "university of psychiatry." Those were days when people with severe mental illness were warehoused and treated abominably; antipsychotics and other tranquilizing drugs had yet to be invented.

Jones was immediately drawn to the graffiti and scrawled imagery on the hallways and walls of the tunnels at the lower levels of the institution, and even more, to the lost souls who had created it. Even when working with patients who were aggressive or destructive, he was able to perceive their humanity. He consistently treated them with "com-passion," as he wrote of it, and painted portraits of many of them in tribute to their personhood and suffering. He later published these works, along with some of the patients' own art and his observations and reflections, in a book, *PRN* (1946), and a manuscript, *Tunnel* (1947), which were later seen by staff at Menninger.

After the war, Jones relocated to the village of Rossville, Kansas, just northwest of Topeka, where he taught art classes and served as a pastor at the town's Methodist church. He engaged the community in his creation of murals at the church and town and continued his studies at seminary during the summers. Soon, word of him and the art of the Marlboro inmates reached Karl Menninger. As Jones later reported, Menninger requested the paintings for display at the Menninger Clinic, whereupon "I wrote Dr. Karl a letter saying that you must have Don Jones also if you're going to have his paintings. . . . You need me to do art therapy, whatever that is." And so, in 1951, Jones became the first "art therapist" at the famed institution.

Don Jones's experience with the warehoused patients at Marlboro provided an essential background for understanding patients' experience of their illness. At Menninger, he was encouraged to develop theory and technique to inform the new approach of art therapy and apply it, retaining his concept of com-passion with the residents. Formally, he postulated a "sociotherapeutic" model that insisted on the importance of caring interactions with patients. He questioned the "narrative-interpretation . . . approaches, . . . too quickly shoe-horned into a diagnostic category or uncompromising belief system" (in other words, Freudian ideology).

Under Jones's auspices, the creative arts program at Menninger trained and employed many art therapists, including two other Kansans who became nationally known: Bob Ault and, after Jones had departed, Charles Anderson. Anderson was a lifelong Topekan who would go on to serve forty years at Menninger and twenty years teaching undergraduate art therapy classes at Washburn University. He served on the original Mosaic Committee of the American Art Therapy Association and in 2008 was awarded the prestigious Multicultural Leadership Award for his outstanding service to the profession. For many years after retirement, Anderson worked part-time as the art therapist on the psychiatric unit of a Topeka hospital, there serving as a beloved supervisor to innumerable graduate art therapy interns from Emporia State University. His strong artist identity was given voice in his late retirement with his explorations into digital photography.

Don Jones was a Kansan for only a couple of decades. His stay at Menninger spanned more than fifteen years of groundbreaking growth of the Menninger creative arts program, which paralleled the establishment of art therapy as a legitimate profession in the overall field of mental health. In 1966 Jones moved to Ohio to accept a position as director of adjunctive services at Harding Hospital. In the meantime, he had developed a relationship, both fatherly and mutually invigorating, with a young man named Bob Ault, who had been hired at Menninger about ten years after Jones. These men would later work together at the national level to help lay the foundations for the professional structure of art therapy.

Robert Ault was a Texas native who initially moved to Kansas, hardly out of his teens, for the Master of Fine Arts program at Wichita University (WU, now Wichita State University). As fate would have it, he never again lived outside the Sunflower State. Ault's original career goal was to be an art professor at some quiet college where he would have time to pursue his own painting. During his MFA program, he was assigned an internship to set up an arts program at an institute for children with disabilities, and this proved to be a life-changing event. He allowed himself to be transformed by the experience of helping others through art, and to articulate this process in his academic writing.

Bob Ault pursued another WU recent graduate, a speech therapist named Marilynn Miller, to Topeka where she had taken a job; they soon married. Following a stint of active duty in the Army Reserves, he returned to seek work. He has related that when he first saw the clock tower of the Menninger campus atop a hill in northwest Topeka, a chill ran down his spine. He knew then that his future was tied to this place. Soon enough, he joined Don Jones in the budding art therapy program. They shared an office and would talk for hours about their ideas for using art to work with patients. They had heard of artists who were also trained in psychoanalysis, mostly on the East Coast, who were doing "art analysis" in collaboration with psychiatrists, using patient art to enable the psychoanalytic process. In their quite different Creative Arts Shop, Ault and Jones observed their patients change and get better, and they were convinced that the actual art process itself, when provided with kind and knowledgeable attention in a sociotherapeutic environment, was curative.

In 1969, not long after Jones left Topeka for Ohio, he and Ault were invited to a meeting in Philadelphia with the purpose of forming a national art therapy organization. Initially there was much deliberation and some contention among the attendees of the general convention over whether the field should be identified as being purely concerned with "art psychotherapy" (mostly the East Coast constituents) or whether "art as therapy" could be allowed (mostly the heartland constituents). Jones and Ault were named as two of five practitioners on a founder's committee that went on to hammer out the charter, bylaws, and constitution of the American Art Therapy Association, which in the end allowed for inclusion of the full spectrum of professional identity. Ault served as its second president, and Jones as its fourth, and both were later awarded the prestigious status of Honorary Life Member.

Ault's contributions to the emergent field scarcely stopped with his work at Menninger's or the founding of the national professional association. In 1970 he approached the University of Kansas in Lawrence to see if administrators would be interested in a master's degree program in art therapy; KU had developed the first graduate degree in music therapy. Although the initial response was yes, neither the art department nor the psychology department proved willing to house the program. After three years of teaching a few classes for KU at the Menninger campus in Topeka, Ault gave up in disgust. Soon after, he was invited to Emporia State University (ESU) to discuss starting a master's program there. The first students arrived in 1973, and the ESU program is now the oldest continuously running master's degree in art therapy in the world. Bob Ault taught half-time there until the mid-1990s, when he also retired from Menninger.

Amid those two careers, in 1979 Ault started his own studio and private practice in art therapy, which he named Ault's Academy of Art. Although the location of the studio changed a couple of times over the years, it was always in a comfortable, middle-class part of Topeka and featured Ault's own studio and gallery—he was a prolific lifelong painter—and art classes for adults and children, in addition to individual art therapy. In his chapter for Harriet Wadeson's 1989 book *Advances in Art Therapy*, Ault described "the unidentified patient," a type he often encountered. These clients had signed up for private art classes but were often subconsciously seeking therapy, a need that Ault perceived and could satisfy with an unobtrusive arts-based approach. Ironically, it was through his friendly studio that Ault became as well-known in the Topeka community as he was nationally, and even internationally, among art therapists. He was sought-after by the local media for filler stories many times over the years. Ault's studio was ever his favorite milieu; it was the one career path from which he never retired.

Another Kansan, Wellsville late-in-life artist Elizabeth "Grandma" Layton, found herself in the national news for several years prior to her death in 1993, by which time she had become a dear friend of Ault's. In 1977, after the death of an adult son, Layton had taken a college class in contour drawing. The class used still lifes, but she took a mirror and applied the technique to self-portraiture. She drew avidly at home, and soon realized that this process had resolved her lifelong symptoms of depression, which traditional treatments had failed to do. Layton became prolific for years in her self-portraiture, and Kansas journalist Don Lambert volunteered to serve as her agent; her work went on tour and eventually was exhibited at the Smithsonian. She always used herself as the subject, depicting herself with pathos and humor in a range of personal life events or roles, as well as to represent stakeholders in social causes such as AIDS, domestic violence, and women's rights. Ault studied her process, used it himself, researched it by designing a class with his students at ESU, and presented about it nationally.

Ault once remarked to me that he could never say no. He was a founder of the Kansas Art Therapy Association, a still-active group that holds annual regional conferences. He educated other professionals about art therapy at innumerable conferences nationally and internationally over the years. He worked with programs for children with special needs, served on the Kansas Arts Commission, and was named a Kansas Outstanding Educator. He contributed to the writing of the first draft licensure bill for art therapists to be presented to the Kansas legislature. He was beloved by the veterans and their family members who attended his creative arts clinic at the Topeka VA, which hired him at quarter-time during his retirement. After his death, Ault's work was memorialized with the establishment in Topeka of the Legacy Community Arts Center, which sought to embody his dream of a place of community where anyone could go to make art.

The founding of the Menninger Clinic in Topeka in 1925 provided fertile ground for the development of a profession that has grown steadily ever since. Mary Huntoon, Don Jones, and Bob Ault provided the strong roots for the therapeutic use of artmaking processes to express, explore, and heal. They practiced their own art, articulated their theory and practice of art therapy, and evinced a deep caring for those they served and taught. In so doing, these Kansas pioneers of art therapy left a lasting legacy to the world.

Digging

J. T. Knoll

I hear the clean, rhythmic sound of his sharpshooter—sixteen-inch blade, ash-and-steel handle—easing down into clay, his straining back in a deep hole, descending to a sewer line or water main. Or out back in the garden with a long-handled shovel, stooping and standing in rhythm; boot on steel, wood on knee, the blade sliding in, arms levering dark earth up and over. Digging.

Grandpa could handle a shovel. He consistently dug more coal in a day than any other man in any of the southeast Kansas mines he worked. And following that, he dug graves for horses, footings for buildings, troughs for water, sewer and gas lines, gardens for grandma. And deep ditches in search of broken sewer pipe; heaving sod and clay and rock to one side—or over his shoulder—going down, down, and down. Digging.

How he smiled and whistled between his teeth when digging narrow trenches for new gas lines near our house—happy to be standing and shoveling above ground in clean air and sunshine rather than on hands and knees, 150 feet down, in foul, dark air, picking and shoveling coal from a three-foot seam. And the easy, confident way he carried his tools—long-handled shovel, sharpshooter, pick, and double-bladed axe—from the bed of his pickup to the string line and set about his work. Digging.

The moist smell of new earth, the rasp and thump of clay, the slice of edge through roots. The economy of motion. Sewer line, water line, gas line. Grave, garden, ditch. Digging.

Getting the Story Right

Wes Jackson

We had been back in our house and home on twenty-eight acres just outside Salina for two years, property we had bought and built on when I was teaching at Kansas Wesleyan University in the late 1960s. A faculty position at California State University, Sacramento, which hired me to start an environmental studies department, took the family and me West in 1971, but we held on to the Kansas place. When I took a one-year leave, we went back to Kansas. The one year stretched into two years, and then came the call from Sacramento that I expected but dreaded. I was told unequivocally that I had to either return to my position in Sacramento or resign. It was as simple as that. From a professional point of view, in Sacramento I had a good job with tenure in the academic world. And so the choice: security in California, a decent salary, and health benefits. Security, money, and health insurance benefits were not here in Kansas.

Sacramento, the capital city, had the clear water of the American River, which came right by the campus out of the western slope of the Sierra Nevada. We had several friends and lots of intellectual engagement, and if we wanted to do anything politically, we were in the capital of a large state where the levers of power for both the state and federal offices were within minutes of us. The Sierra Nevada loomed to the east, the Central Valley of California with its variety of agricultural crops lay to the south, and the Pacific Ocean with its public beaches was a short trip west. The University of California, Davis was less than a half-hour away. We could go to San Francisco, the redwoods on the coast, the Central Valley, or Lake Tahoe and hike in the mountains along a trail toward the peaks. Lots going on in California for our family.

When we left for that leave of absence, we said that we planned to return to California after one year. But if that was the plan, why did we sell the house in Sacramento that bordered the American River, with its hiking/biking trail along the levee that bordered our backyard?

What could have been on our minds to want to return to Salina in the first place, even if for only a year? The next large city west of Salina was Denver,

435 miles away. The next larger-than-Salina town to the east was Topeka, some 110 miles away. Kansas City was nearly three hours away by car. No mountains, no ocean. No wide variety of fruits and vegetables. No Central Valley. No UC Davis close by, no UC Berkeley on East Bay, no Stanford on the peninsula.

What Salina had to offer was twenty-eight acres with a flat-roofed 1,300-square-foot house, partly finished, on the bank of the Smoky Hill River. The average rainfall was twenty-eight inches. Not bad, but it had been in the Dust Bowl corridor in the 1930s. Salina had also been a primary nuclear target for the Soviet Union, given that Schilling Air Force Base had until recently had B-47 bombers loaded with nuclear weapons ready every night to head north to Russia, and there were a few intercontinental ballistic missile silos nearby. The base had recently been shut down, but the missile silos remained. The shutdown led to a population decline in Salina and a scramble to keep the economy going. For God's sake, what were we going back to?

We had family in and around Topeka. My mother was still alive, and from time to time we would be able to see her, my siblings, and their families, many of whom had traveled to visit us in California, where we would take them to see the redwoods, Chinatown, Fisherman's Wharf, ride the cable cars, go up Lombard Street. Why was being so close to home an excuse to stay?

As parents, we worried about how we might prepare ourselves and our children to develop the necessary skills for an uncertain future, which is to say, having the know-how to get along during periods of scarcity. We wanted to see what it would be like to live closer to subsistence level. We had the milk cow, the butcher hog, and chickens for meat and eggs, and my then wife, Dana, was a good gardener and became a good beekeeper. We put the kids to work, and all three learned skills without knowing it, the lessons built in to everyday chores. We had two years of this marginal life behind us—lumber buzzed up by a local sawmill and a shop made mostly from scrap lumber—and we somehow managed, and we were young. Sacramento called: "We need to know. Return or resign." What to do? We had no money. I would do a welding job here and there. Dana did some substitute teaching. As we pondered our options, I thought back to the many nights in Sacramento that I had stared at the ceiling, thinking about the ideal school for college-age students. I had read up on the Deep Springs College in California and Berea College in Kentucky, which combined intellectual rigor with hands-on work. I wondered if anything like that could sprout in Kansas. But with no money and little security, starting an alternative school wouldn't be simple.

Enter Kansas state senator John Simpson, an attorney who lived in Salina. He and his then wife, Diane, invited us to a weenie roast in their backyard. As John and I sat roasting our wieners and then marshmallows, he inquired about what we intended to do. I told him about the choice facing me and that I had been thinking of the ideal school. He quickly replied, "If you want to start a school, I'll help you." John offered to pay half the tuition for any student. Now we had an option: Stay and start a school. This required a family discussion, which included talk of the sort of school I imagined, but still there was the insecurity.

With John Simpson's offer on the table, the five of us—I, Dana, and our children, Laura, Scott, and Sara—assembled in the house to discuss the pros and cons of staying. It seemed to me that it would be too risky to stay. If it didn't work out, well, the options would be greatly reduced. And so I said, "We'd better go back." At that point, Laura, age fifteen, burst into tears and said, "I thought you said that we are not called to success but to obedience to our vision." Hooboy! I resigned, and we stayed.

Countless times over the years I have been asked what led to the decision to leave California and start The Land Institute, and countless times I have told that story. There would be the sober acknowledgment that it was the wisdom of youth with high ideals that brought the institute into existence. "My, my, think of that" and "Out of the mouths of babes," "a child will lead us," and so on. For more than forty-three years, I told something close to this story. But as the old commentator Paul Harvey here in the Midwest would say every afternoon on the radio following a commercial break, "Now, the rest of the story."

On June 15, 2019, my wife, Joan, and I are in Cedar Falls, Iowa, in the home of Laura, her husband, Kamyar, and their daughter Ada. Nettie, their oldest at twenty-three and out of college, has come from Minneapolis. We are there to celebrate two birthdays, Kamyar's sixtieth two days later, and my eighty-third that day. It is also Kamyar's fortieth year since leaving Iran. Some twenty-five or thirty friends and guests are seated here and there around the room, on the sofa, at tables, on the steps in groups of two, three, four, five. Someone asks me the question. I motion toward Laura with the back of my hand and say she's the reason. Then I tell the story once more. Once again the listeners seem amazed, offering thoughtful nods and such. There are looks toward Laura, but within seconds she describes a deeper truth that jump-started the past forty-three years of efforts at The Land.

"Well, there is more to that story," she says. "We had moved seven times, and I had gone to seven different schools. I didn't want to move again, and I knew that if I threw one of Dad's lines back at him, I wouldn't have to change schools again."

I was astounded. I had lived with a good story, my incomplete story of almost mythical proportions. It was the first time I had ever told the story with Laura present.

Well, Laura got what she wanted back then. The Land Institute came into existence because a fifteen-year-old girl did not want to change schools again.

There are stories, and there is the story.

I don't imagine that I was a planned child, being the last of six spread over twenty-two years from the same parents. There is reason to believe they wanted to stop at three, but that would have been in 1919. Well, you know how it is. It just kept happening. The next in line before me is eight years older. My father would turn fifty the year I was born, and my mother forty-two. So I was something of a tagalong, arriving midyear in 1936. Mention the 1930s and it brings to mind both the Great Depression and the Dust Bowl for Kansas. Entry into World War II was five and a half years away. I was told that I was born on the farm, on the kitchen table, with the assistance of a twenty-year-old sister on her way to becoming a nurse.

In my early memories, men would come to our farm to give advice and help monitor a five-year experiment involving twenty-some crops. That required considerable data taking, mostly on the part of my dad but I suspect with the help of my older brothers. All of these professionals were, as family members put it, "down from the college," which meant Kansas State College, now a university. These "down from the college" scientists were kindly men, respectful in every way. Beyond those visiting scientists, Kansas State was "our college." My older brother started school there in 1937 but came back home to farm after one semester. Since then several of my nieces, nephews, and cousins as well as a daughter and two grandchildren have been K-State students. My mother had a cousin who was president there for six years. Beyond these personal engagements, there is another reason to respect the land-grant college along with the experiment station and extension service. These three together represent one of the greatest initiatives dedicated to the democratization of knowledge, given that the purpose was to include agriculture and the mechanical arts. In the mid-1960s I earned my PhD in the genetics department of another land-grant institution, North Carolina State. Like other land-grant colleges, North Carolina State was born from the 1862 Morrill Act, which granted public lands for such a college in each state. The story of democratization is complicated, of course, by the dispossession of Indigenous people behind the land grant project.

With all of these family connections, from birth through graduate school, I had reason to be a lover of the land-grant system. But somewhere during that journey, I began a quarrel with the entire institutional structure as I realized that it had become mostly a cheerleader for industrial agriculture. It's a lover's quarrel, and it endures even as The Land Institute—after years of being treated as a marginal enterprise by those folks—is today increasing its engagement with such universities.

But I spend less time arguing about the institutional structure now, as I have come to realize that most of the people are products of the system and are unable to bring about the necessary fundamental change. If they ever did speak out about the destructive consequences of industrial agriculture, they long ago quit. Export policy, the commodity groups—in short, corporate power—will have their way. My daughter Laura identified this situation as a form of Stockholm syndrome (when hostages develop a connection to, and alliance with, their captors) for certain faculty who come to endorse the powers that have captured their university.

Countless painful moments of engagement have accumulated over the years. As I have gone to and fro on my ecological agriculture errands during the past nearly half-century, the arguments have varied in their intensity. Early on I argued mostly with men my age or older. And now for something of the story behind how those inevitable disagreements arose during my forays into the ag schools of those land-grant universities, the story of how I went a different way. Within a year after the start-up of The Land Institute, in the spring of 1977, I had two experiences within a short period of time. I had read the General Accounting Office (GAO) report on the effectiveness of the Soil Conservation Service. It looked to me, in reading that report, as if soil erosion was about as bad in the 1970s as when the service started back in the 1930s, when it was initially called the Soil Erosion Service. I wondered how this could be, given the thousands of miles of terraces, grass waterways, and such that the service had helped put in place. Shortly after that I took my interns to what came to be called the Konza Prairie near Manhattan, which is the home of Kansas State University. Lloyd Hulbert—a K-State biology professor, ecologist, internationally known expert on tallgrass prairies, and friend—led us on a field trip, describing that grassland ecosystem and mentioning the role of fire and grazing. It was a wonderful trip for all.

Back home, with the GAO study on my mind, I thought about how that prairie had no discernible soil erosion, no chemical contamination of the land or water, and no fossil-fuel dependency. The contrast between nature's prairie and human-designed agriculture was clear. Our grain crops, which grow on around two-thirds to three-fourths of our agricultural acreage and provide a similar share of our calories, are annual monocultures. The prairie features perennial species in mixtures, what we call polyculture.

There was a third element in this thought process. In the back of my mind was a single sentence from my graduate days in Raleigh, North Carolina, something my major professor had told me. Late one night, Ben W. Smith walked into my lab while I was at my microscope and said, "We need wilderness as a standard against which to judge our agricultural practices." He turned around and left without elaborating, but that idea stuck with me.

The GAO report could have been just another document on one of my countless unorganized piles, saved to study in more detail when I had the time. Luckily, it was enough on my mind that after the trip to the Konza Prairie, for whatever reason, I drew a branching diagram on the back of a brown paper grocery sack, starting with four paired contrasts: polyculture versus monoculture, perennial versus annual, woody versus herbaceous, and fruit/seed versus vegetative. I was looking for the combinations useful to humans. Four times four yields sixteen combinations. Four combinations were nonsensical (for example, woody annuals don't exist). Of the twelve remaining real possibilities, eleven of the blanks had been filled with plants useful for direct human purposes. But one combination, a polyculture of herbaceous perennials devoted to fruit/ seed, was blank.

Why this was so, I could not get off my mind. I was mindful that nearly all of nature's land-based ecosystems featured perennial mixtures, and I knew something of the history of earth abuse due to agriculture, so it became clear that our failure to fill that blank stood behind the ten-thousand-year-old problem of agriculture (as opposed to the more familiar focus on specific problems in agriculture). The same year I wrote a paper for our Land Report titled "The Search for a Permanent Agriculture." I later changed the title, replacing "permanent" with "sustainable," and published it in the Friends of the Earth journal called *Not Man Apart*. In 1980, Friends of the Earth published my book *New Roots for Agriculture*, an expansion of the idea and the argument supporting the necessity and possibility of a sustainable agriculture as I perceived it.

Well, the word was out, at least in the alternatives network, which was small enough at that time that we mostly all knew each other. The nonprofit organizations had little to no objection to my story. I was invited to give talks and seminars here and there at a few colleges, including some of the land-grant universities. Even though my degree from North Carolina State made me, in some sense, "one of them," I had to think carefully about how to present myself and my ideas, given the dominance of Big Ag at those schools.

Back in the 1970s and 1980s, there were many ag professors my age or older, born before or during the Great Depression, who had experienced the Dust Bowl years on a farm. I quickly learned that in a college of agriculture, professors speaking on a panel often made sure to establish their rural roots. If they had been born and/or raised on a farm, they said so. If they had gone to a one-room or two-room country school, so much the better. If there was no electricity on the farm when they were born and if the family had an outhouse, they would throw that in. If they worked their way through college washing dishes or went to a college of agriculture and milked cows at the state college dairy to cover tuition and living costs, they would by all means mention that.

Though I learned how important it was to establish one's humble rural origins—once again, I was one of them in this regard—that didn't help me all that much either. It turned out that most of those professors went on to explain that leaving those humble beginnings behind was a good thing, and there was no need to challenge the "progress" we had made in agriculture. We certainly didn't need any harebrained scheme that would take fifty years, maybe even a hundred, as I had predicted for perennial grains in my 1970s writings. The dominant view was that such a radical shift in agriculture was either not possible or not necessary.

In the last quarter of the previous century, the Green Revolution was underway, big time. So were Big Ag, chemicals, and high-tech gadgets, which were dominating agriculture. Turns out that all my land-grant connections and rural-roots cultural capital didn't get me very far. I was seen by many as more of a turncoat. The rhetoric of the industrial hero—"We must feed the world!"—rang out. Things were thought to be getting better in spite of a growing dead zone in the Gulf of Mexico due to industrial chemicals applied throughout the watershed, despite the demise of small towns and rural communities, despite more and more (and ever larger) feedlots.

But things do change.

By the early twenty-first century, talking about ecological agriculture had become easier as evidence of the destructive consequences of industrial agriculture piled up. The reception for talk about perennial polycultures warmed a bit. And with a group of highly qualified young scientists, featuring plant breeders and ecologists, The Land Institute's work expanded. In 2019 the institute had forty-one research colleagues at sixteen universities in the United States and around the world (South Africa, Turkey, Italy, China, Germany, Mali, India, Ethiopia, Canada, Sweden, Uganda, Argentina, Australia, France, Uruguay, and Denmark).

And so here we are now, working cooperatively with some of the land-grant schools. Our first perennial grain, Kernza®, a relative of wheat with the common name intermediate wheatgrass (originally identified as a good breeding candidate by Peggy Wagner, who was on the staff of the Rodale Institute at that time), is being grown by farmers and made into beer and other grain products. Still low in gluten, it must be mixed with wheat to get bread to rise, but it is suitable for pancakes, cookies, and other grain products. Our perennial sorghum is grown in Africa. We helped preserve wild perennial rice from the International Rice Research Institute in the Philippines, and that rice is now being grown in China in thousands of acres in paddies, with work going forward for perennial rice that can be grown on the upland slopes. The Chinese, following Vietnam, Laos, and Cambodia, have now started the effort to save their upland soils.

We still have a challenge in making clear that if we stop with perennial monocultures, we will have missed half the point. We want polycultures, plants grown in mixtures. Mimicking the ecosystem, such as the never-plowed native prairie, remains our goal. This is more plausible now that we have the perennials in the pipeline, so to speak, which means we have—pardon me—new "hardware" with the perennials. Now that knowledge coming out of the broad disciplines of ecology and evolutionary biology, which has been accumulating on the shelf for a century and a half, is becoming available, we can begin to more aggressively blend the two cultures—the ecologists who have had the luxury of being descriptive, and the agriculturists who have had the burden of being prescriptive—given that our food supply is on the line for the farmer and the agricultural researcher.

It is wonderful to be able to imagine that the primary way of doing business on our agricultural land for the past ten thousand years can change.

Dragging Wyatt Earp

Robert Rebein

Hear the words Dodge City, Kansas, these days and you're apt to think, depending on your age, either of a long-running television series—the wildly fictitious *Gunsmoke*, featuring Miss Kitty, Festus, and Marshal Matt Dillon—or else of a favorite phrase of screen hacks and gleeful, road-tripping frat boys: *Let's get the hell out of Dodge!* Few are the souls who would hear the town's name and think of the *real* Dodge City, self-proclaimed "Cowboy Capital of the World," with its beef-packing plants and used car lots and the tired tones of boosterism ("Come Grow with Us!") emanating from its chamber of commerce. To know that Dodge, you'd have to have crossed southwest Kansas in a car, an experience road-weary travelers have been known to compare to crossing the ocean by sail. Either that or, like me, you'd have to be from there.

It's been twenty years now since I escaped the place, and in that time, the real Dodge City, with its dry riverbed and red brick streets, grain elevators casting shadows across an empty downtown, the air filled with dust or tinged with a fecal tang blown in from the feedlots, the Dodge of the Red Demons and Conqs (short for Conquistadors) and the now-defunct St. Mary of the Plains Cavaliers, of the dying mall called Village Square, the scarred but still functional South Drive-In, the cheesy tourist traps (Boot Hill and Front Street, Home of Stone, Gunfighters Wax Museum), none of them worth the drive and not meant to be, the Dodge of the diseased Dutch elm and incessant, driving wind, with its country club and taquerias, its chiropractic clinics and farm implement dealerships, and its Farmer's Country Market that used to be a Safeway that used to be the hospital where I was born . . . *that* Dodge City almost ceased to exist for me, having been replaced in my mind by the Dodge of legend and myth, the so-called Queen of the Cow Towns, the Wickedest Little City in America, the Bibulous Babylon of the Frontier.

Almost, but not quite.

For while I confess to a weakness for tales of the Old West, particularly those having to do with my hometown's sordid past, in most important

respects—in memory, imagination, all the infinitesimal allegiances of iden-
tity—I remain tied to that other Dodge, *my* Dodge, the one that raised me
up and forgave my feeble sins and never once asked for a single thing in
return except that I leave and find my future elsewhere.

For a teenager suffering the boredom of the Cowboy Capital circa 1980, the
only thing to do at night, so we all said, was to "drag Wyatt Earp." By this
we did not mean, as the image would suggest, that we'd pull the nineteenth-
century lawman through the streets by his boot heels, but only that we'd
cruise up and down Wyatt Earp Boulevard in our beat-up Chevrolets and
hand-me-down Buicks, searching for that elusive bit of excitement that al-
ways seemed to exist just outside of our reach. Wyatt Earp, to us, was not a
person but a *place*, a mile-long ribbon of asphalt that stretched from Boot
Hill on the east to the Dodge House on the west, containing in that brief
space all of our teeming and awkward adolescence, our collective longings
and flirtations, and our often ridiculous mistakes, few of which we had to
pay for in any meaningful way.

Dragging Wyatt Earp was a ritual and a clearly demarcated rite of pas-
sage, one that began at age fourteen or fifteen, the years when most of us
were issued our first driver's licenses, and that ended two or three years
later, when the pool halls and beer joints and lakeside keg parties began to
absorb us. Had we been city kids, we'd have been hanging out at the mall or
the cineplex. But we weren't city kids, and Dodge was a suburb of nowhere,
hundreds of mostly tedious miles from Dallas, Denver, and Kansas City, and
there was much that we would never do or see before the age of nineteen
or twenty. But we could drive and drink 3.2 brew, both at early ages and
in plain sight of the police. A kind of unwritten law had been established
long ago.

I can recall, at sixteen or seventeen, wheeling into the Kwik Shop at
Twelfth and Wyatt Earp and emerging five minutes later with a six-pack
of Coors cradled in one arm like a football. Often the person selling me
the beer knew exactly who I was, who my father and brothers were, what
position I played on the high school basketball team. Sometimes there'd be
a cop car in the parking lot when I came out, two sheriff's deputies sitting
side by side with their elbows jutting out open windows. I'd nod to them as
I ambled past with my illicit cargo, and they'd nod right back in that slow,
calculated manner of police everywhere.

"You be careful now, you hear?"

"Yes, sir," I'd answer, innocent as you please.

Once on Wyatt Earp, the routine rarely varied. The official speed limit was thirty-five miles an hour, but like the drinking age, we regarded this as more of a suggestion than an actual law. Either you went fifteen or you went fifty, depending on your style and purpose, the level of gas in your tank, the amount of beer or Jack Daniels or peppermint schnapps you'd consumed. Racing from one light to the next was not unheard of, but neither was it a regular occurrence. A pecking order had been established long before, in seventh or eighth grade, so what was the point? Dragging Wyatt Earp was about killing time; it was about hanging out and hooking up, growing up and throwing up (indeed, in the teen vernacular of Dodge City circa 1980, to "erp" was to vomit, usually by hanging one's head out the door of a moving car); it was about chasing dreams and bursting at the seams and endlessly rehearsing for that preordained day when we, too, would get the hell out of Dodge, never to return.

Dodge City in 1876 was a quintessential Western boom town, a nexus for cash and cattle where overlords like the legendary Shanghai Pierce sold their massive herds at a profit and immediately paid off their hired underlings, most of them young Texans away from home for the first time. To say that the merchants of Dodge City saw these greenhorns coming would be an understatement of epic proportions. In a piece published in the Dodge City *Times* in the spring of 1878, editor Nicholas Klaine made no bones about the anticipation with which "this delectable city of the plains" awaited the return of the cattle trade with its "countless herds" and "hordes of bipeds." As many as fifteen hundred of these "bipeds" might hit town in a single season, and as Klaine, licking his chops, pointed out, Dodge City was the single "source from which the great army of the herder and driver is fed":

This "cattle village" and far-famed "wicked city" is decked in gorgeous attire in preparation for the long horn. Like the sweet harbinger of spring, the boot black came, he of white and he of black. Next the barber "with his lather and shave." Too, with all that go to make up the busy throng of life's faithful fever, come the Mary Magdalenes, "selling their souls to whoever'll buy." There is "high, low, jack, and game," all adding to the great expectation so important an event brings about.

If there was a problem in all this, a glitch, so to speak, in an otherwise flawless business plan, it was the town's tendency to erupt in periodic bouts of profit-draining violence. Ordinances against public intoxication and the carrying of firearms in the city limits were duly composed and promulgated, but enforcing them was another matter. That required the deft touch of a man like Wyatt Earp, who had honed his skills as a peace officer in the cow towns of Ellsworth and Wichita and was more than ready to employ them in Dodge, too—provided, of course, the price was right.

The epicenter of my teen years was the parking lot below Boot Hill Museum, a rectangle of concrete the size of a football field that on any given night contained the same tribes and anthropologically interesting subgroups as the high school—jocks, cheerleaders, potheads, Future Farmers of America—the only difference being that here one leaned against the polished hood of one's car, instead of against one's locker. The same atmosphere of boredom, of stoically doing one's time, obtained in both places. If someone had asked our parents why they allowed us to openly drink alcohol in a parking lot in the middle of town, they probably would have said, "At least we know where they are. At least they're *safe*." And yet what irony, that this, the place we gathered most nights to gossip, pose, and drink beer, bore a name synonymous the world over with sin and violent death. The phrases "dead line," "red-light district," and "die with your boots on" all originated here, as did the legends of Wyatt Earp and Bat Masterson, Doc Holliday and Big Nose Kate Elder, Mysterious Dave Mather and Squirrel Tooth Alice.

Did we know? Did we care? But what's the use of asking: we were teenagers, after all. It would have taken something more tangible than mere history to impress us. In the middle of the parking lot was a large cage, perhaps ten feet square, made of two-by-fours and chicken wire. Sometime before, so the story went, the parking lot had become so littered with our crushed beer cans that someone's dad or Eagle Scout older brother had been inspired to build the cage to hold the empties. I couldn't say now if the story is true, but we certainly were proud of it at the time, and most weekends we possessed no higher ambition than to "fill the cage."

This was the kind of thing that mattered to us; not Wyatt Earp, not history.

Boot Hill parking lot was the place I took my first real girlfriend on our first real date. She was a cheerleader with ambitions to be crowned homecoming queen, and I was a jock suffering from the usual jock grandiosity. I can still recall what it felt like to make that slow, head-turning crawl through the cars parked at Boot Hill. You weren't an official couple until you'd run that gauntlet. Later, when the relationship began to crumble under the weight of its own importance, Boot Hill parking lot was also the place I'd go late at night to cheat on this girlfriend (try to, at any rate), so secure was I in the knowledge that no one who saw me at that hour would dare tell the secret. Like the French Quarter of New Orleans, Boot Hill possessed a strange, nearly magical ability to transform itself several times daily, from afternoon tourist haven to evening esplanade to late-night cruising ground; if the vibe reigning at any one time didn't suit, you could always come back later, and, like the weather on the high plains, it would be sure to have changed.

That world! Looking back, I don't see a series of clearly demarcated nights, but rather a blur, a collage. I see the pimpled faces of my friends, our bad haircuts and unfashionable clothes. I hear the over-amped music, Led Zeppelin, AC/DC, Kool & the Gang, Bob Seger. I smell the burned oil and rubber and gasoline and weed, recall the sickly sweet taste of Copenhagen and Skoal, Jack Daniels sipped from a wax-coated paper cup, the sloppy kisses copped in cramped back seats, and the feel of tight jeans and no hat even in the winter and the stiff arms of my new letter jacket. I remember the roadside signs, McDonalds, Burger King, Pizza Hut, but also El Charro, Kirby's Western Store, OK Tire, Muddy Waters, El Matador. I remember the cars, especially the newer, faster ones with their space-age names (RX-7, 280Z) and the lovingly restored older models ('57 Chevy, '64 Mustang, '69 GTO). My own pride and joy was a ghost-green 1970 Firebird Formula 400, a huge, hulking beast with a chrome-studded engine, fat tires with raised white letters, and a six-speaker stereo system that cost more than the car itself.

Most of all, though, I remember the talk, the ceaseless posturing and bragging and trying on of ideas, the feeble put-downs and bad jokes and misty-eyed confessions, the sputtering declarations of love. Like teenagers everywhere, we existed in a bizarre, fog-bound realm in which the present was at once insufferable and all-important. The past did not exist at all, and when the subject of the future flared up, as it did periodically, we were quick to smother it in a series of outlandish predictions. We would win Daytona, take Hollywood by storm, run for the United States Senate, earn our first million by the age of thirty, and so on and so forth. No plans for how we would accomplish these things were ever asked for, and none were given. Unlike our peers in the cities and the suburbs, we didn't sweat the details. We just believed.

What is it about growing up in a small town in the West that breeds such bravado, such innocence and blind faith? Was it our isolation? The vaunted self-reliance of the region? The fact that our parents and teachers praised us inordinately, or that acceptance into any of the state's colleges was a fait accompli? Maybe, but I have another explanation: we were leaving. And not just for a year or five years, but forever. Like the region's cattle, wheat, and corn, we'd been raised for export, and most of us had learned this fact at about the same time we learned that Santa Claus was a fiction. Coming into this knowledge was both terrifying and liberating. It was like looking over the edge of a great abyss or knowing in advance the date of your own death. It steeled us and set us apart. And yet, for all that, there was no need for alarm or haste or even preparation. As far as we were concerned, the day of our departure would come of its own accord, just as morning would come, after a long night of dragging Wyatt Earp.

Other frontier lawmen may have been faster on the draw, better liars, more handsome and flamboyant—Wild Bill Hickok comes to mind in all of these categories—but none was better at handling drunks than Wyatt S. Earp.

According to newspaper articles on file at the Kansas Heritage Center, Wyatt Berry Stapp Earp was a deputy city marshal in Dodge City—a police-man, essentially—from May 1876 to October 1879, the height of the city's cow-town fame, during which time he earned a reputation as "one of the most efficient officers Dodge ever had," a cop with "a quiet way of taking the most desperate characters into custody."

What was this "quiet method" of Marshal Earp's? An item from the August 20, 1878, Ford County *Globe* sheds some light on the matter. "Another shooting affair occurred on the 'south side' Saturday night," the article begins. "It appears that one of the cow boys, becoming intoxicated and quarrelsome, undertook to take possession of the bar in the Comique. To this the bar keeper objected and a row ensued. Our policemen interfered and had some difficulty in handling their man. Several cattle men then engaged in the broil and in the excitement some of them were bruised on the head with six shooters."

Plainly put, during his stint with the Dodge City police, Wyatt Earp became known not for shooting his gun—a Colt .45 specially modified with an extended barrel almost a foot long (the infamous "Buntline Special")—but rather for using it to brain belligerent drunks. "If some obstreperous cowboy resisted arrest," Earp told his biographer, the fawning Stuart Lake, "a marshal could jerk his gun, bat him over the head, and end the argument." Earp had various names for this favorite ploy of his: "manhandling," "buffaloing," "bending a six-gun over a man's head." We moderns employ another term—excessive force—but in Earp's day it was thought that a cop who kept order without actually firing his gun was a very good cop indeed.

So much of what we think we know about Wyatt Earp turns out, on closer examination, to be false or misleading. Having studied the famous photographs, all of them in black-and-white, we naturally imagine a dark man, when by all reports Earp was a strawberry blonde with blue eyes. Having seen the movies and TV shows, we imagine a big man, someone of the stature of John Wayne or, better yet, James Arness of *Gunsmoke* fame, when in truth Earp was rather slight, never weighing more than 160 pounds. Having read the pulps, we picture a classic gunslinger, a man standing alone at high noon, but as a cow-town cop, Earp worked almost exclusively at night and in tandem with other police, who remembered him not as a "quick draw" or "crack shot" but as an accomplished brawler, a bare-knuckles fighter of such skill and tenacity that fellow cop Bat Masterson, later a New York sportswriter, was reminded of none other than the legendary Jim Corbett. "I doubt if there was a man in the West who could whip [Wyatt] in a rough-and-tumble fight," Masterson wrote.

As for the self-doubt and scruples Hollywood so prefers in its cinematic marshals, apparently Wyatt Earp wasn't much troubled by these. The testimony of those who knew him best describes a dour, supremely confident man who inspired fear in his enemies and loyalty in his friends. Earp was calm, experienced, and methodical, and perhaps most important of all, he did not drink. No, not a drop. Add to this the fact, as one biographer has it, that the young Earp "grew up in the same pro-union, Republican, progressive, antislavery atmosphere that spawned Abraham Lincoln," and the portrait is complete. The man Dodge City's saloon owners hired to keep the peace in the Wicked City was neither a hero nor a saint but rather a detached, seasoned, and somewhat sadistic teetotaler who was good with his fists and didn't much care for the Rebel scum he was charged with arresting on a nightly basis.

For his work in Dodge, Earp drew a salary of $100 a month, plus a $2 bonus for every arrest made. According to Stuart Lake, one of Earp's innovations as a Dodge City marshal was to pool these bonuses and share them among all the cops on the force—provided the arrests were made without shots being fired. "I figured that if the cowboys were manhandled and heaved into the caboose every time they showed in town with guns on, or cut loose in forbidden territory, they'd come to time quicker than if we kept them primed for gunplay," Earp recalled.

Earp's idea—to kill no one, but to collect plenty of bounties from buffaloed drunks—worked like a charm from first to last. "We winged a few tough customers who insisted on shooting, but none of the victims died," he recalled. "On the other hand, we split seven or eight hundred dollars in bounties each month. That meant some three hundred arrests every thirty days, and as practically every prisoner heaved into the caboose was thoroughly buffaloed in the process, we made quite a dent in the cowboy conceit."

Dent indeed! Earp's calculation here is as chilling as his methods were brutal, and yet, a century later, it's still difficult to argue with his basic premise, which counted a rap on the skull as a lesser evil than a bullet in the brain.

Admired by those whose pockets he helped fill, hated by those whose skulls he bruised, Wyatt Earp was the greatest bouncer the West ever knew.

Of all the nights I spent cruising the strip that bears Earp's name, only one stands apart from all the rest. It was a hot night the summer before my junior year of high school, and a friend and I had spent it at the South Drive-In, reclining in beach chairs and sipping at a twelve-pack of 3.2 brew we'd managed to smuggle in. I don't remember what movie played that night, or if it was any good. I don't even recall how many beers I consumed, or in what span of time I consumed them. All I really remember is that, in comparison to other nights that came both before and after this one, I wasn't particularly drunk. Certainly I had no business behind the wheel of a car, but that, like so many others, was a lesson I had yet to learn.

The movie over, we tossed the beach chairs into the back of the Firebird and bounced out of the lunar landscape of the theater.

"Wanna drag Earp a few times?" I asked.

"Yeah, why not," answered my friend, who in years to come would earn a degree in nuclear engineering and circumnavigate the globe in a Cold War sub.

We crossed the dry Arkansas at Second Avenue, not far from where the Spanish conquistador Coronado crossed more than four hundred years before, merging quickly into the night traffic on West Wyatt Earp. What were we thinking? Where were we going? It's all lost now, like the motivations of the men and women who stare back at us, bug-eyed, from nineteenth century daguerreotypes.

Approaching Boot Hill, we craned our heads to the right, cataloguing in an instant all of the cars parked there. Vaguely, as though attempting to see through a fog, I recall a disturbance in my rear-view mirror, something only partially blocked by the beach chairs piled haphazardly in the back seat. What was it? A flash of headlights? The streetlight behind us turning from yellow to red? Whatever it was, I veered sharply into the right-hand lane, nearly sideswiping a carload of Utah tourists. To miss them, I hit the gas hard. The Firebird shot forward, jumped a curb, and narrowly missed a phone pole before crashing into a chain-link fence.

"What the hell!" my friend howled. The paper cup he'd been using as a spittoon had overturned in his lap, filling the car with a sharp, wintergreen smell.

"You all right?" I asked, blinking at the red lights aglow in the car's dash.

"Well, I guess," my friend said.

Moments later, a city patrolman who'd witnessed the entire episode rolled to a stop behind us, lights silently flashing.

What happened next could only have happened to kids like us—underage, white, known quantities to every officer on the force—and in that specific time and place, or so I've come to believe. With the whole of Boot Hill parking lot looking on, my friend and I were pulled from the Firebird and deposited in the back of the patrolman's copper-and-cream squad car, there to sweat the minutes while he calmed the tourists and sent them on their way. Afterward, the patrolman, whose name I've forgotten, took up an aggressive position, legs spread wide, behind the Firebird's license plate, and began writing tickets.

"Can you walk heel to toe?" my friend asked, attempting a joke. "Can you recite the alphabet backwards?"

Scared, my throat dry from the Copenhagen I'd swallowed in the crash, I said nothing at all in response, but only sat there watching as the patrolman closed his aluminum ticket box and began a bow-legged amble back to where we waited.

"Get out," he ordered, opening my door.

I scrambled from the back seat of the squad car, my friend following, and together we lined up in the glare of the car's headlights. By now there were twenty or more people looking on, most of them across the road from us and unable to hear what was said.

"Think you can drive that heap of yours?" the patrolman asked, handing me the stack of tickets he'd written.

I nodded, still too scared to say a word.

"All right, then," he said, shaking his head. "Straight home, fellas. No detours. You hear?"

"Yes, sir," I managed to say.

As we sped away from there, my friend performed a quick inventory of the tickets. "Reckless driving, failure to signal. . . . What is this, your lucky day?"

"I guess so," I said.

Before work the following Monday, I walked into the county courthouse and paid the tickets in full, using money I'd been saving for college. The total damage was something on the order of $400, but I paid it gladly.

Two years later, I packed my bags and headed east on US Highway 50, reversing the outbound path of the old Santa Fe Trail. I can still hear the throaty roar of the Firebird as I opened all four barrels of the carburetor. Trust me when I tell you that I worshiped every inch of that ridiculous beast. And yet, six months later, with little forethought and no real regrets, I walked onto a used car lot in North Lawrence, Kansas, and traded straight across for a boxy, puke-green 1975 Volvo. So do we shed our adolescent selves and venture forth into a larger, less forgiving world.

Wyatt Earp left Dodge City for Tombstone, Arizona, in September 1879. In Earp's words, "Dodge's edge was getting dull." In 1885 the wood shanties of Front Street, the model for a thousand Hollywood sets, burned to the ground in a series of fires. The following winter delivered a devastating storm, the great blizzard of 1886, which decimated herds across the West, bankrupted most of the big ranches, and brought the so-called Cattle Kingdom to its knees. But even before the arrival of fire and ice, the writing was already on the wall. "There are silent but irresistible forces at work to regenerate Dodge City," the Topeka *Capital* reported in 1885. "The passage of the Texas cattle bill, the defeat of the trail bill and the rapid settlement of the country south and southwest of Dodge, have destroyed the place as a cattle town. The cowboy must go, and with him will go the gamblers, the courtesans, the desperadoes and the saloons."

With the good-time people gone away, sod busters, precursors of my own humble ancestors, moved in and broke up the prairie into massive, monotonous wheat farms. With them came the temperance unions that had already tamed the eastern half of the state. And so, the town turned its back on its sordid past and accepted a sober if somewhat boring future. When Front Street was rebuilt after the fires of 1885, the work was done in brick—a safer, more permanent choice than wood. Fifteen years later, on the cusp of a new century, the place had changed so much that the editors of the *Globe-Republican* proudly declared the birth of a "New Dodge City," no longer a place of "high carnival," where "rapturous lewdness and bawdiness held sway," but rather a city "clothed in her right mind," "a paragon of virtue, sobriety and industry."

There's an undeniable sadness to all this that resonates even today—the circus gone, the party over, the days of debauched glory all in the past. Innocence gives way to experience, the child grows to adulthood, the young colt goes into harness and is made to pull the wagon of duty. Inevitably, a kind of nostalgia sets in. When word spread that Warner Brothers was planning a movie based on the city's lurid past, a delegation of old timers and chamber of commerce types traveled to Hollywood to invite Jack Warner to stage the film's premiere in Dodge. Photographs of this 1939 event look surreal, with fifty thousand fans crowding the tracks of the Santa Fe depot to await the arrival of Errol Flynn, Jean Parker, and Humphrey Bogart. Twenty years later, in 1958, a replica of the original Front Street was built on a slope below Boot Hill, and the road running below it, formerly Chestnut Street, was renamed Wyatt Earp Boulevard. In 1970, Front Street itself fell to the wrecking ball to make room for more off-street parking and the widening of Wyatt Earp to accommodate the likes of McDonalds and Kentucky Fried Chicken. Thus did Front Street, upon which, as Zane Grey famously wrote, more frontier history was enacted than anywhere else in the West, become a fast-food corridor and the latest outpost of IHOP and Auto Zone.

I returned to Dodge City on the occasion of my parents' fiftieth wedding anniversary, rolling into town from the east behind the wheel of a loaded-to-the-gills SUV in the back seat of which my son and daughter watched *Shrek 2* on their portable flat-screen TV. Driving up Wyatt Earp to Fourteenth Street, I was amused to see that the Kwik Shop where I once bought beer was now Doc Holliday Liquors. Across the street, on the site of an old Sinclair station, stood Wyatt Earp Liquors. Since the beef-packing plants moved in twenty years ago, the town has become more Western and Hispanic, the airwaves full of country music, programming in Spanish, and advertisements for the annual Dodge City Days Roundup Rodeo. This, too, is my Dodge City, although I do not yet know it half as well as I would like to.

In the years since I got the hell out of Dodge, I've lived in three different states and two foreign countries. I've married, fathered children and a career, seen a handful of dreams come true while others have died on the vine, despite all my efforts to keep them alive. To return home after years away is at best a bittersweet thing. It is to encounter ghosts at every stoplight and corner—ghosts of what once was, as well as ghosts of what might have been.

As I turned north on Fourteenth Street, just as I had as a kid heading home after a long night of dragging Wyatt Earp, I was reminded of what that policeman told my friend and me all those years ago.

"Straight home, fellas. No detours."

But it's all detours after a while.

Basket Ball

Andrew Malan Milward

In early December 2010, I came across an article in the *Lawrence Journal World* titled, "Booths Purchase Original Naismith Basketball Rules at Auction for More Than \$4 Million." \$4,338,500, to be exact. In the same Sotheby's auction, a copy of the Emancipation Proclamation that was signed by Abraham Lincoln and owned by Bobby Kennedy went for \$3.7 million. David Booth grew up in Lawrence, graduated from the University of Kansas (KU), but now lives in Austin, Texas, where he is chairman and chief executive officer of Dimensional Fund Advisors, a privately held investment firm that manages about \$206.5 billion in assets. The Naismith family decided to put the rules up for sale because the Naismith International Basketball Foundation, a charity that promotes sportsmanship and provides service to underprivileged children, was running out of money. Apparently, a rich Duke alumnus was poised to buy the rules and take them to Durham, North Carolina, before David Booth stepped in to spare KU the embarrassment. Previously, in 2004, he and his wife, Susan, had donated \$9 million to build the Booth Family Hall of Athletics in Allen Fieldhouse, and now the rules would be housed there on the University of Kansas campus, where the inventor of the game presided as the coach of the first Kansas basketball team.

It's a familiar enough story—to those familiar with the game, anyway. Basketball's creation myth begins in Springfield, Massachusetts, in the freezing winter chill of 1891. The entire Big Bang can be traced back to one man, James Naismith, a Canadian-born physical education instructor of Scottish stock, who was given the seemingly inconsequential task of creating an indoor game that would keep occupied the young men of the YMCA International Training School (now Springfield College) during New England's interminable winter months. He thought on it for two weeks and then wrote the rules in one sitting on the morning of December 21, 1891, shortly before the start of the 11:30 a.m. class in which he introduced the new game he called "Basket Ball" to his eighteen students. He claimed to have drawn inspiration from a childhood game called "Duck on the Rock," which sounds frighteningly medieval, essentially involving a group of boys attempting to chuck rocks past some poor soul who was forced to stand guard—in effect *trying* to be stoned by his pals—in front of a larger rock, and which to my mind bears little resemblance to basketball, but to each his own muse.

Naismith's primary aims were to create a game that was easy to play and rooted in skill and accuracy rather than force. "Basketball, in my opinion, is one of the few games that emphasizes agility, speed, and accuracy, and is directly opposed to bodily contact," he wrote in his book *Basketball: Its Origin and Development.* "There is no necessity for the bodily shock that is part of football, hockey, and some of the other games."

Basketball's invention came at a time when the role of sports was changing in the culture. In his book *A People's History of Sports in the United States,* the sportswriter David Zirin notes that prior to the Civil War sports were viewed as wicked, a temptation away from religious devotion, and while it might seem laughably, well, puritanical today to think of baseball as wicked, there were certainly enough horrors like rat-baiting, cockfighting, and bare-knuckle boxing to bolster the claim. This sentiment carried over even after the war. Naismith recounts the following anecdote of his time playing football while majoring in theology at McGill University: "For seven years I played without missing a game and enjoyed the sport, even though it was not thought proper for a 'theolog.' Football at that time was supposed to be a tool of the devil, and it was much to my amusement that I learned that some of my comrades gathered in one of the rooms one evening to pray for my soul."

While sports may have long been viewed as a pathway to sin, however, a competing concern among Protestant church leaders in the mid-nineteenth century was that religion was becoming increasingly feminized, the domain of women and effete males. From this anxiety was born a philosophy known as Muscular Christianity. In his history of sports in America, Duncan Jamieson writes that "Muscular Christianity reflected the interrelationship between religion, sports, health and physical fitness, and contemporary changes taking place in Victorian society caused by the industrial and scientific revolutions." Founded in England and imported to the United States, the movement sought to re-brand Christianity by tracing the importance of sport back to the apostles.

The goal of Muscular Christianity and of its institutions like the YMCA and YWCA was to encourage both physical and spiritual health, while bringing more people into the church. Jamieson writes, "Churches, which sometimes had the best recreational facilities in town, built gymnasiums and summer camps for altruistic and practical reasons. Athletics taught young people appropriate Protestant values while reinforcing the image of the body as a temple. In addition to saving city children, gymnasiums and summer camps also attracted members, which improved the church's finances and standing in the local community." Zirin notes that political leaders and ruling elites quickly took notice and saw that sports could be useful in combating their own concerns about social unrest after the Civil War. With the industrial North having defeated the agrarian South, people immigrated to the country in huge numbers, which helped meet the labor demands of the growing economy, but it also created a host of social problems like overcrowding in the cities, garbage, poverty, and crime in the streets, as well as the eternal ruling-class fear of what might happen if a large number of highly exploited people get together and try to do something about being highly exploited. The wealthy and powerful saw that sports was a way of assimilating and socializing poor, working-class immigrants into American culture, and they were quick to lend financial support, underwriting and funding sports leagues and institutions like the "Y" as philanthropic endeavors.

"Muscular Christianity was the intellectual base for the Young Men's Christian Association," writes Jamieson, and with Naismith having invented the sport in a YMCA, it might best be said that basketball literally came out of that tradition that believed sports were not just salubrious but could teach important values.

Naismith and his wife Maude arrived in Lawrence, Kansas, in September 1898. He'd been hired to head KU's new Department of Physical Education, recommended by a colleague who described him as "the inventor of basketball, medical doctor, Presbyterian minister, teetotaler, all around athlete, non-smoker, and owner of a vocabulary without cuss words." Basketball had gained popularity quickly, spreading throughout the northeast, but was slower to reach the rest of the country, and upon his arrival in Lawrence, Naismith found the university had no basketball team. He sought to rectify the situation immediately, and soon the game caught on.

Naismith would live out the next forty-one years of his life in Lawrence. He is buried in Oak Hill Cemetery, where most of the victims of Quantrill's Raid are buried, and his grave is a popular destination for those wishing to pay their respects to the inventor of the game. Though he'd be involved with the University of Kansas until the end of his life, he coached the basketball team for only nine seasons, the last of which was 1906–1907 when it finished

7–8. He turned the coaching reins over to one of his most gifted players, Forrest Allen, who would lead Kansas to winning records the following two seasons before taking a ten-year sabbatical to study and practice medicine. Allen returned to coach KU in 1919, a post he would hold until 1956, when the compulsory retirement age at KU (seventy) forced him to retire just as he had recruited the greatest player ever to play for Kansas: Wilt Chamberlain. During his time, Allen would coach Kansas to twenty-four conference titles, two Helms Athletic Foundation national titles in 1922 and 1923, and an NCAA title in 1952. Along the way he became known worldwide by his nickname, "Phog."

Phog Allen is often referred to as the "Father of Basketball Coaching," and it's easy to illustrate the accuracy of the title. He retired with 746 career coaching wins, a record that would later be broken by Adolph Rupp—who played for Phog at KU—whose record in turn would be broken by Dean Smith, who also played for Phog at KU. Other great Hall-of-Fame coaches, including Dutch Lonborg, Ralph Miller, and Frosty Cox, also played for Phog. To give you a sense of scale: the three winningest basketball programs in the history of the sport are Kentucky, Kansas, and North Carolina, and their greatest coaches Adolph Rupp, Phog Allen, and Dean Smith all played at Kansas, with Rupp and Smith learning the game from Phog, who in turn learned the game from Naismith himself. It's a tingly, shivers-inducing thing to ponder if you love the game.

And what's fascinating about looking back at the relationship between these two patriarchal totems of the sport, the Father of the Game and the Father of Basketball Coaching, is that you see the way Naismith and Allen were in effect debating the nature and purpose of the game, engaging in a veritable Obi Wan vs. Darth Vader–style lightsaber fight for the soul of basketball.

Naismith and Allen were never terribly close, though they maintained a respectful working relationship, which was necessary since Naismith was the director of the physical education department, a position different from what we'd call an athletic director today in that Naismith had little role in overseeing or managing the university sports teams, but nonetheless he and Allen ran in the same circles at KU. Their sense of what basketball was and their vision for what it should be would come into conflict, but their key differences revolved around how authority, competition, and commercialism affected the game.

It is widely remarked upon, usually with a chuckle, that of the eight coaches in Kansas basketball history Naismith, with an overall record of

55–60, is the only one with a losing record. This had less to do with the fact that he wasn't good at coaching or teaching—he was one of KU's most beloved professors and instructors—than that it didn't interest him, and it didn't interest him because he believed the game belonged to the players, not coaches. What authority he did exercise was less as coach than as referee (he often had to referee his own team's games before the sport got big, exercising a sense of judicious objectivity that surely drove his players crazy at times), trying to enforce the rules and keep the game from becoming too rough and unsportsmanlike. It was the players who would direct the flow of the game and who together would determine the outcome. He writes of watching a game in which players had been "mechanized" through the repeated drilling of a coach to run specific plays: "These players were not allowed to think for themselves." Later in the same game a player on this team stole the ball and scored a layup at the other end of the court. Naismith and the "crowd wildly acclaimed this feat, but the boy was removed from the game for failure to follow exactly the instructions of the coach. . . . It was to practices like these that I objected. Why should the play of a group of young men be entirely spoiled to further the ambitions of some coach?"

James Naismith's bottom-up, decentralized approach to coaching was the complete opposite of Phog Allen's highly centralized, coach-as-benevolent-dictator approach; if measuring success in terms of wins and losses, Allen's approach was superior to his mentor's, though it's obvious Naismith used a different arithmetic to calculate victory. In his biography of Naismith, Rob Rains writes:

> It was obvious that Naismith and Allen had different approaches to their jobs, a difference in attitude about their work. Allen's most publicized slogan was that he taught his teams to "play to win," while Naismith always maintained that he wanted his athletes to do their best, but it didn't really matter to him whether they won or not. Naismith often said that sports should fulfill three purposes: to play for the fun of playing, to engage in physical activity to aid the overall development of the body, and to learn sportsmanship through being a member of a team. Winning was never mentioned as a goal by Naismith.

There is a story, perhaps apocryphal, that perfectly captures the different stances the two men took toward coaching. In 1906 administrators from Baker University, a small college outside of Lawrence, wrote Naismith to inquire whether his young star Phog Allen, then only a sophomore, would be interested in coaching the team the following year. Naismith called Allen into his office and was apparently amused to inform him of Baker's interest. Defensive, Allen asked what was so funny about that. But Naismith wasn't casting doubt upon his pupil's knowledge of the game. His answer to Allen was simply: "You can't coach basketball, you just play it."

It's necessary to tease a line of thought on the relationship between winning and competition. Though Naismith didn't prize the former, he believed there was a place for the latter. It's an important distinction, one I've often struggled with myself because I have an aversion to competition in most areas of life, and yet, it's the lifeblood of sports. Even for a basketball nut like me, it would take an amazing act of self-discipline to watch a basketball game where the players weren't trying and there was no time and score, neither team winning or losing. Time and score are ways of marking the boundaries of the game, giving it shape and structure, but they are also indicators of and incentivizers to give maximal effort, which is to say, to compete. And competition gives the game what my writing instructors used to say that meaningful and consequential conflict gives fiction: stakes, the sense that you're playing for something that matters. The reason it works in sports is that, as in fiction, the stakes are largely an illusion. Unlike most areas of competition in our society, winning a basketball game does not come at the expense of depriving the losing team of something materially significant, like an education or livelihood.

This is not to say that competition in sports can't have negative consequences. Problems and confusion abound when we overinvest the essentially meaningless with absolute and singular meaning, when we trust the reality of the illusion too much, when we insist on turning fiction to fact—which has certainly been encouraged by the ever-increasing commercialism of the game. But before moving on, we need to make clear that although both Naismith and Allen valued competition in basketball, they valued it in very different ways. Allen's winning-is-the-only-thing-that-matters take on competition was different from Naismith, who saw it as a mechanism or trigger that would enable the players and the game to reach its full potential. Put another way: for Allen you competed to win the game, and for Naismith you competed to play the game in its most artful and meaningful way. In the last chapter of his book, titled "The Values of Basketball," Naismith gives us a good sense of what full potential might mean, outlining the twelve attributes he believes the game strives to engender: initiative, agility, accuracy, alertness, cooperation, skill, reflex judgment, speed, self-confidence, self-sacrifice, self-control, and sportsmanship.

From today's vantage, it's hard to imagine a time when elite sports teams weren't essentially businesses, either nakedly so as at the professional level or as potential revenue-makers at the collegiate level. But it wasn't always so, though the transition from sports as purely recreational to professional advanced quickly. Naismith saw what was in the offing, and as early as 1911 he gave an address on the matter. A transcription of the speech was published in the May 1911 issue of the *Graduate Magazine* of the University of Kansas under the title "Commercialism in Sports." It's a well-written and carefully argued polemic about "insidious growth of commercialism" and its ability to "destroy one of the greatest forces of education."

Drawing heavily on the work of E. Norman Gardner, Naismith opens by going back to "the time of Homer," arguing that the ancient Greeks faced the same problem we would face two-and-a-half millennia later. Initially sports weren't organized affairs, he says. In pre-Olympic times they were

> spontaneous activities of the leisure class celebrated chiefly at the funerals of great men. The rewards at this time were given in memory of the dead rather than for the reward of the victor, and were given to the losing contestants as well as to the winners. The worth of the prizes indicated the amount of honor to the dead and these gifts were in many cases of great value.

From there, he moves to the Olympics, which carried on this spirit through the first several Olympiads but gradually became more popular and competitive, spurring the development of a professional class of athletes that brought with it the simultaneous debasement of the sport and competitors, from Olympians who bribed opponents to lose, to the extreme specializations and training that destroyed the body.

Me quoting Naismith quoting Gardner: "'The popularity of the athletics, the growth of competition, and the rewards lavished on successful athletes completely changed the character of sport. The events remained the same, but a change came over the attitude of the performers and spectators.'" That last bit warrants repeating: the sports didn't change; the attitudes toward them did.

Naismith transitions from the antiquity to modernity, drawing parallels between the "evils that wrecked the ancient games" and what he saw happening with sports in the twenty years since he invented the game of basketball. He begins this final movement of his talk by comparing the arguments in favor of commercializing the sport with his own counterarguments. Of the seven pro arguments, the two most persuasive and that umbrella most of the others are that people should have the freedom to "turn skill into coin," and that doing so will raise the quality of play across the board.

The sixteen counterarguments that close Naismith's speech are too numerous to quote in full, but among them are concerns that commercialism leads to overtraining and the breaking down of athletes' bodies, it makes work of sport and turns it into a spectacle instead of recreation, and it puts the emphasis on winning instead of enjoyment and personal development and thus encourages breaking the rules and stimulates betting. He also says it leads to "worship of the dollar" and "class distinction, for when a man is paid for his services in athletics he is on a different level from the man who buys him."

Over one hundred years after Naismith gave that speech, I imagine him going absolutely centrifugal in his grave, given the current landscape of sports, particularly basketball and football, in universities. As William J. Baker writes in his introduction to Naismith's book, "Whatever its later commercial developments, basketball was made for principled play, not for profit. . . . Naismith designed his new game for athletes to enjoy, not for coaches, television networks, or corporate sponsors to control."

Phog Allen, in contrast, was quick to realize the monetizing potential of the game. One of the issues he and Naismith clashed over was whether tickets should be sold for KU games, which by the time Allen had returned to coach KU in 1919 had become quite popular. Again, Rains: "Allen wanted to use the strong interest in basketball that was developing on campus to generate as many sold tickets as possible, while Naismith considered selling tickets an exploitation of the student athletes. Allen argued that bringing money in to the university through the sale of basketball tickets would benefit the other university sports as well." There's compelling logic in both positions, but the chancellor agreed with Allen. That same chancellor, Ernest Lindley, demoted Naismith from director of the physical education department a couple of years later. The person he appointed to replace him was Phog Allen. And so, while Allen had consolidated total control of the athletic department, Naismith receded to the background, focusing on his teaching, mentoring, and ministering. There are accounts of Naismith occasionally attending KU basketball games, sitting alone in the stands impassively while the crowd went wild around him.

I do not mean to paint Phog Allen as a villain. The truth of the matter is that even had he shared Naismith's views on the sport, basketball would have ended up where it is today. Simply put, the values and purpose of the game, as envisioned by Naismith, are so at odds with the values and purpose of American business. Allen was shrewdly adapting the game to the larger societal forces going on in the world at the time, the explosion of American capitalism and the commodification of our lives in ways never before known. For this reason Naismith was derisively viewed as behind the times or out of step or unrealistic or simply nostalgic. With every rule change and adaptation, every small step toward commercialism, he would warn to not stray too far from the game and rules he'd invented. "It was the best game," he would continue to asseverate, even as he felt it slipping through his fingers.

F. Scott Fitzgerald was right: it's a hard thing to hold two seemingly contradictory things in your head at once. Yet, somehow I know that when I'm cartwheeling down the block after a KU victory or pensively staring out a window after a loss, when I'm watching YouTube clips of a player KU is recruiting two years down the line or spending an hour on the phone dissecting KU's performance against a Division II team in the preseason, I'm swearing allegiance to the game that Phog Allen helped create and perfect, and part of me loves these aspects of the game, the insane carried-away-ness of fandom. But I also know that when I look back on my time playing the game, the thing I most appreciate was not the fun I had on the court, but the values basketball instilled in me, the bullshit platitudes that happen to be true: teamwork, discipline, cooperation, effort, solidarity, commitment to something bigger than yourself. Those were the kinds of values Naismith had in mind when he imagined basketball into existence, and he knew it was the game itself, not coaches, that could instill them in participants.

"Saints should always be judged guilty until they are proved innocent," wrote George Orwell in an essay on Mahatma Gandhi, adding, "but the tests that have to be applied to them are not, of course, the same in all cases." At times I've been tempted to see Naismith in a saintly light, despite Orwell's cautionary bonbon. The truth, however, is that I don't know enough about him to be able to issue an opinion on his case for canonization. But does it even matter? Isn't it enough that there's so much we do know that can be admired?

Naismith refereed some of the earliest women's basketball games and supported women's right to play sport, which sounds laughable now but was a highly controversial notion at the time. So too was his stance on race. He spends most of his book *Basketball: Its Origin and Development* detailing to the point of tedium his surprise and pleasure at seeing basketball played by so many different countries, cultures, and skin colors. At home, he was an antisegregationist and enacted those beliefs. Rains, in his biography, devotes an entire chapter to Naismith's mentorship of John McLendon, a black KU student in the phys-ed department whom Naismith helped navigate through the virulent racism of the time to become a very successful teacher at integrated schools as well as a coach. Ultimately McLendon was elected to the Basketball Hall of Fame in 1979. In an interview at the time, forty years after his mentor's death, McLendon said: "Dr. Naismith didn't know anything about color or nationality. He was so unconscious about your economic or religious background. He just saw everyone as potential."

And furthermore, Naismith did his good works without any expectation of reciprocation. He understood, like a skillful assist to an open teammate, that giving was the gift. He writes about this in his book. Of his younger self, he states: "For several years I had been wondering what I wanted to accomplish; finally I decided that the only real satisfaction that I would ever derive from life was to help my fellow beings." His personal motto was: "Leave the world a little better for having lived in it." Elsewhere he writes, "Thousands of times, especially in the last few years, I have been asked whether I got anything out of basketball. To answer this question, I can only smile. It would be impossible for me to explain my feelings to the great mass of people who ask this question, as my pay has not been in dollars but in the satisfaction of giving something to the world that is a benefit to masses of people."

I'll grant that a lot of that sounds like something you'd read on a cross-stitch sampler in the Cracker Barrel gift shop. Naismith's bromides provoke suspicion, sounding like the sort of thing a very calculating person would want remembered for posterity. He's almost so good and humble that you distrust it because it feels like the humility of one consciously participating in his own deification. And I would remain doubtful, cynical even, except that his beliefs are bolstered by fact and action. Consider that he could have patented the game he invented—imagine the boatloads of money—but chose not to because it didn't "belong" to him. Consider that he never really made a dime off basketball, turning down countless endorsement opportunities. Consider that the book in which these quotes appeared was written with great reluctance and not as a moneymaker, but because his children knew the story of the game needed to be recorded and preserved. He and his family bore the material cost of not cashing in on basketball. The Naismiths were not wealthy, but they weren't poor the way many were poor in those years. It is enough to say they got by, at times barely, on his modest professor's salary.

Naismith derived satisfaction not from material comforts so much as knowing that he had passed the gift on.

I am sure no man can derive more pleasure from money or power than I do from seeing a pair of basketball goals in some out of the way place—deep in the Wisconsin woods an old barrel hoop nailed to a tree, or a weather-beaten shed on the Mexican border with a rusty iron rim nailed to one end. These sights are constant reminders that I have in some measure accomplished the objective that I set up years ago.

That was enough for him.

I came across a story in Rains's biography about how Naismith began missing mortgage payments after KU cut professors' salaries when the Great Depression hit. The bank threatened to foreclose, but someone intervened to make arrangements on Naismith's behalf. That person was Phog Allen, stepping in to offer help when his old mentor needed it. A few years later, in 1936, when basketball was officially added to the Olympics, Allen began a nationwide campaign to raise funds so that Naismith could attend the games in Berlin, a successful effort that afforded Naismith one of his most cherished memories: tossing the ball up at the very first Olympic basketball game.

SpiritDancer
Dennis Rogers

I will always be known as the SpiritDancer, named for a song written and sung by BlackHawk. I dance with determination and cause. My steps become fluid motion. Natural movements. My dances give the appearance that my feet are not touching the ground. That I am in the presence of a Spirit. That my elders are pleased by me. When I am dancing I do not see people or audiences. I'm only focused on the drum beat and the song that's being sung. Like a chameleon, I change my appearances. I become a Warrior, a Spirit, an elder, a healer, a teacher, a storyteller in motion.

I have always danced in some form or another, but the beat of the pow-wow drum resonated within me and drew me into the circle. In my early childhood years my family attended a pow-wow where I became entrenched in movement, in feathers, colors, culture, and history. As a student at Haskell Indian Junior College from 1989 to 1991, I received my eagle feathers and began making dancing regalia. Thinking of where I would dance next. Or for what cause. Seeing the possibilities that by dancing I could eke out a livelihood while still being an active substitute teacher. I've danced everywhere—from school classrooms to Boy Scout and Girl Scout gatherings, from local fairs and events to churches and assisted living facilities, from museums, libraries, and universities to historical sites and cemeteries. Dancing has become my way of life; most everyone knows me as a Native dancer, artist, and educator. Each of these labels requires knowledge, research, study, practice, and presentation. Dancing on stage at concerts is very different from at a school auditorium or a concert venue. Wherever I dance, I do my best to project pride and honor through my dancing.

I have chosen to make Kansas my home. My state has 105 counties. Twelve are named after a Native American tribe, and four others have a Native word or meaning, for a total of sixteen. Their names dance on the tongue, from Kiowa to Cherokee, from Comanche to Shawnee, from Wyandotte to Ottawa. Four tribal reservations reside in Kansas: the Iowa, the Sac & Fox, the Kickapoo, and the Prairie Band of Potawatomi. These tribes were relocated from their traditional homelands, removed to Kansas as a result of the 1830 Indian Removal Act drafted by President Andrew Jackson. The forced removal of Native populations caused great loss of lives. As a result of cultural assimilation, Native children were forced to speak English, to read and write in English, to learn the Christian religion, and to suffer separation from family as they were coerced into attending Indian boarding schools.

My father was one such child who suffered under the hands of church leaders and school administrators. I believe my parents chose to remain in Kansas so that my brother and sister and I could attend public schools in Topeka. In 1964 I attended an *all*-white school in West Topeka. Our family were the *only* dark-skinned children in the school, and my educational upbringing was different from other students' experiences. I was bilingual, and by the time I reached the third grade, I faced learning difficulties with reading, spelling, and math—multiplying and dividing. I did not learn how to tell time on a standard wall clock until I was in the ninth grade. In middle school and then high school, I was a standout athlete. Wrestling was my way of expressing my skills and abilities. I went undefeated for two years. In 1971 I started judo lessons. This would prove to be a life direction for me. I went to tournaments monthly in various states and across Kansas. I rose in the ranks and dominated the first-place trophy standings. I earned my Shodan (first-degree) black belt in 1984. While a student at Washburn University I was a student ambassador to Japan, in 1993 and 1994. In Japan, I was promoted to Sandan (third-degree) black belt. I am an eight-time Kansas state champion.

What does a Japanese martial art form have to do with being a Native American? Well, it taught me that the more I learned about other cultures, the more I learned about myself. I learned to speak Japanese. In 1993 I attended both Kanagawa University and Fukuoka University. Both were positive experiences, and I was honored to be the student ambassador leader representing Washburn University.

I have continued to be an ambassador. As SpiritDancer, I realize that many of my audiences know very little of Indian culture. When dancing for students, I know these kids are seeing Indian dances for their first time. When I'm dancing at pow-wows, I realize that I am among seasoned dancers. Dancing and traveling go together, and my dancing has been requested at many events and functions as an "edu-tainer." I am not an act, or a choreographer, or entertainment. I am an edu-cultural specialist of dance, traveling all across Kansas, where not so many years ago I might have been taken prisoner and punished, starved, beaten, even killed. But in today's world I am welcomed, invited in, and treated with respect and consideration. I do not need to fear for my life. I value what my eyes can see when I travel across Kansas. The crop fields, trees, Flint Hills, rivers, cliffs, even the dry hot temperatures.

I often reflect on the responsibilities bestowed upon me as a dancer. Through my travels to distant places my eyes behold the beauty of Mother Earth and Father Sky. Creation stories told to me as a child make sense now as I tell them to my grandchildren. I tell the story of how I became a dancer, explain what I am dancing for and what goes through my mind, my body, my heart. I want young kids to meet me, listen to me, watch me, and learn from my teachings. Today, I dance as honorably as I did when I started thirty-five years ago.

I live in the same neighborhood I grew up in, fifteen houses from my mother, who still lives in my childhood home. I have always believed that doing community service is a privilege, not a punishment. I encourage Native students to follow their hearts, to learn about themselves, and to get involved in activities that promote healthy lifestyles and way of life. Being an American Indian in today's society is still a struggle and challenge for many. I think I have succeeded because my parents supported me in my endeavors. I draw strength in knowing my Navajo grandparents never learned to speak English. Never attended school. Could not write their names, never drove a vehicle or used a telephone. They lived without modern utilities, in a remote location in northern Arizona. I spent my summers every year with them. My Navajo was not that fluent, and neither was their English. But we managed to communicate and enjoyed life without the technology deemed so important and necessary to prosper and achieve wealth and success.

At sixty-five years of age, I find myself at ease and at peace with my surroundings. I have achieved many goals and milestones that others only see as a dream. What will become of my dance regalia, my eagle feathers, my legacy when I walk into the happy hunting grounds? I do not know. Will one of my grandchildren continue my life's work? Will my life's efforts go untold to future Kansans? I am a Native living in the twenty-first century but utilizing nineteenth-century methods of teaching. I live a simple, stress-free life, and my dancing keeps me active. I do not seek fame or fortune. I remain humble and grateful that our Creator has guided me upon a good path in life, a spiritual path that has afforded me many wonderful gifts: a life with family, a home, and a community I believe in. It is my hope and belief that when someday I walk on, my moccasins will be laced up and carried forward, or my works and efforts to teach students will become part of Kansas history: the story of a little Indian boy from Topeka, Kansas, who lived in a different generation with his own guidelines and rules.

And it is so. . . . Amen.

How Kansas Gave Texas the Boot

Jim Hoy

Mounted herders, and their footwear, have existed since the dawn of recorded history, but it was the Texas-to-Kansas trail drives of the late 1860s that gave birth to the American cowboy. Naturally enough, the earliest cowboy bootmakers are also associated with these two states, as suppliers for the cattle trade set up shop in the towns where the drives ended, or where the herds were shaped up for the trek north. The 1870 and 1880 censuses indicate that Kansas bootmakers were more numerous than their Texas counterparts, and they appear to have been more influential in the development of the cowboy boot, particularly in the early years. Determining just when and where the first real pair of cowboy boots was made, however, is an unanswerable question, not only because of the scarcity of historical records, but also because it is difficult to determine what was considered a cowboy boot in the 1870s.

The cowboy boot has obviously undergone numerous transformations and incarnations since T. C. McInerney opened his shop at the end of the trail in Abilene in 1868 and began to cater to the cowboy trade. The early-day drovers wore everything from laced work shoes to military boots, which had a high stovepipe top, a low flat heel, and a broad round toe. Like other bootmakers who operated in Kansas during the first decade of the cattle drives, McInerney apparently built a drover's boot from a military model.

Kansas bootmakers have long been credited with firsts, bests, and biggest in the folklore of the West. Kansas folklore tells us that one of the first boot styles associated primarily with the cowboy was the Coffeyville boot, which seems to have been developed sometime in the late 1860s to mid-1870s. Named after the Kansas town, the Coffeyville boot had such a reputation that it was mentioned in a cowboy folksong, "The Dad-Blamed Boss": "I'll buy a new slicker and some Coffeyville boots." The boot may have been available as early as 1876, when bootmaker J. W. Cubine moved to Coffeyville. Cubine's boot seems to have represented a transition between the military style and the cowboy boot. Its high top was straight across the back and rounded in front, and it had a high heel and a broad, round toe. Sometimes a red leather star was sewn onto the top front in a successful effort to attract the Texas cowboy. Cubine's Coffeyville shop produced some of the country's best boots from 1876 until it closed in 1931. The Coffeyville boot was contemporaneous with Charles Hyer's boots built in Olathe, Kansas.

Conflicting accounts credit both Hyer and Cubine with an innovation in boot making that seems rather obvious: making a right-footed boot on a last shaped to the right foot, and a left-footed one on a similar last for the left foot. The belief is that before the days of the cattle drives, each boot in a pair was identical to the other and was shaped to the right or left foot by wear alone. This legend appears to have remarkable persistence. In 1847 British shoe historian J. Sparkes Hall vainly attempted to clear up the confusion concerning "the idea that right and left shoes are a comparatively modern invention." Nearly 180 years later, the story still circulates. It is true that for centuries most shoes and boots were not shaped to the contours of the left and right foot. However, in 1818 a process to manufacture wooden lasts by machine was invented, and factories turned out left and right lasts routinely. Even though the truth may well lie somewhere else, folklore confers the honor of this innovation to one of these two Kansas bootmakers.

Tradition also credits Charles H. Hyer with inventing the first distinctive cowboy boot in the mid-1870s. Hyer was born to German parents in New York before the family moved to Illinois, where Hyer's father was a practicing shoemaker. A job with the railroad brought Hyer to Leavenworth. After quitting the railroad, he found work as foreman of the shoe shop at the Kansas School for the Deaf in Olathe.

According to a story passed down through newspapers, company promotional materials, and the Hyer family, the cowboy boot was developed when a Colorado cowboy, on his way home from the Kansas City stockyards, stopped by Hyer's Olathe shop sometime in 1875. He wanted a pair of new boots but built differently from his Civil War military-style footwear. He preferred a pointed toe that would slide more easily into a stirrup; a high, slanted heel that would hold a stirrup on a pitching horse; and a high top that was scalloped in front and back rather than a smooth stovepipe style. As other cowboys saw and admired Hyer's handiwork, orders started coming into the shop. Before long, not only was Hyer operating a boot-making factory that employed scores of workers, but other bootmakers were being influenced by his innovations, including a mail-order system in which the customer provided his own foot measurements.

How valid is this traditional account? There is no reason to doubt that the basic outline is factually correct, according to Dean Hyer. But even though he likes the idea of his grandfather having invented the cowboy boot, Dean Hyer also believes that by the mid-1870s the cowboy boot was an idea whose time had come, and other bootmakers throughout cattle country were independently creating similar innovations. Texas bootmaker Henry Leopold, for instance, has said that his father, Frederick William Leopold, was employed in Coffeyville to make slant-heeled boots for cowboys perhaps as early as 1869. German-born John Mueller opened a boot shop in Ellsworth in 1872, then moved it west to Dodge City two years later following the cattle trade. A man named Aley had a boot shop in Coffeyville as early as 1875. We also know that H. J. Justin moved to Spanish Fort, Texas, in the 1880s (1879 according to Texas tradition) to set up shop and catch the cowboy trade at the starting point of the cattle drives. Undoubtedly there was much polygenesis in the development of drovers' footwear.

However, wherever and whenever the first cowboy boots were made, Kansas bootmakers played an important role in their overall development. The Coffeyville boot was important enough to be recorded in song, whereas the Hyer Boot Company soon became one of the leading boot manufacturers in the country. Moreover, Blucher boots, considered by many working cowhands to be the best cowboy boots ever made, were produced for many years in an Olathe shop across the street from Hyer. G. C. Blucher was a Missouri bootmaker and shoemaker who was hired to run the shop floor for the Justin Company in Texas. After several decades in Texas, Blucher moved to Cheyenne, Wyoming, in 1915 and opened his own shop.

The winters there proved too severe, both for himself and for some of the workers who had accompanied him from Texas, and in 1918 he moved to Olathe. Among the innovations folklore attributes to him are the undershot heel and the streamlined toe, which combines the appearance of a round and a square box toe. When Gus Blucher died around 1930, an associate named Flournoy bought the business and continued operations until his death in the mid-1960s. At that point John Payne became the owner, and in 1969 he moved everything to Fairfax, Oklahoma. The company has since changed hands and locations several times, but it is currently in Beggs, Oklahoma, producing high-quality boots in traditional Blucher designs. The Hyer Boot Company closed in 1977 but was relaunched by great-great-grandson Zach Lawless in 2010.

Much of the Hyer equipment, however, and many of its designs, have remained in Olathe. During the late 1970s, Ron Orscheln bought many of the lasts, dies, and machines and started a new company, Olathe Boot

Company. The first boots came out of the company in mid-1978; fifteen years later, fifty employees were producing 180 pairs of good-quality factory boots per day. About 80 percent of this number were custom ordered, although not custom made. That is, the customer selected features such as style, leather, and stitching, but the boots are made in standard sizes, not individually lasted to the customer's measurements. Sales are nationwide, with some international outlets in Canada and England. In addition to cowboy boots, Olathe Boot Company caters to some smaller niche markets such as English-style polo boots and jodhpur boots.

In their heyday, when Hyer was the country's leading cowboy boot manufacturer and Blucher did the best custom work, both companies had a long list of celebrity clients. The daddy of all Western heroes, Buffalo Bill Cody, was a Hyer customer. Early movie stars such as William S. Hart, Harry Carey, Ruth Roland, Buck Jones, Ken Maynard, Gene Autry, Joel McCrea, Will Rogers, and Clark Gable all wore Hyer boots, as did presidents Coolidge, Eisenhower, and Teddy Roosevelt. So too did showmen Tex Austin, Zach Miller, and Pawnee Bill; rodeo cowboys Yakima Canutt and Booger Red; and author Will James. Tom Mix wore both Hyers and Bluchers, while John Wayne, Monte Montana, and Ben Johnson were Blucher customers, along with outlaw Emmett Dalton and, more recently, country singer Reba McEntire.

Considering that the cowboy boot was derived from a military model, it is not surprising that some boot companies made boots for both markets. Company representatives known as fitters, some from as far away as England, would travel from military post to military post measuring feet and taking orders from cavalry officers for custom boots. Two of the major suppliers were based in Kansas: Hyer and Teitzel-Jones. Military boots were Teitzel-Jones's main business.

J. C. Teitzel was originally headquartered in 1884 at Junction City, adjacent to Fort Riley, which had one of the largest, and the last, horse cavalry units in the country. In 1916 he and his partner C. C. Dehner moved the company to Wichita so they could concentrate on making boots instead of repairing them and be close to a steady supply of labor. At that time Schuyler Jones bought into the company, then took over sole ownership in 1930. When the horse cavalry was phased out during World War II, so was the steady market for English riding boots. Thus Teitzel-Jones began making cowboy boots, a venture that lasted only until 1950.

In the meantime, a former Teitzel-Jones employee, Carl McDowell, had opened his boot shop in Wichita. McDowell got his start in 1933 just out of high school as a general handyman for Teitzel-Jones; when he left in 1946, he was foreman of the bottoming room, where the vamps are attached to the soles.

In the interim, McDowell had experienced every aspect of boot making. Sensing the coming drop in demand for military boots, he quit the company. He set his sights on supplying boots for the ranchers and working cowboys of the Gypsum Hills and Flint Hills in Kansas and the Osage Hills in Oklahoma, many of whom were more or less steady customers at the Wichita Livestock Exchange, across the street from his shop.

Thus, McDowell's boots, although well-crafted and fine in detail, were never as fancy as some of those from the better-known Texas shops. Nor did he try to expand his business into a mass production factory. At its peak the McDowell Boot Company never had more than three employees, made only a few hundred pairs of boots per year, and never sought customers from beyond a two-hundred-mile radius of Wichita. Rather than get rich, McDowell was content to earn a living making fine boots, with the help of his wife, Martha, who stitched tops and handled orders.

A number of husband-and-wife teams are found among Kansas bootmakers, including Bob and Jolene Baker of Garden City. Both are graduates of the boot- and saddle-making curriculum of Oklahoma State Technical University at Okmulgee, and both are former rodeo competitors. Once they started a family, however, they decided that a boot shop might be more financially secure than rodeoing. In 1977, about the time they were finishing at Okmulgee, they bought the entire shop contents of an octogenarian cobbler in Cimarron and moved everything to Garden City. In addition to making boots, they repair saddles, boots, and shoes and sell tack.

The late Fred Hammon and his wife, Carolyn, comprised another husband-wife team of bootmakers. Fred was Hyer's floor manager when the company sold in 1978. Like Carl McDowell, Hammon had begun work just out of high school in 1953 as a general handyman. During his years with Hyer he learned the entire two-hundred-plus-step process of boot making. When the new owners moved the company to El Paso, the Hammons bought some of the equipment and set up shop in Gardner, a few miles southwest of Olathe, in the spring of 1981. With two employees, one to last bottoms and the other to stitch tops, Fred and Carolyn began turning out about thirty pairs of boots a week. Fred's major contribution was measuring feet, building lasts, and performing finish work. Carolyn would skive (trim) the leather, mark patterns, and sew in beading and counters; everything that the laster and stitcher did not do. Unfortunately, Fred died in the fall of 1986, and Carolyn sold the business five years later. Olathe saddle maker George Steinberger bought the company, and Carolyn taught him to make boots. Thus, through the Hammons, the Hyer tradition continues. Carolyn has also passed on her boot-making knowledge to James Holmes, Bill Gomer, and her children, Gregg and Christine.

Jim Holenbeck learned to make boots from a trade school and from the more traditional apprenticeship method. Jim worked for several Utah saddle makers in the mid-1970s, then in 1979 took a job with legendary Texas bootmaker Charlie Dunn. His workbench was directly behind Dunn's, so Holenbeck could observe the master at work. Dunn insisted on quality. The smallest error in stitching had to be corrected, even if the mistake would have been hidden in the final product. And Dunn was meticulous in measuring feet, a lesson Holenbeck learned well: if you get the measurements wrong, the boots do not fit and you have to make a new pair, or the customer finds another bootmaker. By having served as Dunn's apprentice, Holenbeck maintained a dual tradition: his ancestor Bill Blasing was a bootmaker during the 1890s in the same area of the Flint Hills (between Manhattan and Alma), and Charles Dunn himself was apprenticed to a bootmaker in 1898 at age eight. As do the Bakers, Holenbeck finds that the lucrative repair business can inhibit making new boots and saddles.

In addition to professional bootmakers who began through technical school programs, such as Dave Treptow of Lawrence, Darrel Krug of Russell, and Brian Chambers of Salina, several Kansans have made a few pairs of boots as sidelines. The late Murray Edwards, for example, was a working cowboy from Atwood who could make boots and saddles as well as spin a rope and play the fiddle. Marvin Ferguson of Preston, who retired to Kansas from the military in 1965, is a saddler who also has made boots. Archie Leach of Sedan is another Kansas bootmaker who took up the trade in retirement. He learned boot and shoe repair from his father in the 1920s, and he had bought a number of lasts and other equipment in the 1930s when he ran a small repair service. When he took a job with the Caney Valley Electric Cooperative, he closed his shop and sold the lasts. Then in 1982 Leach retired and bought the lasts back from the man who had purchased them nearly a half-century earlier. Rather than take up golf, Leach installed boot-making equipment in his garage. He began turning out several pairs of boots a month, partly because he enjoyed working with leather and partly because it was a link to his heritage.

Today, Kansas has cowboy boot manufacturers for the mass market and a number of individual artisans who custom-make boots one pair at a time.

These bootmakers are keeping alive a tradition of craftsmanship that goes back, through Blucher and Cubine, to what some like to think of as the very origin of the cowboy boot in Charles Hyer's boot shop in 1875. One hopes that this tradition will continue as part of the Kansas cultural heritage.

I'll end this essay on a personal note: Kenneth, my late father, wore Blucher boots his whole adult life, with the exception of one pair of Mc-Dowells, which he undoubtedly bought because his brother, Marshall, wore only McDowells. Neither man was wealthy, but like many old-time cowboys, they would skimp on necessities in order to afford the luxury of custom-made boots.

My parents drove me from Cassoday to Olathe when I was fourteen to get my first pair of Bluchers. I have since worn out three or four pairs, and still have some ten pairs on my boot shelf.

Digital Homesteading, or The Traveler's Home

Rolf Potts

On January 29, 1997, I threw a Kansas Day party at a house I shared with five other North American expatriates in the mountain-fringed Oncheon neighborhood of Busan, South Korea. I'd been in Asia for two months, and it was the first time I'd lived anywhere outside of the United States.

Everyone who lived in the house worked as English as a Foreign Language (EFL) teachers at *hagwons*, private afterschool academies that augmented the nation's hyper-competitive educational system. Since a newly industrialized and outward-looking South Korea had embraced the ethos of *segyehwa* (roughly, "globalization"), *hagwon* jobs were easy to come by for native English speakers with any sort of university degree. *Hagwons* didn't typically require teaching experience or certification, so most of us, as young expatriate teachers, made up the curriculum as we went. Our teenage students already had a competent grasp of English grammar, which meant that our job as teachers was simply to generate conversations and guide them in the ways of pronunciation and vernacular.

My initial conversation starters involved broad topics like global politics and pop culture, but I soon discovered that students became especially engaged whenever I talked about the place I came from. Both of my parents taught in Wichita public schools, so I often made use of their own materials and subject matter. A copy of my science-teacher dad's 1993 book *Watching Kansas Wildlife* sparked classroom conversations about the world's fauna; Kansas-themed bison and meadowlark stickers donated by my elementary-teacher mom served as prizes for pop quizzes. Most popular of all was a VHS video I'd made of my septuagenarian Kansas grandfather giving a jolly, swear word–inclusive tour of his Coffey County farm. In a matter of weeks, my students alluded to the Flint Hills and Quivira National Wildlife Refuge with the same enthusiasm they had when speaking of Disneyland or Times Square.

This amused my roommates so much that they cheerfully assented to my Kansas Day beer bash. Part of the fun was that none of them knew much about my home state. Cathy from Ontario brought a bag of snacks honoring the "Kansas state flower," only to be told that they were pumpkin, and not sunflower, seeds. Stan from New Brunswick showed up costumed in a leather military jacket, but when he began to hold forth about the amphibious landings at Incheon, it became clear that he'd confused Dwight D. Eisenhower with Douglas MacArthur. I oversaw the evening's trivia contest, which proved popular with my beer-sodden roommates, mainly because the answers to all the questions ("What is the birthplace of the first African American person to win an Oscar?" "Where did Albert Einstein's disembodied brain reside for most of the 1980s?") were some variation on "Kansas."

Two years later, my Busan-teaching savings funded an open-ended, low-budget vagabonding journey across Asia into Europe and the Middle East. By this point Kansas had become more essential to my sense of identity than when I'd left the state a few years earlier—in part because, at a time when I had no real physical home, the *idea* of Kansas had a way of both grounding me and imbuing me with a sense of authenticity. Much like the acclaimed Independence-born playwright William Inge, who once quipped that "it wasn't until I got to New York that I became Kansan," living and traveling overseas had rejuvenated my relationship to the landscape in which I'd been raised. At a time in my life when I belonged to no single landscape, the simple pride I took in my Kansas roots allowed me to belong to the world in a grounded way.

As I made my way across Asia and points beyond, I began to submit travel-themed articles to various digital magazines that had sprung up amid the 1990s dialup-internet boom. I soon found that the specifics of my Kansas upbringing had left me with two useful strengths as a fledgling travel writer. First, being raised by Midwestern schoolteachers taught me that earnest, open-hearted curiosity about new places made it easier for me to discover intriguing travel stories than did any combination of erudite postulation, insider recommendations, or trend-driven fashion sense. Second, spending my youth in the under-touristed prairie landscape of Kansas had sharpened my instincts for intrigue and beauty in non-obvious places.

When Bill Bryson chose my Salon.com Thailand essay for inclusion in *The Best American Travel Writing 2000* alongside a bevy of accomplished journalists (including David Halberstam, P. J. O'Rourke, and William T.

Vollmann), I could more easily pitch unorthodox stories about under-traveled places to well-paying glossy magazines. In the years that followed, several of my essays landed on the *Best American* "Notable Mention" list. Most were stories reported from provincial regions of Laos, Myanmar, India, Australia, and Peru, that—much like Kansas—weren't on the radar of conventional tourism. To paraphrase what one *Conde Nast Traveler* editor said when I told her where I'd grown up, my prairie upbringing had somehow instilled in me "a talent for exploring landscapes that people don't really see until they slow down and take a closer look."

Much like the internet had offered me a venue to break into travel writing from the far side of the world, it also allowed me to develop my career while traveling overseas full-time. My business office was located wherever I'd stopped for the night (invariably in tandem with visits to the local internet café), and the increasing ubiquity of email—be it sent from France or Lebanon or Brazil—allowed me to respond to urgent editorial requests as readily as colleagues based in New York or San Francisco. In time, I began to share tips and philosophies about nomadic life on my rolfpotts.com website. With a big assist from a fellow Wichita North grad who'd landed an editorial job at Random House, I then published my first book, *Vagabonding: An Uncommon Guide to the Art of Long-Term World Travel*, in 2003.

Not long after *Vagabonding* was published, journalists and bloggers began to approach me for my perspective on what was then called "location-independent living." Young, digitally savvy web developers, marketers, and graphic designers had begun to use *Vagabonding* as a philosophical handbook as they endeavored to mix digital work with full-time travel. This trend, which blew up into a full-on global movement with the rise of remote-office software and smartphones in the decade that followed, eventually became known as "digital nomadism."

Ironically, I had grown weary of not having a physical place to call home. One of the core principles of the digital nomad movement was "geo-arbitrage"—the idea that one's income can create a more enjoyable lifestyle if one works remotely from cheaper parts of the world. According to that concept, income that barely affords the rent for a four-hundred-square-foot, fifth-floor walkup in New York City might easily pay for a three-bedroom penthouse in a building with a gym and a pool in Lisbon or Medellin or Chiang Mai. At various points in my global wanderings, I had lingered for several months in pleasant regions of Egypt, Argentina, and Thailand—not because travel writing had earned me copious amounts of money, but because food and lodging in those places hadn't cost much.

The thing was, none of those places ever felt like home to me, and for all my global wandering, I still, at heart, felt like a Kansan.

One day, I was stateside visiting family. My sister Kristin and her Hong Kong–raised husband, David, had returned to Kansas after a decade of living on the West Coast. Kristin had found work as an American Literature professor at Bethany College in Lindsborg, and David had landed a plant biologist position at The Land Institute near Salina. They now lived on a forty-acre farmstead in rural Saline County, and day-to-day life there proved much cheaper than the more urban life they'd led in California. Kristin presented me with a tantalizing insight: *If you're already leveraging your income by living in affordable global places rather than New York or San Francisco*, she posited, *why not embrace Kansas as an affordable global place as well? If Kansas really has helped you feel grounded in distant places, why not back that up by investing in actual Kansas ground?*

Within a matter of months, I'd initiated the process to acquire a thirty-acre plot of rural land that Kristin and David spotted for sale just two miles from their own farmstead. Because the property had two houses (and because I didn't have the financial means to buy it solo), my newly retired schoolteacher parents became my real-estate partners. Mom and Dad moved into the sturdy earth-contact house on the north edge of the property, and—with the help of everyone in my family, elementary-age nephews included—I began to renovate the decrepit double-wide that sat on the western fence line. Thanks to my years of travel, I regarded this collective-kindred undertaking not as a quaint provincial anomaly but as a resolutely global act—a variation on the communal family approach to land ownership that was still seen as the norm in places as far-flung as Mexico and Vietnam, Uganda and Sweden.

Much as my Canadian roommates had done one decade before in Korea, my New York– and San Francisco–based travel-writing colleagues regarded my embrace of Kansas with friendly bemusement. Whereas they'd considered my remote-work setups in Asia and Latin America as very much in keeping with the global ethos of travel, basing myself in rural Kansas struck some of them as a harbinger of defeat, or, at the very least, diminished possibility. At the time, returning to live in one's "flyover" home state was still equated with an inability to measure up to the standards of the metropole. While digital technology was redefining how media elites viewed the importance of place, digital nomadism never seemed to apply to life in nonurban America, even as the term was being applied to people living in rustic corners of Bali, Belize, and Estonia.

So it was that I became something of a "digital homesteader" over the course of the late aughts and 2010s, living a life that still felt global, even as it became more committed to a single piece of land. I continued to write travel stories (traveling overland to Ethiopia's Omo Valley for the *New York Times Magazine*, sailing from island to island in the Greek Cyclades for *Outside*, viewing wildlife in the remote South Atlantic for *National Geographic Traveler*), but each journey was bookended by activities like watching my nephews show 4-H pigs at the Tri-Rivers Fair, installing laminate flooring in my double-wide, or going for dirt-road runs along the rural pasturelands near my home.

In time, the intensified attention I gave to distant places as a writer came full-circle to Kansas itself. I reported a *New Yorker* "Talk of the Town" article about military reading lists from the US Army Command and General Staff College in Leavenworth; I reported a *Sports Illustrated* story about the murder of a college football player in McPherson; and I wrote an essay for *The Atlantic* about how social media had globalized Kansas City Royals fandom—transforming the very factors that made baseball communities "local"—amid the team's inspired 2014 run to the World Series.

The most fascinating magazine reporting project from my initial years back in Kansas was researching a biographical essay for *The Believer* about Emanuel Haldeman-Julius, the activist publisher who, in an idealistic effort to promote populist self-education, printed and sold hundreds of millions of inexpensive "Little Blue Books" out of Girard, Kansas, in the 1920s. As the subtitle to my *Believer* story noted, Haldeman-Julius's Little Blue Books endeavor created "a mail-order information superhighway that paved the way for the sexual revolution, influenced the feminist and Civil Rights movements, and foreshadowed the Age of Information." The prolific success of Little Blue Books lent Girard something of a cosmopolitan air, as mail orders arrived from around the world (Ethiopian emperor Haile Selassie was a customer), and the likes of Upton Sinclair, Will Durant, and Clarence Darrow journeyed to the little southeastern Kansas town to meet Haldeman-Julius and tour his printing plant.

Researching 1920s Kansas made me realize that the state had been in innovative and engaged conversation with a globalizing world for the better part of a century. Indeed, while Haldeman-Julius was revolutionizing populist publishing in Girard, William Allen White was influencing national opinion (and winning Pulitzer Prizes) from his newspaper office in Emporia. The nomadic Oscar Micheaux (for whom Great Bend was one of many homes) was pioneering independent filmmaking for Black

American audiences, around the same time Walt Anderson was pioneering the concept of fast food with his White Castle sliders in Wichita. Anderson's hamburgers proved popular with the factory workers of Travel Air Manufacturing Company, whose founders Clyde Cessna, Walter Beech, and Lloyd Stearman went on to have a huge influence on commercial aviation in the decades that followed. The single most storied aviation pioneer to emerge from Kansas during that era, of course, was Atchison-born Amelia Earhart.

For me as a travel writer, the most intriguing embodiment of the 1920s dialogue between Kansas and the world at large was the husband-and-wife filmmaking team of Martin and Osa Johnson. Originally from Independence and Chanute, the duo became international celebrities by depicting themselves having real-life onscreen adventures in the South Pacific, Borneo, and East Africa. Their 1928 documentary *Simba: King of the Beasts* influenced a century of nature films by introducing techniques like slow-motion photography and synchronized cameras to wildlife cinematography. So wide was the Johnsons' reputation that the Duke and Duchess of York (later King George VI and Queen Elizabeth) joined them on safari in Kenya, and Ernest Hemingway alluded to their movies in his Africa-based short story "The Short Happy Life of Francis Macomber."

From the outset of their career, the Johnsons promoted themselves not as flinty aristocratic expeditioners but as a relatable, unpretentious Kansas couple whose partnership just so happened to play out along the jungle rivers of Borneo and the wilderness beaches of Melanesia. During a four-year stint at a remote northern Kenya outpost known as "Lake Paradise," Osa delighted in planting her garden with vegetable seeds she'd brought with her from Chanute—harvesting basketfuls of sweet corn, carrots, beans, peas, potatoes, cucumbers, turnips, squash, and cantaloupes when she wasn't out helping Martin build camera blinds and film herds of elephants. By design, the Johnsons sought in their films to erase the distinction between local and global, portraying themselves as inarguably cosmopolitan and unapologetically Kansan.

Martin Johnson dedicated his 1924 book *Camera Trails in Africa* to Osa, calling her "the best pal a man ever had." While I enjoyed reading this, it also reminded me that my own travel career had played out as a largely solitary endeavor. Indeed, for all the pleasure I'd found in establishing myself as a Kansas-based, globally focused travel writer, my ongoing desire (and vocational necessity) to journey overseas for weeks or months at a time had left me with a bifurcated personal life. Digital nomads often cite loneliness and the difficulty of maintaining romantic relationships as a core hazard of their lifestyle, and it felt like my own venture as a digital home-steader had left me with a similar conundrum. Over the course of the 2010s, my most serious romantic relationships were shared with accomplished, urban-minded women who lived in London or New York and didn't take much interest in Kansas.

This changed in the early months of 2020, when the coronavirus out-break was approaching pandemic status, and rumors of a global travel lock-down sent scores of internationally based Americans back home to be near their families. One of these erstwhile expatriates was a Sterling-born actress named Kiki, who'd returned to her Kansas hometown from Berlin to wait out the pandemic near her parents. I met Kiki on a smartphone dating app in May of that year, and we had our first date on my rural property. Nobody was sure at the time how COVID-19 was transmitted, so we spent the day socially distanced outside on the prairie. When it got late, I didn't want the conversation to end, so I asked her if she wanted to sleep with me—and, when she said that she did, we spent the night ten feet apart, in separate sleeping bags, on top of my deck.

As we lay there under the stars, one of our conversational tangents was speculating about where in the world our paths might have crossed before. Despite having been born and raised in Kansas nine years and sixty miles apart (roughly the same interval as Martin and Osa Johnson), we may have been near each other in places besides Wichita and Sterling. In the winter of 2017, we surmised, it's possible we'd crossed paths in north London's Hamp-stead Heath when Kiki was there socializing with her friends from drama school and I was there taking my English girlfriend's cocker spaniel out for twice-daily walks. Five years prior, in the summer of 2012, we may well have brushed shoulders in Manhattan's Union Square, which I habitually traversed en route to my New York girlfriend's apartment and she often cut through on her way to meetings at her acting agency. Perhaps most fanci-fully, it was possible that we'd randomly high-fived each other the night of April 7, 2008, when we both found ourselves in rowdy, pro-Jayhawks Los Angeles sports bars the night Kansas point-guard Mario Chalmers drained a three-pointer with 2.1 seconds left in regulation against Memphis, leading Bill Self's KU squad to the team's first national basketball title since 1988.

Four and a half months after our socially distanced first date, I awakened

Kiki before dawn, led her down to the cottonwood grove that swayed next to the ponds on the eastern edge of my Kansas property, and asked her to marry me. She said yes.

A curious irony of the COVID-19 pandemic was that remote work—a skill that digital nomads had been fine-tuning for well over a decade—rapidly became the global norm. Few industries were untouched by the shift to virtual offices and video teleconferencing, including Kiki's work in the entertainment industry. Kiki, who acted under her birth name Kristen Bush, had been steadily accumulating stage and screen credits since graduating from London's Guildhall School of Music & Drama in the mid-2000s. She didn't have the kind of career that compelled random people to accost her on the street (unless for some reason they'd seen her guest appearances on *Suits* or *The Good Wife* or *Law & Order: SVU* the night before), but she'd found work at the highest levels, appearing onstage at Lincoln Center and The Public, onscreen for HBO and Showtime, and in movies directed by Barry Levinson and Charlie Kaufman.

With theater and TV auditions on hold, Kiki installed a makeshift recording studio with a broadcast-quality microphone and sheets of acoustic foam in our spare closet. She created English-language voice-overs for European clients she'd met through her connections in Berlin. When TV shows instituted pandemic safety protocols and went back into production in New York and Los Angeles, in-person cattle-call auditions were replaced by remote "self-tapes" that could be recorded and uploaded from anywhere.

One of Kiki's 2021 self-tapes landed her a guest role on the NBC medical-procedural drama *New Amsterdam*. We drove our Toyota Tundra the fourteen hundred miles to Brooklyn—not just to get Kiki to the *New Amsterdam* set in time to shoot her scenes, but also to move her furniture and belongings out of the apartment she'd been using for New York gigs (subletting it to others when she wasn't there) for most of the past decade. During our New York visit, Kiki's agents sent her an audition script for the Paramount+ supernatural drama *Evil*, and there was a curious joy in seeing her shoot the self-tape against a white Brooklyn living-room wall that looked no different from the wall we'd used for her self-tapes in rural Saline County. Previously beholden to maintaining a physical presence in global cities with ongoing theater and film productions, Kiki could now—like me—live as a digital homesteader, mixing work in distant places with a meaningful connection to our own parcel of land in north-central Kansas.

Digital homesteading in Kansas has proved enjoyable, if not always easy.

Romantic as it might sound, a writer/actress couple seeking to sustain their artistic life (a difficult task anywhere) comes with its own set of challenges when based out of a double-wide on a rural stretch of prairie. In addition to the fact that our Kansas homelife means we don't have ready access to the opening-night parties and publishing conferences that allow our urban colleagues to network with industry gatekeepers, other challenges abound. Most of the glossy travel magazines I sought to write for in the 2000s, for example, either no longer exist or are now focused on poorly compensated online content. I've shifted my focus to podcasting and books (my fifth, *The Vagabond's Way*, came out in 2022). Kiki landed the lead role in the drug-addiction drama *People, Places, and Things* at DC's Studio Theatre on the strength of a remote Zoom audition, but while the press raved (the *Washington Post* calling her performance "commanding" and "buzzworthy"), she returned to Kansas after closing night and resumed self-tape auditions for the "mother of more-important young characters" type TV roles the entertainment industry reflexively relegates to women above the age of forty.

As we do our best to balance our far-flung artistic careers with a settled life in Kansas, we've come to see Martin and Osa Johnson as inverted role models. Whereas they met when they were young (Osa was just sixteen years old when they eloped in 1910), we met in middle age. Whereas their Kansas identity was relegated to geographical abstraction as they set up temporary homes in places like Africa, our home life is centered on the thirty acres to which we return after our overseas travels, including a 2023 journey to the Johnsons' old Lake Paradise camp in Kenya. Whereas they didn't have the option of living in their home state while continuing to do the work for which they were known, we are determined to use the tools and technologies of the twenty-first century to embrace a global, cosmopolitan creative life while based out of Kansas.

Part of our task as digital homesteaders is showcasing the idea that leaving Kansas to improve one's professional opportunities need not be seen as a one-way road. If certain creative fields necessitate an inevitable "brain drain" from places like Kansas, remote work can allow those same Kansas creatives to eventually come full circle and give back to the communities that formed them. In February 2023, Kiki testified before the House Commerce Committee in Topeka, urging its members to pass tax incentives that would make it easier for Kansas filmmakers to create work in their home state. Four months later, Kiki and I did just that, co-writing and co-producing *The*

Game Camera, a short film about grief, starring Kiki, that featured a mostly female, mostly Kansas-born cast and crew working on sets in Marion and Saline Counties.

Though we're not always sure what will come of our Kansas-based ventures, optimistic uncertainty has always been a feature of living in this place. In the 1850s, the Vegetarian Settlement Company staked out land in Allen County and created Octagon City, whose residents signed a pledge to "abstain from the flesh of animals." In the 1870s, working-class activists settled in Nemaha County and established the Workingmen's Cooperative Colony, which emphasized collective land ownership. Perhaps most famously, formerly enslaved African Americans established as many as eleven different settlements (including Dunlap in Morris County and Votaw Colony in Montgomery County) in various parts of Kansas in the late nineteenth century. Few of these idealistic experiments lasted long, but it could be argued that the creative flourishing that resonated in 1920s Kansas had its roots in the notion that this was a landscape that welcomed people who were willing to expand the notion of what home might entail.

As digital homesteaders seeking to enhance our place in the greater world by basing ourselves in rural Saline County—deepening our relationship to everything global by sharpening our own sense for what is local—Kiki and I endeavor to expand the notion of what home can be.

An Evolution of Spirit

Leslie VonHolten

For me, Kansas is the damp smell of the creek bed behind one of my childhood homes. The water was an offshoot of the Marais des Cygnes River that usually flows laconically through Ottawa, Kansas, but goes wild every so often, spilling and roaring through downtown, forcing the city to close the floodgates across Main Street, a feat of engineering.

If this creek has a name, though, I've never known it. With my younger brother, I mucked along exposed tree roots collecting freshwater mussel shells, crawdads, frogs, or bones. In winter we pushed on ice to watch bubbles travel underneath, or threw rocks from the bank. Everywhere we explored, we were accompanied by a pack of mutt dogs, most of them offspring from our beloved rescue Suzie.

This Franklin County home was a maximal space with a massive, unruly garden, litters of barn cats, and a coop of hens viciously guarded by two mean Rhode Island Red roosters. Great horned owls, coyotes, a bobcat, rattlesnakes, and deer were abundant. Possums showed up to chow with the dogs. It was a fecund and untamed place, alive and volatile, both inside and outside the house.

But then the lean times got leaner, and my young father—a Vietnam combat veteran with undiagnosed, severe PTSD—rejoined the army when I was ten. Suddenly our lives of wildness were contained in apartment housing and military protocol. And meeting new people who asked where we were from. My roots needed a name: Kansas. Until then, Kansas had been an abstraction, a place on the map, a concept I had never considered. But moving away forces home's hand, and here I was discovering what Kansas—my home—means to me.

Fast-forward seventeen years, after we returned to Kansas, where I graduated high school and tumbled finally through college. I had married and left Kansas again, this time for Chicago. I remember the moment clearly: 1998, a cold slushy day on my lunch break wandering the shelves at Powell's

Used Books at Fifty-Seventh and South Harper, just past the Metra tracks. There it was: *What Kansas Means to Me*, edited by Thomas Fox Averill. I bought it. I was desperately homesick. And two years later I was a Kansan again.

Kansas gives me some of the things I love most about the world: thunderheads, the sound and smell of shirring wheat, long empty highways. If you're from here, you have been poked at, called Dorothy, treated like a hayseed, dismissed, considered ignorant or at least "too nice," whatever that means. For some reason, people like making sport of Kansas, which is often a place they haven't visited, or they've lazily judged from a car window on I-70.

I say, let these folks fly over. After a life of defending this place, I no longer do it. Kansas, to me, is a litmus test of character. When I meet someone who is curious about Kansas, or one who sees the subtle beauty of this place, I tend to like them immediately.

But I am not a booster. Love and life are complicated, even when that love is a loyalty to place or an ever-shifting concept, which I consider Kansas to be. In the mystery of it all, some things have gone against my very soul. As I write this in early 2025, many of our fellow Kansans—even some within the pages of this book—fear for their rights, their ability to stay, their bodily safety. Their stories and their histories are being erased. I scold myself for believing that those days were in our past. Just like in 2005 when Kansas voters approved an amendment to the state constitution that banned marriage equality and I went into a tailspin of faith, today I struggle to reconcile who we are. How could a state of such reservedly kind people do this? I still cannot come to terms with it, just like I will never understand the political careers of a few hate-based politicians in a state where a large sector of our economy would collapse without the hard work of immigrants, people who have enlivened our communities and added to the ongoing narrative of change and opportunity here.

And yet, change is evident. In recent years and across all corners of the state, LGBTQ clubs proudly carry the pride flag in their local Fourth of July parades—some in towns as small as two thousand residents. Many Kansas communities have their own Pride Month celebrations every summer. In 2023, Juneteenth, or Emancipation Day, became a state holiday to remember and commemorate the end of slavery and the nation's slow path to healing. Incredible to think that fewer than a hundred years ago, Ku Klux Klan members marched in these very same Independence Day parades, abhorrent and hiding their faces under their dumb hoods. I like this version of Kansas better.

I choose to believe in this evolution of spirit. Many anecdotal episodes support this. A colleague ran out of gas on a desolate rural highway and was helped by two friendly women who never once mentioned her hijab. Hundreds have shown up to city commission meetings to defend their librarians. Town groups are building relationships with Native nations to deepen their histories. Land owners toil in the sun and humidity to restore prairie and strengthen habitat for pollinators.

This, to me, is what Kansas means. It's complicated and messy and will knock your teeth out sometimes. But it is also a land of kindness and quiet generosity. Many take—we're human and deeply flawed—but many more of us give. Keep an eye on the politicians and the sycophants who run their social media, but don't let them define us. That isn't real life; often this is not even where they live.

The work of defining Kansas is up to us. That is why I am deeply honored that Tom invited me to coedit this book with him. The writers on these pages have laid the foundation for our future: each essay, poem, and story reveals the unexpected, or fights the assumptions, or broadens the narrative of this special place. Collected, they also show Kansas as exactly how I remember it during my childhood: a place wild with stories, overrun with strange and unexpected creatures; a place of discovery and heart.

About the Authors

Thomas Fox Averill is professor emeritus of English at Washburn University in Topeka, Kansas, where he taught creative writing and Kansas studies. He is an O. Henry Award short-story winner and author of ten books. His introduction to *What Kansas Means to Me: Twentieth Century Writers on the Sunflower State* (1991) was titled "Afflicted with Affection," and he remains so. In 2010 he created the Thomas Fox Averill Kansas Studies Collection at Washburn's Mabee Library.

Traci Brimhall is the author of five collections of poetry, most recently *Love Prodigal*. Her poems have appeared in many publications, including *The New Yorker*, *Poetry*, *New Republic*, *Orion*, and *Best American Poetry*. She has received fellowships from the National Endowment for the Arts, National Parks Service, and the Academy of American Poets, and a Pushcart Prize. A professor and director of creative writing at Kansas State University, she served as the poet laureate of Kansas from 2023 to 2026.

Rex Buchanan grew up in Rice County, Kansas, on the edge of the Smoky Hills. He is director emeritus of the Kansas Geological Survey, based at the University of Kansas. He is the editor or coauthor of five books, including *Roadside Kansas*, *Kansas Geology*, and *Petroglyphs of the Kansas Smoky Hills*, all published by the University Press of Kansas. He does occasional commentaries for Kansas Public Radio.

Marcia Cebulska's critically acclaimed plays, many of them Kansas themed, have been performed at thousands of venues worldwide, and her screenwriting aired on PBS. She has received the Jane Chambers International Award, the Dorothy Silver Award, and several Master Artist Fellowships. In recent years, she has written a guided journal (*Skywriting*, 2019), a novel (*Watching Men Dance*, 2020), and a memoir (*Lovers, Dreamers, & Thieves*, 2023). She lives in Topeka, Kansas, with her husband, historian Tom Prasch.

Rachel Seth Coleman has lived in Liberal, Kansas, with her husband for thirty years. During that time she has been a newspaper writer, homeschool teacher, and community college public relations director, all with the goal of working for truth, justice, and beauty. In this, she finds the Kansas motto apt: *ad astra per aspera*.

Kelly Erby is professor of history and dean of the College of Arts and Sciences at Washburn University in Topeka, Kansas. She received her BA in history and English from the Ohio State University and MA and PhD in nineteenth-century US history from Emory University. Now she is a proud Kansan and Ichabod.

B. H. Fairchild was born in 1942 in Houston, Texas, and grew up in small towns in Texas and Kansas. The son of a lathe operator, his poetry explores the landscapes of the region of his birth and the lives of its working-class residents, including his own family and friends. His honors and awards include fellowships from the National Endowment for the Arts and the Guggenheim Foundation, the William Carlos Williams Award, and the Kingsley Tufts Poetry Award.

Ian Frazier is the author of *Travels in Siberia*, *Great Plains*, *On the Rez*, *Lamentations of the Father*, and *Coyote v. Acme*, among other works. A frequent contributor to *The New Yorker*, he graduated from Harvard University and now lives in Montclair, New Jersey.

Jeffrey Ann Goudie is an award-winning freelance writer and book critic. Her book reviews have appeared in the *Boston Globe*, *Minneapolis Star Tribune*, *Kansas City Star*, and *New York Times Book Review*. A former newspaper columnist for the *Topeka Capital-Journal* and *Topeka Metro News*, she has also written opinion pieces for the *Kansas Reflector* and the *Huffington Post*. She grew up in West Texas but considers herself a Kansan by choice.

Davis Hammet is the president and executive director of Loud Light. In 2015 he founded the organization to address the disparity in youth civic engagement with the goal of developing a critical mass in youth voter turnout that transforms Kansas. Prior to this, he was the director of operations for the international nonprofit Planting Peace and co-created the rainbow-colored Equality House across from the Westboro Baptist Church hate group.

Raylene Hinz-Penner, who resides in North Newton, Kansas, taught in the English departments of Bethel College and Washburn University. Publications include *Searching for Sacred Ground: The Journey of Chief Lawrence Hart, Mennonite* (2007) and *East of Liberal: Notes on the Land* (2022). She is drawn to stories of place and learning how humans might live with the land from an Indigenous worldview.

Jim Hoy (1939–2025) was professor emeritus of English and director emeritus of the Center for Great Plains Studies at Emporia State University. He was a native of Cassoday, Kansas, in the Flint Hills, where his great-grandparents settled in 1877. In 2022 he was granted the Chester A. Reynolds Memorial Award by the National Cowboy and Western Heritage Museum. Most of his nineteen books have dealt, to a greater or lesser degree, with the folklife of ranching.

Rachel Constance Jackson is an enrolled member of the Cherokee Nation of Oklahoma and assistant professor of English at the University of Oklahoma, where she teaches Native American literature and Indigenous rhetoric courses. She is a Ford Foundation Fellow, a Newberry Consortium on American Indian Studies Research Fellow, and a member of the National Consortium on Rhetoric and Environmental Writing. She is currently revising her first monograph, *Red State Reclaimed: The Transrhetorical Recovery of Resistance in Oklahoma.*

Wes Jackson is cofounder and president emeritus of The Land Institute in Salina, Kansas, and the author of numerous articles and books, including *With Digressions, Nature as Measure: The Selected Essays of Wes Jackson, Consulting the Genius of the Place: An Ecological Approach to a New Agriculture,* and, most recently, *Hogs Are Up: Stories of the Land.*

C. J. Janovy is a veteran journalist with deep roots in the Midwest. Her book *No Place Like Home: Lessons in Activism from LGBT Kansas* (University Press of Kansas, 2018) won the 2019 Stubbendieck Great Plains Distinguished Book Prize, was nominated for a national Lambda Literary Award in LGBTQ nonfiction, joined the list of Kansas Notable Books for 2019, and inspired a 2023 documentary by Oscar-winning Kansas filmmaker Kevin Willmott.

Megan Kaminski is a poet and professor of environmental studies at the University of Kansas. She is the author of three books of poetry, most recently *Gentlewomen* (2020), and two artists books, *Prairie Divination* (2022) and *Quietly Between* (2022). Her place-based sound, poetry, and art installations have appeared at museums, public gardens, and libraries across the country, and her poetry and essays regularly appear in literary magazines and journals.

Michael Kleber-Diggs was born, raised, and educated in Kansas and currently makes his home in Saint Paul, Minnesota. He is a poet, essayist, literary critic, and arts educator. His debut poetry collection, *Worldly Things* (2021), won the Max Ritvo Poetry Prize and the 2022 Hefner Heitz Kansas Book Award in Poetry, among other awards. He often writes about togetherness and community. Learn more about his work at www.michaelkleber-diggs.com.

J. T. Knoll, founding member of White Buffalo and award-winning columnist for *The Morning Sun*, is the author of *Paperboy*, *True Stories*, *Entry / Exit Point*, *Chorus Line*, *Where the Pavement Ends*, *Fetch Crazy*, and *Counterpart*. The collection *Ghost Sign*, coauthored with Al Ortolani, Adam Jameson, and Melissa Fite Johnson, was selected as a Kansas Notable Book for 2017. He lives with his wife, Linda, and Arlo the Labradorian on Euclid's curve in Pittsburg, Kansas.

Becky Mandelbaum is the author of the novel *The Bright Side Sanctuary for Animals* and the story collection *Bad Kansas*, which received the Flannery O'Connor Award for Short Fiction and the High Plains Book Award for First Book. Her work has received a Pushcart Prize and has appeared in *The New Yorker*, *One Story*, *The Sun*, *The Georgia Review*, *McSweeney's Internet Tendency*, and elsewhere. Born and raised in Kansas, she now lives in Bellingham, Washington.

Kate McIntyre grew up in Salina, Kansas, and now teaches at Worcester Polytechnic Institute in Massachusetts. Her story collection *Mad Prairie* won the Flannery O'Connor Award, selected by Roxane Gay. The collection was longlisted for the PEN/Robert W. Bingham Prize for best debut and was named a Kansas Notable Book. She coedits the speculative flash journal *hex* (hexliterary.com).

Valerie M. Mendoza is a public historian and burgeoning folklorist whose research focuses on the Latinx community in Kansas and beyond. She serves as host of the Big Idea, sponsored by Humanities Kansas, and is co-owner of The Other Roads Consulting, Inc. She has worked with the Kansas State Historical Society, the Kansas Oral History Project, the Kansas Creative Arts Commission, the National Folklife Network, and the Duty to Country Education Project.

Andrew Malan Milward was born in Lexington, Kentucky, and grew up in Lawrence, Kansas. He is the author of the story collections *I Was a Revolutionary* and *The Agriculture Hall of Fame*, a novella collection called *You Are Loved*, and a book of narrative nonfiction, *Jayhawker: On History, Home, and Basketball.* He lives in Lexington and teaches in the MFA program at the University of Kentucky.

Armando Minjárez Monárrez is a Mexican interdisciplinary artist, designer, and community organizer. His practice is guided by themes of displacement, collaboration, and empowerment to open space for the development of social change strategy, creative expression, and liberation for racialized communities. He has presented work and conducted research on racism, displacement, migration, and creative expression in Canada, the United States, Mexico, and throughout Europe, and his creative and community work has been featured on major news publications and published in peer-reviewed scientific journals.

Caryn Mirriam-Goldberg, PhD, the 2009–2013 Kansas poet laureate, is author of two dozen books, including *How Time Moves: New & Selected Poems* and *The Sky Begins at Your Feet: A Memoir on Cancer, Community, and Coming Home to the Body.* Founder of Transformative Language Arts, she offers writing workshops, coaching, and collaborations. Her poetry has been widely published in dozens of journals and anthologies. See her blog, "Everyday Magic," and more at her website, CarynMirriamGoldberg.com.

Jesse Nathan grew up on a wheat farm in southcentral Kansas and studied history at Bethel College, in North Newton, Kansas, and poetry at Stanford University. He cut his teeth as a writer writing music criticism for the *Kansas City Pitch* and now teaches literature at UC Berkeley and edits poetry at *McSweeney's.* His book of poems, *Eggtooth,* won the 2024 New Writers

Award. His work has been published in the *New York Times*, *The Nation*, *New Republic*, *New York Review of Books*, and the *I-70 Review*.

Al Ortolani is a winner of the Rattle Chapbook Prize and has been featured in Garrison Keillor's *Writer's Almanac* and Ted Kooser's *American Life in Poetry*. He is a two-time recipient of the Kansas Notable Book Award. *Bull in the Ring*, a novel, and his collection of poetry, *Controlled Burn*, were recently published.

H. C. Palmer was a battalion surgeon for the First Infantry division during the American War in Vietnam. His poems and short stories have appeared in *New Letters*, *Narrative Magazine*, *War, Literature and the Arts*, and other literary journals and anthologies, and his poetry collection *Feet of the Messenger* was a finalist for the Balcones Poetry Prize. His spiritual place is the Flint Hills of Kansas. He lives in Lenexa, Kansas, with his wife, Valerie, and their Boykin Spaniel, Julip.

Matt Perrier lives outside Eureka, Kansas, and is a fifth-generation cattleman from the Flint Hills. When not tending to his family ranch, Dalebanks Angus, or his five kids, he produces a biweekly podcast, *Practically Ranching*. He and his wife, Amy, communicate the wonderful story of modern beef production and rural Kansas values through their various social media platforms, in-person speaking engagements, and tours.

Rolf Potts is the author of five books, including the bestseller *Vagabonding: An Uncommon Guide to the Art of Long-Term World Travel* (2003). His essays and reportage have appeared in *National Geographic Traveler*, *Outside*, *The New Yorker*, and *Sports Illustrated*, and on National Public Radio and the Travel Channel. He is based in north-central Kansas, where he keeps a small farmhouse on thirty acres with his wife, Kansas-born actress Kristen (Kiki) Bush.

Robert Rebein is professor of English at Indiana University Indianapolis. He is the author of a novel, *The Last Rancher* (2024); two collections of memoir essays, *Headlights on the Prairie: Essays on Home* (2017) and *Dragging Wyatt Earp: A Personal History of Dodge City* (2013), both named Kansas Notable Books; and a work of literary criticism, *Hicks, Tribes, & Dirty Realists: American Fiction after Postmodernism* (2001).

Dennis Rogers, a lifelong Topekan, is a graduate of Haskell Indian Nations University. A full-time Native American visual and performing artist and educator, he tours nationally and internationally. His knowledge of American Indian culture and history is based on fact, thought, research, and of living on and off the Navajo reservation. He shares, "I wish for all Kansans to be mindful of our state's rich Native history."

Libby Schmanke is an associate professor in the Emporia State University graduate art therapy program. She worked clinically for more than two decades in addictions and art therapy. The author of *Art Therapy and Substance Abuse* (2017) and *The Life and Legacy of Robert Ault, Art Therapy Pioneer* (2024), and coauthor of *Graphic Guide to Art Therapy* (2022), she considers artmaking and her friendship with the late Robert Ault to be foundational aspects of her life.

Joshua Svaty is a former Kansas legislator and state secretary of agriculture from rural Ellsworth, Kansas, where he and his family have been farming since the 1860s. He and wife Kimberly are raising their four children in Topeka, where he works with his wife in her firm, Gencur Svaty Public Affairs. He speaks and advises nationally and internationally on matters related to agriculture, energy, and natural resources.

Leslie VonHolten writes about land and culture in the prairie and Great Plains regions. She is a 2022 Tallgrass Artist Residency fellow and long-time commentator on High Plains Public Radio in Garden City, Kansas. Her recent essays have been published in *The New Territory*, *Literary Landscapes*, and *The Dark Mountain Project*. She lives in Lawrence, Kansas, with her husband, Tim, and their misbehaving dogs and garden.

Kevin Young is the author of fifteen books of poetry and prose, including *Stones*, shortlisted for the T. S. Eliot Prize; the children's book *Emile and the Field*; and *Bunk*, a *New York Times* Notable Book also longlisted for the National Book Award. He is the editor of eleven other volumes, including *African American Poetry: 250 Years of Struggle & Song*, and is the poetry editor of *The New Yorker*, where he hosts the Poetry Podcast.

Acknowledgments

I thank the University Press of Kansas for soliciting a new anthology of writing about the Sunflower State. Joyce Harrison and Alec Loganbill are encouraging, supportive, insightful editors. Thanks to all at the press who worked diligently to make *Kansas Matters: Twenty-First-Century Writers on the Sunflower State* possible.

Coeditor Leslie VonHolten has shown her artful skills in all aspects of this book: from brainstorming, to soliciting material, to working with writers, to shaping contents, to contributing her own evocative writing. Her expertise, her knowledge of the state, and her connections to diverse writers of all ages and occupations and regions across Kansas have improved the reach of *Kansas Matters*. Thank you for signing on, Leslie.

To all the writers who allowed us to reprint previously published work, thank you. To those who answered our solicitations for new material, thank you for creating such fine work under deadline.

Martha Imparato, Washburn University archivist and Special Collections librarian, was always willing to pull books from the Kansas Studies Collection, to scan material, and to help Leslie and me gather resources toward making *Kansas Matters* an inclusive, far-reaching representation of Kansas.

My spouse, Jeffrey Ann Goudie, generously allowed us to reprint her Kansas commentary, but was also present throughout the making of this book. I am lucky to have her as an insightful conversationalist, careful thinker, and crackerjack editor. Her honest criticism has always improved my work.

Last, my adult children, Ellie and Alex, have enlarged and enhanced my understanding of the world with their intelligence, care, good humor, and enthusiasm. Thank you.

—*Thomas Fox Averill*

My great thanks to Tom Averill for inviting me to coedit this labor of love with him. To meet a writer who has impacted the way I see the world, and then to later work with him, at his invitation, is a dream. Getting to know Jeffrey Ann Goudie and reap the benefits of her wise edits has been an added joy. Thank you to Joyce Harrison and Alec Loganbill at the University Press of Kansas for their guidance. And deep thanks to all of the writers within these pages who freely shared their stories and expanded what Kansas means to me.

My life as a Kansan has been enriched by the work of my curious, kind, and respectful colleagues at Humanities Kansas. I thank Julie Mulvihill, Tracy Quillin, Murl Riedel, Leslie Daugharthy, Abigail Kaup, Kaitlyn Savage, and Ruth Madell for their insight and friendship.

On a country walk when I was twelve, my mother woke me up to the beauty of the neighbor's wheat field and the gentle sound it made in the evening breeze. Janet Bowyer always kept Kansas in the heart of our family.

Marrying an Illinois farm boy who jumps into everything he does with both feet—including making a home in Kansas—is the best thing I've ever done. Tim VonHolten, my deepest well of gratitude is for you. Atticus and Bea, thank you for the fresh perspectives and good humor along the way. Sorry for so many miles "just to see." And Forrest Bowyer, my nephew, let's plan that trip to Garfield County soon.

Our diverse and rich cultural identity is strengthened by the labor of underpaid professionals and volunteers who are passionate about history and place. Support your local historical society. Support your librarians. Kansas is made better by the work they do.

—*Leslie VonHolten*

Permissions and Credits

Thomas Fox Averill, "Digging with Darwin," *Cottonwood 68* (Fall 2010), pp. 83–98.

Traci Brimhall, "Ad Astra," poem written for the inauguration of Governor Laura Kelly, January 2023.

Marcia Cebulska, excerpted lines from *Rooted: The Greensburg Odyssey*, 2012.

B. H. Fairchild, "The Second Annual Wizard of Oz Reunion in Liberal, Kansas," *Early Occult Memory Systems of the Lower Midwest* (New York: Norton, 2002), pp. 52–53.

Ian Frazier, "The Day the Great Plains Burned," *The New Yorker*, October 29, 2018.

Jeffrey Ann Goudie, "Let Kansas Be Kansas" appeared in slightly different form in the June 21, 2022, *Kansas Reflector* (kansasreflector.com), a member of the States Newsroom network.

Davis Hammet, "How I Fell in Love with Kansas—and Spent the Next Five Years Trying to Change It" appeared in slightly different form in the *Washington Post*, November 27, 2018 (washingtonpost.com).

Raylene Hinz-Penner, "Girls on the Land," *East of Liberal* (Telford, PA: Dreamseeker Books, 2022), pp. 169–176.

Jim Hoy, "How Kansas Gave Texas the Boot," originally published as "Kansas and Cowboy Boots: Folklore, Fact, and Fancy," and "Custom-Made Boots: A Traditional Process Continues," in *Cowboy Boots: the Kansas Story*, by Barbara Brackman, Jennie A. Chinn, and James F. Hoy (Topeka: Kansas State Historical Society, 1994).

Wes Jackson, "Getting the Story Right," introduction to *Hogs Are Up: Stories of the Land, with Digressions* (Lawrence: University Press of Kansas, 2021), pp. 1–14.

C. J. Janovy, "Rainbow Flag's Creator Didn't Celebrate His Home State, but Kansans Keep His Memory Alive," KCUR, June 6, 2020.

Megan Kaminski, "Amazon Army," commissioned for and first exhibited as part of the installation *Forgotten Stories* at the Mid-America Arts Alliance, curated by Quraysh Ali Lansana and the Tulsa-based Tri-City Collective, Kansas City, Missouri, September 2021.

Megan Kaminski, "They say," originally published in *Written in the Stars*, Humanities Kansas, October 2024.

www.ingramcontent.com/pod-product-compliance
Lightning Source LLC
Chambersburg PA
CBHW021035310726
48969CB00006B/1668